ACCELERATE YOUR IT CAREER JOURNEY

Save 13% on Exam Vouchers*

Head to the last page of this book for more details.

*Certain restrictions apply.

CompTIA A+ Practice Test Core 2 (220-1102)

Achieve certification by practicing with hundreds of mock questions and tests for each exam topic

Mark Birch and Ian Neil

BIRMINGHAM—MUMBAI

CompTIA A+ Practice Test Core 2 (220-1102)

Copyright © 2023 Packt Publishing

All rights reserved. No part of this book may be reproduced, stored in a retrieval system, or transmitted in any form or by any means, without the prior written permission of the publisher, except in the case of brief quotations embedded in critical articles or reviews.

Every effort has been made in the preparation of this book to ensure the accuracy of the information presented. However, the information contained in this book is sold without warranty, either express or implied. Neither the authors, nor Packt Publishing or its dealers and distributors, will be held liable for any damages caused or alleged to have been caused directly or indirectly by this book.

Packt Publishing has endeavored to provide trademark information about all of the companies and products mentioned in this book by the appropriate use of capitals. However, Packt Publishing cannot guarantee the accuracy of this information.

Authors: Mark Birch and Ian Neil

Reviewers: Sahil Kumar and Sylvio Musto

Senior Editor: Ketan Giri

Production Editor: Shantanu Zagade

Editorial Board: Vijin Boricha, Megan Carlisle, Ketan Giri, Alex Mazonowicz, Aaron Nash, Abhishek Rane, and Ankita Thakur

Production reference: 1231023

Published by Packt Publishing Ltd.

Grosvenor House

11 St Paul's Square

Birmingham

B3 1RB

ISBN 978-1-83763-889-5

www.packtpub.com

Contributors

About the Authors

Mark Birch is an experienced courseware developer and teacher in both information systems and cyber-security. Mark has been developing content and teaching CompTIA A+ classes for more than 20 years and understands the subject area in great depth. Mark began his career working within the aerospace industry (for a major defense contractor) and has over 30 years' experience consulting, engineering, and deploying secure information systems. He has spent over 20 years working with the United States Military and United Kingdom Armed Forces, helping many students attain their learning goals. Mark has ensured that soldiers, officers, and civilians have had the best opportunities to gain cyber-security accreditation.

Ian Neil is one of the world's top trainers of Security+. He is able to break down information into manageable chunks so that people with no background knowledge can gain the skills required to become certified. He has recently worked for the US Army in Europe and designed a Security+ course that catered to people from all backgrounds (not just IT professionals), with an extremely successful pass rate. He is an MCT, MCSE, A+, Network+, Security+, CASP, and RESILIA practitioner that has worked with high-end training providers over the past 23 years and was one of the first technical trainers to train Microsoft internal staff when they opened their Bucharest Office in 2006.

About the Reviewers

Sahil Kumar is a software engineer driven by an unwavering passion for innovation and a keen aptitude for problem-solving. With an impressive career spanning eight years, Sahil has honed his expertise in various domains, including IT systems, cybersecurity, endpoint management, and global customer support.

His experience in the tech industry is marked by a commitment to continuous learning and professional growth, as evidenced by his numerous certifications. Sahil holds coveted certifications such as CompTIA A+, CompTIA Security+, ITIL V4, OCI 2023 Foundations Associate, Microsoft SC-200, AZ-900, and a Certificate in Cyber Security (ISC2). This extensive certification portfolio reflects his dedication to staying at the forefront of technology and security trends.

Sahil's proficiency extends beyond the realm of cybersecurity; he is also well-versed in DevSecOps, demonstrating his versatility in tackling multifaceted challenges within the IT landscape. Currently, Sahil is pursuing a master's degree in cybersecurity at New York University, a testament to his commitment to academic excellence and staying at the top of his field. He holds a bachelor's degree in electrical and electronics engineering from Kurukshetra University.

Sylvio Musto is a technical trainer with over 13 years of experience in Information Technology, Information Security, Cyber Risks, and Auditing. He holds MBAs in Information Security Management as well as Leadership and Strategic People Management.

Sylvio currently works as the Supervisor of Internal Audit at MercadoLivre, one of the leading companies in the e-commerce and technology market in Latin America.

Throughout his career, Sylvio has made significant contributions to the field of Information Technology, working with renowned companies in software development, healthcare, insurance, and financial markets.

In addition to his professional accomplishments, Sylvio is also a dedicated educator. He currently serves as a professor at the Fundação Vanzolini and CompTIA, sharing his knowledge and experience with the next generation of IT professionals.

Sylvio Musto is recognized for his solid credentials, including ITIL v3, Cobit v5 Foundation, CompTIA Security+, CompTIA CySA+, and ISO 27001 Foundation certifications. His commitment to enhancing information security and strategically leading teams makes him a respected authority in the field of Information Technology.

Outside of work, Sylvio has a strong interest in automobiles and recently devoted his time to restoring a collector's vehicle he owns in Brazil.

Table of Contents

Preface	**xi**
How to Use This Book	**xv**
Approach for Navigating Multiple-Choice Queries	xv
Exercising Caution in Testing	xv
Advice on Additional Resources – Practical Exercise	xvi

1

Operating Systems 1

Introduction	1	1.6 Given a scenario, configure Microsoft Windows networking features on a client/desktop	17
Practice Exam Questions	2		
1.1 Identify basic features of Microsoft Windows editions	2	1.7 Given a scenario, apply application installation and configuration concepts	19
1.2 Given a scenario, use the appropriate Microsoft command-line tool	4	1.8 Explain common OS types and their purposes	21
1.3 Given a scenario, use features and tools of the Microsoft Windows 10 operating system (OS)	9	1.9 Given a scenario, perform OS installations and upgrades in a diverse OS environment	23
1.4 Given a scenario, use the appropriate Microsoft Windows 10 Control Panel utility	12	1.10 Identify common features and tools of the macOS/desktop OS	25
1.5 Given a scenario, use the appropriate Windows settings	15	1.11 Identify common features and tools of the Linux client/desktop OS	28

2

Security · 33

Introduction · 33	2.5 Given a scenario, manage and configure basic security settings in the Microsoft Windows OS · 45
Practice Exam Questions · 34	
2.1 Summarize various security measures and their purposes · 34	2.6 Given a scenario, configure a workstation to meet best practices for security · 47
2.2 Compare and contrast wireless security protocols and authentication methods · 38	2.7 Explain common methods for securing mobile and embedded devices · 50
2.3 Given a scenario, detect, remove, and prevent malware using the appropriate tools and methods · 39	2.8 Given a scenario, use common data destruction and disposal methods · 52
2.4 Explain common social-engineering attacks, threats, and vulnerabilities · 42	2.9 Given a scenario, configure appropriate security settings on small office/home office (SOHO) wireless and wired networks · 53
	2.10 Given a scenario, install and configure browsers and relevant security settings · 55

3

Software Troubleshooting · 57

Introduction · 57	3.3 Given a scenario, use best practice procedures for malware removal · 64
Practice Exam Questions · 58	
3.1 Given a scenario, troubleshoot common Windows OS problems · 58	3.4 Given a scenario, troubleshoot common mobile OS and application issues · 66
3.2 Given a scenario, troubleshoot common personal computer (PC) security issues · 62	3.5 Given a scenario, troubleshoot common mobile OS and application security issues · 69

4

Operational Procedures · 73

Introduction · 73	4.2 Explain basic change-management best practices · 77
Practice Exam Questions · 74	
4.1 Given a scenario, implement best practices associated with documentation and support systems information management · 74	4.3 Given a scenario, implement workstation backup and recovery methods · 79
	4.4 Given a scenario, use common safety procedures · 81

4.5 Summarize environmental impacts and local environmental controls	83	4.7 Given a scenario, use proper communication techniques and professionalism	89
4.6 Explain the importance of prohibited content/activity and privacy, licensing, and policy concepts	86	4.8 Identify the basics of scripting	91
		4.9 Given a scenario, use remote access technologies	94

Mock Exam 97

Solutions 121

Index 251

Other Books You May Enjoy 260

Coupon Code for CompTIA A+ Exam Vouchers and Labs 263

Preface

Welcome to the practice test book on CompTIA A+ Core 2 (220-1102), meticulously crafted for those seeking to pass the exam and gain a clear, concise understanding of the foundational concepts, technologies, and practices that underpin modern computer systems.

Who This Book Is For?

This A+ practice test book has been written for individuals who are preparing to take the CompTIA A+ certification exam. This certification is often sought after by individuals aiming to start or advance their careers in the field of IT and technology support. The book caters to a wide range of individuals, including the following:

- **Aspiring IT professionals**: Those who are new to the IT industry and looking to gain the necessary knowledge and skills to enter the field
- **Entry-level technicians**: Individuals who are already working in IT support roles and wish to validate their skills and knowledge by obtaining the A+ certification
- **Career changers**: People coming from other industries who are interested in transitioning into a career in IT and require a foundational understanding of computer hardware, software, and troubleshooting
- **Students**: Students studying computer science, information technology, or related fields who want to enhance their learning and increase their employability
- **Self-learners**: Individuals who prefer self-paced learning and want to improve their technical skills in their own time, potentially with the aim of changing careers or advancing within their current role
- **IT enthusiasts**: Hobbyists and technology enthusiasts who wish to deepen their knowledge and skills in computer systems and hardware
- **Job seekers**: Those actively seeking employment in IT support or technician roles, as the A+ certification is often a prerequisite or advantage in job applications
- **Military personnel**: Military personnel transitioning to civilian roles in the IT sector, as the A+ certification can aid in their reintegration into the workforce

- **Professional development**: Individuals already in IT roles who are seeking to enhance their skills, stay updated with industry trends, and potentially pursue higher-level certifications in the future

Overall, this CompTIA A+ Core 2 (220-1102) practice test book serves as a valuable resource for anyone looking to prepare for the CompTIA A+ certification exam and establish a solid foundation in IT hardware, software, troubleshooting, and customer service skills.

What This Book Covers

Chapter 1, Operating Systems, tests your skills regarding installing and supporting the Windows operating system, including the command line and client support. We will also test the skills you will need for system configuration imaging and troubleshooting on macOS, Chrome OS, Android, and Linux OS.

Chapter 2, Security, evaluates your readiness for the exam by focusing on identifying and selecting controls used to mitigate security vulnerabilities for devices and their network connections. Wireless security, threats, and vulnerabilities including common methods of social engineering are also covered in this chapter.

Chapter 3, Software Troubleshooting, assesses your knowledge when troubleshooting PC and mobile device issues, which can include common operating systems, malware, and security issues.

Chapter 4, Operational Procedures, assesses your competence in adhering to best practices related to safety, environmental impact, communication, and professionalism. Important elements such as change management, backup and recovery, and privacy concepts are also covered in this chapter.

Mock Exam provides you with a thorough evaluation of your grasp of the A+ Core 2 (220-1102) exam objectives. You can test your problem-solving skills and exam readiness against a realistic selection of CompTIA A+ exam questions.

Conventions Used

New terms and important words are shown like this: "Common environments that need to be secured include wireless networks, **small office/home office** (**SOHO**) networks, enterprise networks, and situations where securing remote access is crucial."

Get in Touch

Feedback from our readers is always welcome.

General feedback: If you have any questions about this book, please mention the book title in the subject of your message and email us at *customercare@packt.com*.

Errata: Although we have taken every care to ensure the accuracy of our content, mistakes do happen. If you have found a mistake in this book, we would be grateful if you could report this to us. Please visit www.packtpub.com/support/errata and complete the form.

Piracy: If you come across any illegal copies of our works in any form on the Internet, we would be grateful if you could provide us with the location address or website name. Please contact us at *copyright@packt.com* with a link to the material.

If you are interested in becoming an author: If there is a topic that you have expertise in and you are interested in either writing or contributing to a book, please visit authors.packtpub.com.

Share Your Thoughts

Once you've read *CompTIA A+ Practice Test Core 2 (220-1102)*, we'd love to hear your thoughts! Scan the QR code below to go straight to the Amazon review page for this book and share your feedback.

https://packt.link/r/1837638896

Your review is important to us and the tech community and will help us make sure we're delivering excellent quality content.

How to Use This Book

The purpose of having a practice test book is to facilitate your preparation for the CompTIA A+ Core 2 (220-1102) exams. Prior to attempting a practice test, it's advisable to have either a digital document or a blank sheet of paper at your disposal. While taking the test, it's beneficial to jot down any subjects that are unfamiliar to you or questions you've answered incorrectly. This practice will help pinpoint areas where your understanding is lacking. Following the test, it is recommended that you revisit your study guide to address the identified gaps.

Approach for Navigating Multiple-Choice Queries

Embrace this strategy to effectively tackle multiple-choice queries:

- **Thorough reading**: Immerse yourself in the questions and absorb their nuances
- **Elimination game**: Discard incorrect choices, systematically narrowing your options
- **Refinement process**: Evolve from a 50-50 stance to a 60-40 perspective through a meticulous review
- **Unveil the optimal**: Opt for the finest or most plausible choices when multiple correct answers exist
- **Precision in choice**: Align your selection with the specific query at hand

Exercising Caution in Testing

Avoid these counterproductive actions during your testing endeavor:

- **Overthinking pitfall**: Steer clear of overanalyzing; maintain a balanced mindset
- **Rushing dilemma**: Eschew hasty scanning or racing through the test; maintain a composed pace
- **Doubt's detriment**: Refrain from second-guessing or doubling back; trust your initial instincts
- **Choice constancy**: Resist altering your answers; initial choices often prove sound
- **Comprehensive consistency**: Spare yourself from re-reading the entire test; stay focused on the task at hand

Advice on Additional Resources – Practical Exercise

An additional preparatory resource that could prove valuable is the CompTIA Official Labs. These cloud-based labs offer a practical approach to exam readiness by directly addressing the topics covered in the exam. Particularly beneficial for individuals with minimal or no prior IT experience, these labs serve as excellent tools for gaining hands-on familiarity.

In the context of CompTIA A+ Core 2 (220-1102), a solid grasp of hardware concepts is essential, and the labs effectively facilitate this understanding. A noteworthy aspect is the 12-month access granted, allowing ample time for exploration and learning. Notably, Packt Publishing has secured a substantial discount on the CompTIA official labs and the exam voucher, the details for which are at the back of the book.

What You Will Learn in the CompTIA Official Labs

Once you have paid and signed up for the CompTIA CertMaster Labs for A+ Core 2 (220-1102), you will have access to hands-on practice and skills development using real equipment and software accessed through a remote, browser-based lab environment. Aligned with Official CompTIA courseware and the CompTIA A+ Core 2 (220-1102) exam objectives, CertMaster Labs make it easy for learners to practice and apply their skills in real workplace scenarios in preparation for the certification exam. All lab activities include gradable assessments, offer feedback and hints, and provide a score based on learner inputs, ultimately guiding you to the most correct and efficient path through job tasks.

There are two types of labs in the course:

- **Virtual Workbench Labs** provide learners with valuable hands-on practice installing, configuring, and troubleshooting computer hardware in an immersive 3D environment. Each scenario features a Tutorial Mode to guide the learner through step-by-step instructions, allowing learners to understand and practice 3D controls; an Explore Mode that enables learners to identify and manipulate hardware components in a sandbox environment; and an Assisted Mode that takes learners step by step through a procedure, offering help when needed. This hands-on environment gives learners the ability to learn the tangible aspects of IT and gain real-world experience. Learners can explore how the different components of a desktop, a laptop, and peripherals work together, and will get experience of working through different processes for installing and configuring computer components.

- **Virtual Machine Labs** utilize virtual machines built to simulate a server network so a learner can gain real-world, hands-on experience with tools, applications, and operating systems they would utilize in a job environment, such as Microsoft Windows or Kali Linux. Learners can compare network hardware using the GNS3 network simulator and configure a home router using OpenWRT.

Virtual Machine Labs are also available in different modes:

- **Assisted Labs** guide the learner step by step through tasks, offering assessment and feedback throughout a 10-15 minute experience, allowing the learner to correct any misunderstandings as they proceed through the activity.
- **Applied Labs** present a series of goal-oriented scenarios in a 20-30 minute experience covering multiple topics, scoring the learner's work at the end of the activity based on their ability to successfully complete each scenario. As a result, learners are forced to think critically about how to approach problems without a prescribed set of steps. Currently, Applied Labs are only available for Virtual Machine Lab activities.

The following labs are available:

- Assisted Lab: Manage User Settings in Windows
- Assisted Lab: Support Windows 11
- Assisted Lab: Configure Windows System Settings
- Assisted Lab: Use Management Consoles
- Assisted Lab: Use Task Manager
- Assisted Lab: Monitor Performance and Event Logs
- Assisted Lab: Use Command-line Tools
- APPLIED Lab: Support Windows 10
- Assisted Lab: Perform Windows 10 OS Installation
- Assisted Lab: Perform Ubuntu Linux OS Installation
- Assisted Lab: Install and Configure an Application
- Assisted Lab: Troubleshoot a Windows OS Issue
- Assisted Lab: Configure Windows Networking
- Assisted Lab: Configure Folder Sharing in a Workgroup
- Assisted Lab: Manage Linux using Command-line Tools
- Assisted Lab: Manage Files using Linux Command-line Tools
- APPLIED Lab: Support and Troubleshoot Network Hosts
- Assisted Lab: Configure SOHO Router Security
- Assisted Lab: Configure Workstation Security

- Assisted Lab: Configure Browser Security
- Assisted Lab: Troubleshoot Security Issues Scenario #1
- APPLIED Lab: Troubleshoot Security Issues Scenario #2
- Assisted Lab: Use Remote Access Technologies
- Assisted Lab: Implement Backup and Recovery
- Assisted Lab: Implement a PowerShell Script
- Assisted Lab: Implement Bash Script
- Assisted Lab: Manage a Support Ticket

Accessing the Course Materials

You will receive an access key and registration instructions via email once you have paid and signed up for the CompTIA CertMaster Labs for A+ Core 2 (220-1102).

1
Operating Systems

Introduction

It is important that the exam candidate understands typical usage scenarios for different mainstream operating systems and specialist mobile operating systems. In an enterprise environment, it is important that support technicians can support and troubleshoot many different devices. Modern enterprise networks need to tailor their approach for many different end-user scenarios, from on-premises support to remote and mobile users. Devices may connect to applications and services using various network media, including Bluetooth, cellular and wired connections, and Wi-Fi.

It is important that technicians can configure and troubleshoot all types of network connections. There is a need to upgrade hardware and software solutions over time, and knowledge of any constraints or requirements when planning for upgrades is important. To offer a speedy response to customer support requests, the technician should be able to choose the correct tool or techniques, so a good understanding of the different configuration settings and menu options is important.

In order to be successful on the CompTIA A+ Core 2 (220-1102) certification exam, candidates must ensure they are familiar with the following objectives:

- 1.1 Identify basic features of Microsoft Windows editions
- 1.2 Given a scenario, use the appropriate Microsoft command-line tool
- 1.3 Given a scenario, use features and tools of the Microsoft Windows 10 operating system (OS)
- 1.4 Given a scenario, use the appropriate Microsoft Windows 10 Control Panel utility
- 1.5 Given a scenario, use the appropriate Windows settings
- 1.6 Given a scenario, configure Microsoft Windows networking features on a client/desktop
- 1.7 Given a scenario, apply application installation and configuration concepts
- 1.8 Explain common OS types and their purposes
- 1.9 Given a scenario, perform OS installations and upgrades in a diverse OS environment

- 1.10 Identify common features and tools of the macOS/desktop OS
- 1.11 Identify common features and tools of the Linux client/desktop OS

The rest of this chapter is committed to practice. For each of the concepts defined above, you will be given a series of questions designed to test your knowledge of each Core 2 exam objective as defined by the official certification exam guidance for this domain. These questions will test the candidate's knowledge of how to troubleshoot and configure common operating systems.

Practice Exam Questions

1.1 Identify basic features of Microsoft Windows editions

1. A user receives a new laptop computer that runs Windows 10. Upon first use, they are prompted to provide a password prior to the regular login prompt. What feature would likely cause this prompt?

    A. Password-protected BIOS

    B. Windows Privacy and Security

    C. Windows Accessibility

    D. BitLocker Drive Encryption

2. A senior manager is insisting that their personal laptop be joined to the company's domain so that they can use their preferred operating system and hardware. Which operating systems would NOT be supported for this role? (Choose two.)

    A. Windows 10 Home

    B. Windows 8.1 Pro

    C. Windows 10 Pro

    D. ChromeOS

3. A technician is attempting to enable BitLocker Drive Encryption on company laptops, but the option is only available for some of the laptops. Which versions of the Windows operating system support BitLocker Drive Encryption? (Choose two.)

    A. Windows 10 Pro

    B. Windows 10 Home

    C. Windows 7 Pro

    D. Windows 10 Enterprise

    E. macOS

4. A small company is looking to upgrade all company workstations from Windows 8.1 Pro to the equivalent Windows 10 edition. The systems are managed, and all conform to the company's baseline image. The company would like to use the least administrative effort to make this transition, migrating all applications and user data at the same time. Which of the following would be the best solution?

   A. In-place upgrade
   B. Fresh installation from a central server
   C. Fresh installation from optical media
   D. Fresh installation from USB media

5. A technician is responding to a support ticket from a manager who cannot enable BitLocker on their personal computer while working from home. What is the MOST likely cause of this problem?

   A. The system only has 2GB of RAM installed
   B. The system is running Windows Home edition
   C. The system is running a 32-bit edition of Windows
   D. The system has a 128GB hard drive

6. A service desk technician is tasked with connecting remotely to a Windows desktop computer. The technician needs to change configuration settings using a secure connection. It is important that the user must be logged off during this process. Which of the following tools would the technician MOST likely use?

   A. RDP
   B. Virtual network computing
   C. Microsoft Remote Assistance
   D. SFTP

7. A company is proposing in-place upgrades for all the current Windows platforms that are running on a 32-bit OS. If these are performed, what would the memory limitation of the 32-bit OS be?

   A. 16MB
   B. 2048GB
   C. 4GB
   D. 128GB

Operating Systems

8. A deskside support technician has shown the marketing manager how to use BitLocker To Go. The technician MOST LIKELY encrypted which of the following?

   A. A DVD-RW disk
   B. A network drive
   C. An internal disk drive
   D. A USB drive

9. A technician plans to install the latest version of the Windows OS on a user's device. The user insists all of their data files and configuration settings are retained during this process. Which of the following installation types should the technician use?

   A. Network installation
   B. Clean install
   C. In-place upgrade
   D. Image deployment

10. A home user has raised a support ticket requesting remote assistance for a problem they are experiencing with a locally installed application. When a technician attempts to connect to the remote system using RDP, there is a connection error. What is the MOST LIKELY reason for the error?

    A. The system only has 2GB of RAM installed
    B. The system is running a Windows Home edition
    C. The system is running a 32-bit edition of Windows
    D. The system is running a Windows Pro edition

1.2 Given a scenario, use the appropriate Microsoft command-line tool

1. A network engineer must troubleshoot a section of a business network in which marketing users cannot access printers, e-mail, or websites. The network infrastructure equipment appears to be working correctly, so the engineer is looking to eliminate misconfigured user workstations as a possible cause of the problem. Which command-line tool would provide the best information regarding workstation configuration?

   A. ping localhost
   B. ipconfig /all
   C. netstat -a
   D. hostname

2. An administrator is responsible for the operating system migration of 300 Windows users. As part of the migration, the administrator must save the end-users' data to a temporary shared drive. The data must retain all security permissions and support hidden files. Which of the following commands will achieve this result by default?

   A. robocopy
   B. copy
   C. xcopy
   D. cp

3. A technician is troubleshooting network connectivity and receives the following output:

   Server: UnKnown
   ```
   Address:   10.10.0.1
   Non-authoritative answer:
   Name:    www.google.com
   Addresses:  2a00:1450:4009:81e::2004
            142.250.187.196


     1    <1 ms    *        *        <1 ms    WIN2022-DC [10.10.0.1]
     2    *        *        *        *        Request timed out.
     3    3 ms     1 ms     1 ms     172.17.48.1
     4    3 ms     3 ms     3 ms     192.168.0.1
     5    6 ms     6 ms     6 ms     151.231.252.44
     6    16 ms    72 ms    16 ms    2.120.11.144
     7    15 ms    14 ms    109 ms   72.14.219.96
     8    17 ms    *        *        216.239.40.71
     9    16 ms    16 ms    16 ms    142.251.54.35
    10    17 ms    18 ms    17 ms    lhr25s33-in-f4.1e100.net
   [142.250.187.196]
   ```

   Which of the following tools is the technician MOST LIKELY using? (Choose two.)

   A. ping
   B. ipconfig
   C. netstat
   D. nslookup
   E. tracert
   F. nbstat

4. A support ticket is raised by a senior manager having computer-related problems while working from home on their personal Windows 10 computer. They are attempting to access e-mail prior to attending an important business event. The support technician is unable to access the system using remote desktop, so, as a workaround, they use a third-party desktop sharing application. The technician identifies a solution to the manager's problem and proposes that they make configuration changes using Group Policy Editor (gpedit.msc). However, when they attempt to run the tool, they find it is not available on the manager's computer. What is the most likely reason that these tools have not been present on the manager's computer?

    A. The computer is running Linux
    B. The computer is running Windows 10 Enterprise
    C. The computer is running Windows 10 Home
    D. The computer has a corrupt registry

5. A customer powers on their laptop and discovers that, though their device displays the normal Windows desktop, they are unable to access any network-based resources. Which of the following tools should be used at the command line to troubleshoot this scenario?

    A. ping
    B. msconfig
    C. nbtstat
    D. nslookup

6. A network technician investigates an ongoing incident in which a desktop computer makes a connection to an IP address across the network. The technician needs to resolve the computer's name associated with the IP address. Which of the following commands should the network technician use?

    A. gpresult
    B. ipconfig
    C. nslookup
    D. net user

7. A malware infection has spread across a company's network via several USB storage devices. The support team must identify a method to prevent users from using storage devices that connect to USB ports. The team has been notified that this must be done quickly with minimum disruption to users. Which of the following is the BEST way for the support team to address this requirement?

   A. Push a group policy to all users
   B. Assign a local security policy
   C. Create a network login script
   D. Update the company AUP

8. A support technician has added a Windows 10 workstation to the domain companydomain.com. The technician needs to verify that the workstation has received security policies from the domain. Which command will confirm whether the policies have been effective?

   A. ipconfig /all
   B. netstat -e
   C. gpresult /Z
   D. nslookup -query=a server1.companydomain.com

9. A technician is using a command-line interface to perform tasks on a Windows 10 computer. The technician needs to determine which ports have active TCP connections to local or remote hosts. Which of the following commands should the technician use?

   A. netstat -p TCP
   B. net use -p TCP
   C. nslookup -p TCP
   D. netstat -p UDP

10. An administrator has tested a new Group Policy Object (GPO) and now wants to deploy it into the production environment. After deployment, the finance users do not appear to be receiving the new GPO. The administrator thinks the problem may be related to other GPOs that have been deployed at the same time. Which of the following command-line tools would be MOST USEFUL for the administrator to verify which GPOs are being deployed to the accounting department?

    A. nbtstat
    B. gpresult
    C. nslookup
    D. gpupdate
    E. tasklist

11. A technician is creating a logon script that needs to automatically assign a drive mapping to a public folder shared on server1. The new drive letter on the user's workstation will be allocated the P drive letter. Which of the following commands will achieve the desired result?

    A. net use P: \\server1\public
    B. tracert \\server1\public local drive P:
    C. net use \\P = Server\public
    D. tracert P: \\server1\public

12. After a malware incident, a Windows system displays evidence of operating system files that have been modified. Anti-malware definitions were updated, and a full scan was performed. What needs to be performed next to verify the integrity of the Windows operating system files?

    A. chkdsk /scan
    B. SFC /SCANNOW
    C. diskpart> RESCAN
    D. netstat -s

13. An administrator has created a new group policy and deployed it into the production environment. The administrator would now like to verify that the new group policy settings have been downloaded and are now enforced on user workstations. Which of the following commands will allow the administrator to verify that the group policy is working?

    A. shutdown -r
    B. dcdiag
    C. gpresult
    D. gpmc.msc
    E. gpupdate

1.3 Given a scenario, use features and tools of the Microsoft Windows 10 operating system (OS)

1. Prior to beginning an online certification exam, a user must run an agent to manage the online exam. The agent reports that an application named "Dell Diagnostics" is preventing the online exam from starting. How can the user quickly identify the background application and end the task?

    A. Go to Task Manager | Processes and End task
    B. Go to Task Manager | Startup and disable the startup process
    C. Go to Task Manager | Performance and End task
    D. Run Registry Editor and modify Computer\HKEY_CURRENT_USER

2. A technician is working on a computer when the PC suddenly experiences a Windows blue screen and restarts, apparently normally. To resolve the issue, the technician needs to determine which error message was displayed during the blue screen event. Which of the following should the technician use to help troubleshoot the issue?

    A. sfc
    B. msconfig
    C. regedit32
    D. eventvwr
    E. msinfo32

3. A recently terminated employee had made several undocumented changes to a manager's laptop computer. These changes are preventing Office 365 applications from receiving updates in a timely manner and have halted the automated disk defragmentation service. In order to ensure these services run automatically, which tool will BEST remediate the problems?

   A. Task Scheduler (taskschd.msc)
   B. Device Manager (devmgmt.msc)
   C. Performance Monitor (perfmon.msc)
   D. Certificate Manager (certmgr.msc)

4. Ann, a payroll manager, has complained of poor system performance on her company laptop computer. Applications are running slowly during certain parts of the day and occasionally in the evening, when she stays late to finish a task. The support technician allocated the ticket would like to monitor Ann's computer in an effort to identify the problem. Which of the following tools should the technician use to BEST analyze the computer's behavior?

   A. Computer Management
   B. Event Viewer
   C. Performance Monitor
   D. Task Manager

5. An employee returns from a six-month assignment working with a business partner. A computer technician would like to check whether the hardware vendor's BIOS updates were installed on the employee's laptop during the six-month period. Which tool would BEST display this information?

   A. System Information (msinfo32.exe)
   B. Resource Monitor (resmon.exe)
   C. System Configuration (msconfig.exe)
   D. Registry Editor (regedit.exe)

6. A service desk technician is allocated a ticket when a user's Windows workstation is running slowly. The computer boots up slowly and has long delays when executing large files. After checking the local hard disk, it appears to be near capacity. The technician needs to free up space and optimize access times for large files. Which two commands will BEST address this requirement? (Choose two.)

    A. Boot into safe mode
    B. Reboot the computer
    C. Defragment the hard drive
    D. Install device drivers
    E. Run Disk Cleanup

7. Due to a misconfigured workstation build template, workstations used by the sales team have a very small amount of storage space available. Technicians would like to view the currently allocated space for the main operating system drive and, if possible, extend the size of the drive. What graphical-based tool would be BEST for this task?

    A. Diskpart
    B. Disk Management
    C. Device Manager
    D. Disk Cleanup

8. A support technician is troubleshooting a helpdesk ticket raised by a sales executive. Applications that load on Windows startup are resulting in a wait time of nearly five minutes before the user is able to use the computer. What can be done to help the user avoid this long wait time?

    A. Use the System Configuration | Startup options to disable startup applications
    B. Delete entries listed under the registry key
    C. HKEY_LOCAL_MACHINE\SOFTWARE\Microsoft\Windows\CurrentVersion\Run
    D. Use Task Manager to disable all startup tasks currently set as enabled, then reboot the computer to ensure the issue has been resolved
    E. Open Task Manager | Startup and identify applications with High start-up impact. Disable these apps causing excessive boot times on startup.

9. A user from the human resources department raises a support ticket. The reason for the ticket is their desktop computer has been running slowly. The user reports that there have been no changes made to the PC. Which of the following tools should the support technician use to determine the cause of the speed reduction?

   A. Task Scheduler
   B. Windows Memory Diagnostic
   C. The Performance tab in Task Manager
   D. Disk Defragmenter

10. A department manager was accidentally assigned privileges that allowed them to make several unauthorized changes to their company laptop. One of the changes made was to add additional certificates to their laptop's Trusted Root Certificate Authorities store. The company is a government contractor, and these new certificates are not trusted as they do not meet government compliance regulations. How can a support technician ensure these certificate authorities will not be trusted by applications run on the manager's laptop?

    A. Remove the certificates from the Trusted Root Certificate Authorities store using certmgr.msc on the laptop
    B. Remove the certificates from the Trusted Root Certificate Authorities store using regedit.msc on the laptop
    C. Remove the certificates from the Trusted Root Certificate Authorities store using devmgmt.msc on the laptop
    D. Request the external certificate authorities put all of their certificates on a certificate revocation list (CRL)

1.4 Given a scenario, use the appropriate Microsoft Windows 10 Control Panel utility

1. A support technician is helping a user to solve a printing problem on their desktop computer. To test for a possible fix, it is necessary for the technician to disable the printer. Which of the following tools should the technician use to do this?

   A. Devices and Printers
   B. Sync Center
   C. Device Manger
   D. Power Options

2. A user calls the service desk after discovering they are unable to open a JPEG file in their pictures folder. When the user double-clicks on the file, instead of being able to view the picture, a command prompt window flashes up for a few seconds and then disappears. A technician views the file and sees the following:

   ```
   Name            Date modified Type          Size
   Sunshine.jpg    22/10/2020    Application   78KB
   ```

   Which of the following Windows Control Panel utilities should the technician use to resolve this issue?

   A. Default Programs

   B. Display Settings

   C. Device Manager

   D. Internet Options

3. Technicians must ensure that all users' web browser traffic is forwarded to the new proxy server. Select the Control Panel utility that will allow the relevant settings to be configured.

   A. Network and Sharing Centre | Change Adapter Settings

   B. Internet Options | Connections

   C. Device Manager

   D. Windows Defender Firewall | Advanced Settings

4. A support technician is resolving a support issue for a visually impaired user who is having issues with default colors and screen resolution. Which of the following utilities should the technician use?

   A. Device Manager

   B. System

   C. Ease of Access Center

   D. Programs and Features

5. A support technician installs a new webcam and downloads the drivers from the manufacturer's site, but the webcam fails to operate as expected. Which of the following options will BEST allow the technician to troubleshoot problems associated with the newly installed hardware?

   A. Services

   B. Device Manager

   C. Event Viewer

   D. Programs and Features

6. A project manager allowed a colleague to use their computer. Afterward, they notice that webpages are not being displayed as intended in the web browser. A technician troubleshoots the issue and discovers that many settings have been changed from their defaults. The technician must find a way to reset the web browser back to its default settings. Which Control Panel utility should the technician use?

    A. System
    B. Programs and Features
    C. Network and Sharing Center
    D. Internet Options

7. A technician needs to manually set a temporary IP address for five workstations in a branch office due to the DHCP server failing. Where will the technician find the controls to manage manual IP address assignment?

    A. Network and Sharing Center
    B. Sync Center
    C. User Account Control
    D. Credential Manager

8. A service provider supports a small organization with less than ten users. The organization is informed by their Internet Service Provider (ISP) that the email server has been changed to a different DNS name. A technician needs to visit the small organization to update configurations for all the local users. What Control Panel utility will allow the technician to make the changes?

    A. Internet Options
    B. Windows Defender Firewall
    C. User Accounts
    D. Mail

9. A research scientist user wants to connect a Windows 10 laptop computer to an external desktop monitor, keyboard, and mouse. When the scientist shuts the lid, the system shuts down. How can the system be configured to remain powered up whenever the lid is closed?

    A. Control Panel | Power | Do nothing
    B. Control Panel | Power | Sleep
    C. Control Panel | Power | Hibernate
    D. Control Panel | Power | Shut down

10. A user responsible for creating rich digital media has installed an additional sound card into their tower computer system. However, the audio output still uses the default built-in hardware. How can the user ensure the default playback device is configured for the new sound card?

    A. Device Manager | Audio inputs and outputs
    B. Control Panel | Sound
    C. Devices and Printers
    D. Speech Recognition

1.5 Given a scenario, use the appropriate Windows settings

1. A legal firm has recently installed a new word-processing application on all user desktops. Some users have raised support tickets, complaining that they do not get what they expect when trying to input special characters. Where should the support technician go to remediate this problem?

    A. Settings | Time & language
    B. Settings | Accessibility
    C. Settings | Personalization
    D. Settings | Apps

2. A support technician has been tasked with configuring a multiple-display setup for several members of the marketing team. After connecting all appropriate power and display cables, where should the technician go to configure the displays?

    A. Settings | Time & language
    B. Settings | Personalization
    C. Settings | System
    D. Settings | Bluetooth & devices

3. A sales manager has returned from a company event and complains that their laptop computer is displaying warning messages about a lack of disk space. The manager saved a lot of new data on the local storage and was required to install some software during the event. A technician must now try to fix the problem. Where should they go NEXT to support the user?

    A. Settings | Time & language
    B. Settings | Personalization
    C. Settings | System
    D. Control Panel | File History

4. A new company policy is being implemented and, prior to this policy being pushed out company-wide, the security settings must be configured and tested. One of the policy requirements is that when the screensaver locks the screen, a password must be used to unlock the screen. Where can this setting be accessed?

   A. Settings | Personalization | Lock screen
   B. Settings | Screen Timeout settings
   C. Control Panel | User Accounts
   D. Settings | Privacy & security | Lock screen

5. A company would like to use BitLocker to secure all Windows mobile devices, which will be centrally managed through group policy. In the pilot phase, a small number of laptops will be manually configured with this security feature. To do this, the Device Encryption settings will need to be accessed through which of the following paths?

   A. Settings | System
   B. Settings | Apps
   C. Settings | Privacy & security
   D. Settings | Network & internet

6. A small publishing company would like to configure all devices to connect through a newly purchased proxy server before accessing internet resources. Which Settings menu option will allow technicians to access the proxy server settings?

   A. Settings | System
   B. Settings | Apps
   C. Settings | Privacy & security
   D. Settings | Network & internet

7. A research and design company has a Corporate Owned Personally Enabled (COPE) policy in place. The Acceptable Use Policy (AUP) allows users to access personal email accounts, as well as their business email. Where can these settings be accessed?

   A. Control Panel | Internet Options
   B. Settings | Apps
   C. Settings | Privacy & security
   D. Settings | Accounts

8. A company is testing a new gaming application and seeks to gauge customer feedback by recording the customer experience during gaming sessions. What Windows settings would allow them to record customer reactions and feedback during a game?

   A. Settings | Gaming | Captures
   B. Control Panel | Autoplay
   C. Settings | Apps | Video Playback
   D. Control Panel | Sync Center

1.6 Given a scenario, configure Microsoft Windows networking features on a client/desktop

1. A network technician must add a new workstation to the Windows domain. What Windows settings would be used to switch from workgroup configuration to a domain-joined configuration?

   A. Settings | Accounts | Sign-in Options
   B. Control Panel | Region Settings
   C. Settings | System | About | Domain or Workgroup
   D. Control Panel | Credential Manager | Domain or Workgroup

2. A user contacts the service desk and reports that they cannot access any network resources. A support technician asks the user to open Command Prompt and type in IPCONFIG /ALL. The resulting output contains the 169.254.23.66 IP address. What is this address type and what is most likely the problem on the network?

   A. Private IPv4 address
   B. Automatic Private IP Addressing (APIPA)
   C. IPv6 link-local address
   D. DHCP service failure
   E. Active Directory service failure
   F. DNS service failure

3. A support ticket is raised by a user who is unable to share a newly installed departmental printer. The user has been assigned privileges to share folders and printers. The user is part of a workgroup NOT on the Windows domain. The user reports that email and internet browsing are working correctly. What setting is likely causing sharing error?

   A. The user does not have permission to share the printer
   B. The Network profile is set to public
   C. The Network interface is disabled
   D. The Network profile is set to private

4. What Windows feature can be configured to prevent P2P file-sharing applications from being used by members of the sales department?

   A. Windows Defender Firewall
   B. Windows Virus & threat protection
   C. Windows Secure Boot
   D. Windows BitLocker Drive Encryption

5. A user raises a support ticket after being prevented from adding an exception to Windows Defender Firewall. The user has an application launcher that they are attempting to run from their Downloads folder. Which type of user account allows for the modification of firewall rules?

   A. Guest Account
   B. Power Users
   C. Administrator
   D. Standard users

6. A technician is troubleshooting a user's workstation that has no network connectivity. After confirming that the current IP address is set to 169.254.44.89, what is the next action that the technician should take?

   A. Attempt to obtain an IP address using ipconfig /flushdns
   B. Attempt to obtain an IP address using ipconfig /all
   C. Attempt to obtain an IP address using ipconfig /renew
   D. Attempt to obtain an IP address using ipconfig /flushdhcp

7. A company has recently switched to a remote workforce model. The company supports many users in remote locations with expensive cellular and satellite connections. In order to minimize the costs for these links, the company would like to restrict monthly data usage. Which TWO configuration options will BEST allow the organization to restrict data use?

   A. Settings | System | Storage settings
   B. Advanced Network Settings | Data usage
   C. Advanced Network Settings | Network Interface | Metered Connection – On
   D. Advanced Network Settings | Advanced Sharing
   E. Advanced Network Settings | Network Interface | Flight Mode – On

8. A business unit has had a new network printer installed and directly connected to the Local Area Network (LAN) switch, and a technician must now configure several workstations to connect directly to the network printer. When adding a printer on the client workstations, which of the following options will allow the technician to connect the network printer?

   A. Select a shared printer by name
   B. Add a printer using an IP address or hostname
   C. Add a Bluetooth or wireless discoverable printer
   D. Connect directly with a USB cable

1.7 Given a scenario, apply application installation and configuration concepts

1. A technician is supporting a customer who has a Windows 10 x86 computer with 4GB of RAM. The customer needs to increase the available memory to 16GB RAM in order to install an engineering application. What should the technician recommend to the customer in order to meet this requirement?

   A. Install Ubuntu Linux
   B. Install a larger SSD
   C. Use a 64-bit architecture
   D. Install 16GB DDR4 RAM

2. Several members of the engineering design team have raised service tickets due to latency issues and poor performance when using a Computer-Aided Design (CAD) application. A hardware scan of the workstations reveals the following:

   - 64GB DDR4 Memory
   - 2GB Integrated Graphics
   - 1TB SSD HDD
   - Intel XEON 3.4GHZ 16-Core CPU

   What change can the engineers make that would be most beneficial when using the CAD application?

   A. Increase memory
   B. Install dedicated graphics cards
   C. Install faster CPUs
   D. Install faster HDDs

3. A marketing team is using a Customer Relationship Manager (CRM) system on their 32-bit Windows 8.1 workstations. After upgrading the workstations to Windows 11 64-bit edition, the team wants to use the same CRM application. Which of the following restrictions will they encounter when using a 32-bit application on a 64-bit OS?

   A. 32-bit applications will be restricted to 32GB of RAM
   B. 32-bit applications do not support multi-threading
   C. 32-bit applications will be restricted to 4GB of RAM
   D. 32-bit applications do not support multi-tasking

4. Following the upgrade of a customer's Windows 8 operating system to Windows 10, an application now fails to launch. An error message is displayed, stating that the application was written for Windows 8 and is incompatible with the current operating system. What can a support technician offer as a quick fix for this problem?

   A. Contact the application vendor to investigate whether an updated version can be purchased
   B. Set the application compatibility setting to Windows 8
   C. Boot Windows into safe mode to run the application
   D. Set the application compatibility setting to Windows 7

5. A software development company has designed a Computer-Aided Design (CAD) application at great expense. They need a control to ensure that each copy of the application will only run from a licensed workstation. What would be the MOST effective way to protect the application from theft?

   A. Make each customer agree to strict licensing requirements during installation

   B. Deploy an external hardware token for each copy of the application

   C. Make each customer sign an Acceptable Use Policy (AUP)

   D. Only sell the application to trustworthy customers

1.8 Explain common OS types and their purposes

1. An engineer needs to format a USB storage device in preparation to copy 20GB of data from an Ubuntu Linux server to a Windows system. Which of the following filesystems will the engineer MOST likely use?

   A. FAT32

   B. ext4

   C. NTFS

   D. exFAT

2. A recent risk assessment has highlighted a security issue, wherein legacy equipment has a 32-bit edition of Windows XP as its embedded OS. The company does not receive any quality or security updates for this operating system. What term would BEST describe this operating system?

   A. End of Life (EOL)

   B. Incompatible operating system

   C. 32-bit operating system

   D. Vendor-supported operating system

3. A school is looking to invest in easy-to-support technology for student workstations. The chosen devices will run a lightweight operating system based on a browser interface. What would be the BEST choice to meet these requirements?

   A. Linux

   B. macOS

   C. ChromeOS

   D. Windows

4. A company wants to streamline its customer support after a recent inventory assessment reported that four different operating systems were in use by servers, workstations, and mobile devices. To compound the issue, there were also five different versions of Android OS and three different versions of iOS in use. The company would like to choose a single operating system to support servers, workstations, and handheld devices. Which of the following is the BEST choice?

   A. Linux
   B. iOS
   C. Windows
   D. ChromeOS

5. After installing the most recent version of Red Hat Linux on a datacenter server, additional storage is added. The new hard drive must be formatted with a filesystem that supports 40TB of storage, and it is also anticipated that the storage will need to be regularly defragmented. Which of the following is the BEST choice of filesystem?

   A. FAT32
   B. ext3
   C. NTFS
   D. ext4

6. A marketing company is looking to deploy smartphones to their workforce. The smartphone must support an operating system based on Linux, as developers will create applications for the company and have experience with Linux operating systems. Which of the following Os's would be the BEST choice for this?

   A. iOS
   B. SUSE Linux
   C. Android OS
   D. Windows mobile

1.9 Given a scenario, perform OS installations and upgrades in a diverse OS environment

1. A support engineer is tasked with upgrading multiple desktop computers to Windows 10. However, they are only able to obtain a single copy of the installation media, and so they propose that they perform the upgrade over the network. Which of the following boot methods allows such an upgrade?

    A. SSD
    B. Optical drive
    C. Flash drive
    D. PXE

2. A pharmaceutical company needs to deploy 500 new Windows 11 desktops in the most efficient way. The process needs to be automated so that the technicians' time spent on this installation is minimized. What installation would be the BEST choice?

    A. Remote network installation
    B. Repair installation
    C. Clean installation
    D. Unattended installation

3. During a manual installation of Windows 11 x64 on a brand-new desktop computer, a technician must select a partitioning scheme for the 12TB hard disk drive. Which partition format would make the best use of the available storage?

    A. ext4
    B. MBR
    C. GPT
    D. APFS

4. A technician is helping a remote customer upgrade their Windows workstation to the latest edition. The customer would like to retain all their applications and settings. Which option will upgrade the system and meet the customer's requirements?

    A. Clean install
    B. Repair install
    C. Unattended install
    D. In-place upgrade

5. Which was the first Microsoft Windows operating system with a mandatory requirement for feature upgrades?

   A. Windows 11
   B. Windows 8.1
   C. Windows 10
   D. Windows 7

6. A large multinational manufacturer has a user base of 6,000 Windows desktops and would like to create a baseline configuration so that all desktops have identical features and applications. What would be the BEST solution for this organization?

   A. Upgrade
   B. Clean install
   C. Image deployment
   D. Repair installation

7. An installation team is deploying new images using pxe boot. In order to minimize the load on the deployment server, they are deploying images to only 30 workstations simultaneously. There is a possibility that this process may cause bottlenecks. What should the team most closely monitor?

   A. Impact on users
   B. Impact on the network segment
   C. Impact on the DHCP scope
   D. Impact on workstations

8. A technician is helping the company upgrade a mixture of laptops and desktops to run Windows 11. In order to support larger volume sizes and multiple partitions, it has been decided that hard drives will be configured using GPT partitioning. In order to support Windows 11 and GPT disks, what MINIMUM hardware specifications must be in place? (Choose two.)

   A. 32GB RAM
   B. UEFI
   C. TPM 2.0
   D. LEGACY BIOS
   E. 8-core CPU

9. A Windows desktop computer fails to boot following a power loss and unexpected system shutdown. What should the technician try FIRST to see if the system can be recovered?

   A. Unattended installation
   B. Repair installation
   C. Image deployment installation
   D. Remote installation

10. Technicians are preparing to upgrade departmental workstations to the latest Windows OS. In order to avoid problems during the upgrade, they would like to see a report listing potential missing hardware features that may prevent an upgrade.

    A. Microsoft Windows HCL (hardware compatibility list)
    B. Microsoft Windows PC Health Check App
    C. Microsoft Windows System Information
    D. Microsoft Windows Task Manager

1.10 Identify common features and tools of the macOS/desktop OS

1. Several users in the publishing department would like to have access to Skype, as this is the standard tool within the organization for conducting meetings and making calls with colleagues. The users in the publishing department all use macOS and cannot find the Skype application in the Apple App Store, but it is available as a download from the official Microsoft site. What file format should the users select to ensure the Skype application can be installed on their macOS computers?

   A. MSI
   B. EXE
   C. DMG
   D. APK

2. A support technician is helping a user to restore deleted files from a recent backup. The user's workstation runs on macOS, and the user needs to take a look through the files on the backup before restoring some of the files. Which macOS utility will be MOST useful for this task?

   A. Keychain
   B. Finder
   C. Mission Control
   D. Explorer

3. A user raises a support ticket as they are unsure how to create automated backups onto an external hard disk that they have purchased. The client workstation is running the latest version of macOS. What tool or application would be the BEST choice for scheduling automatic backups onto the drive?

    A. File History
    B. Time Machine
    C. Windows Backup
    D. Mission Control

4. A technician is providing support to the user of a macOS computer on which the e-mail application is unresponsive. What feature will allow the technician to view a list of currently active applications and shut down the unresponsive application?

    A. Force Quit menu
    B. Task Manager
    C. Task List
    D. Control Panel

5. A research department recently purchased MacBook computers for departmental users. Due to highly sensitive data being stored on these computers, management is asking for additional security for locally stored content. What feature would be a good choice to secure the local data drive?

    A. iCloud
    B. Keychain
    C. FileVault
    D. BitLocker

6. macOS is based upon what source code?

    A. Linux
    B. Android
    C. Unix
    D. ChromeOS

7. A user visits several different internet sites where a user account and password must be entered to access the site. The user would like to automate this process so that, when they sign in to their macOS computer, they will not need to enter additional passwords to access these sites. What macOS feature will allow the use and management of multiple credentials?

    A. Mission Control
    B. Spotlight
    C. Keychain
    D. Dock

8. A technician has been asked to uninstall a large application that is no longer used on a manager's MacBook Pro. How can they uninstall the application?

    A. Use Finder to locate the application and delete the application folder
    B. Use Mission Control to locate the application and delete the application window
    C. Use the App Store to remove the unwanted application
    D. Use Finder to locate the application and move it to Trash

9. A marketing manager raises a support request when their macOS laptop fails to boot, displaying the following error message:

    ```
    No bootable device - insert boot disk and press any key
    ```

    What should the technician do FIRST?

    A. Access the Recovery menu by holding Command + R during boot and choose the Disk Utility
    B. Access the Recovery menu by holding Command + R during boot and choose Reinstall macOS
    C. Access the Recovery menu by booting from DVD installation media and choose the Disk Utility
    D. Boot into safe mode using Command + R during the boot and choose Restore from the Time Machine Backup

10. After installing a number of applications on a user's MacBook Pro, the technician deletes a number of DMG and PKG files from the downloads folder. Upon running Activity Monitor, there does not appear to be much free disk space. What can the technician do to free up disk space?

    A. Use the Trash application to permanently delete the files
    B. Use the Recycle Bin application to permanently delete the files
    C. Use the Disk Cleaner application to identify unwanted files
    D. Use Disk Utility to split the hard drive into separate partitions

11. A user would like to customize the list of available utilities and applications that they see after successfully logging on to their MacBook Pro. What feature should they customize?

    A. Mission Control
    B. Dock
    C. Start menu
    D. Toolbar

12. A technician must perform a number of tasks to configure a macOS workstation before assigning it to a user. They need to configure network settings, set up a printer, and configure backups. Which folder will host these configuration utilities?

    A. Mission Control
    B. System Preferences
    C. Dock
    D. Disk Utilities

13. A user wants to use multiple desktops on their macOS workstation. Which of the following methods will allow the user to switch between desktops? (Choose two.)

    A. Control + right or left arrow keys
    B. Select the desktop from the Dock using the mouse or trackpad
    C. Enter Mission Control and choose the desired desktop using the mouse or trackpad
    D. Command + spacebar

1.11 Identify common features and tools of the Linux client/desktop OS

1. A technician is assisting the HR manager in protecting a number of sensitive files that had been saved in the HR documents folder. The technician is able to see the following output:

    ```
    -rw-r-----  1 mark HumanResources 0 Jan 9 14:37 Employee-Conduct
    -rw-r-----  1 mark HumanResources 0 Jan 9 14:37 Employee-Details
    -rw-r-----  1 mark HumanResources 0 Jan 9 14:36 Employee-Health
    -rw-r-----  1 mark Sales          0 Jan 9 14:37 Employee-Reports
    ```

    A. Which command did the technician use to view the output, and which command would BEST secure sensitive file(s)? (There are TWO answers.)
    B. dir /L
    C. sudo chown :HumanResources Employee-Reports

- D. ls -l
- E. sudo chmod 664 Employee-Reports
- F. pwd
- G. sudo mv Employee-Reports ../Sales

2. A technician must log into the Linux print server and restart the print service. What command-line syntax will they use if they want to make use of root privileges during the session?

- A. pwd
- B. grep
- C. samba
- D. sudo

3. A technician is investigating user complaints of latency when accessing applications on the Ubuntu Linux server. The technician reviews the following output in an attempt to see what might be causing this latency:

```
Tasks: 140 total,   1 running, 139 sleeping,   0 stopped,   0 zombie
%Cpu(s):  4.0 us,   2.6 sy,   0.0 ni, 93.4 id,   0.0 wa,   0.0 hi,   0.0 si,   0.0 st
MiB Mem :   3930.4 total,   2531.8 free,    643.7 used,    754.9 buff/cache
MiB Swap:    975.0 total,    975.0 free,      0.0 used.   3041.8 avail Mem

    PID USER      PR  NI    VIRT    RES    SHR S  %CPU  %MEM     TIME+ COMMAND
   3841 root      20   0  404048  44664  34388 S   3.0   1.1   0:03.42 xfce4-taskmanag
    534 root      20   0  372876 137032  53220 S   2.3   3.4   0:12.53 Xorg
     12 root      20   0       0      0      0 S   0.3   0.0   0:00.27 ksoftirqd/0
   3473 root      20   0       0      0      0 I   0.3   0.0   0:00.45 kworker/0:0-events
   3633 root      20   0  351168  28412  20912 S   0.3   0.7   0:00.39 panel-13-cpugra
   3864 root      20   0  405764  82144  63056 S   0.3   2.0   0:00.46 qterminal
   3878 root      20   0   10244   3708   3096 R   0.3   0.1   0:00.24 top
      1 root      20   0  164388  10780   7988 S   0.0   0.3   0:01.50 systemd
      2 root      20   0       0      0      0 S   0.0   0.0   0:00.01 kthreadd
      3 root       0 -20       0      0      0 I   0.0   0.0   0:00.00 rcu_gp
      4 root       0 -20       0      0      0 I   0.0   0.0   0:00.00 rcu_par_gp
      6 root       0 -20       0      0      0 I   0.0   0.0   0:00.00 kworker/0:0H-events_highpri
      9 root       0 -20       0      0      0 I   0.0   0.0   0:00.00 mm_percpu_wq
     10 root      20   0       0      0      0 S   0.0   0.0   0:00.00 rcu_tasks_rude_
     11 root      20   0       0      0      0 S   0.0   0.0   0:00.00 rcu_tasks_trace
     13 root      20   0       0      0      0 I   0.0   0.0   0:00.24 rcu_sched
     14 root      rt   0       0      0      0 S   0.0   0.0   0:00.38 migration/0
     15 root      20   0       0      0      0 S   0.0   0.0   0:00.00 cpuhp/0
     17 root      20   0       0      0      0 S   0.0   0.0   0:00.00 kdevtmpfs
     18 root       0 -20       0      0      0 I   0.0   0.0   0:00.00 netns
```

Figure 1.1: Linux performance data example

What command did the technician use to view this performance data?

A. nano
B. dig
C. top
D. ps

4. What command can be used to delete a file or folder on a Linux operating system?

A. chmod
B. man
C. df
D. rm

5. A developer is worried that they may be running short of available disk space on their local system. They run a command at the prompt that results in the following output:

```
Filesystem    1K-blocks    Used        Available   Use%    Mounted
on
/dev/sda1     263174212    230887666   32286546    87%     /
```

What Linux command have they used?

A. ps
B. top
C. df
D. ip

6. A technician provides support to a remote user who is operating on an Ubuntu Linux workstation with NO graphical interface. The technician needs to access a terminal session securely as the system contains sensitive intellectual property. They will need to use a number of command-line tools during the session. What will allow the technician to perform this task?

A. RDP (Remote Desktop Protocol)
B. SSH (secure shell)
C. telnet (teletype network)
D. cp (copy command)

7. What is the purpose of the man command when it precedes a command-line interface (CLI) command in Linux?

   A. It elevates the users' privileges so they can perform administrative tasks
   B. It automatically assigns the manager privilege to the command
   C. It displays help in the form of a manual
   D. It enters maintenance mode for the command

8. A department would like their Windows 10-based workstations to be able to access shared files on an Ubuntu Linux server using mapped drives. What service would allow for this functionality?

   A. Install the telnet service on the Ubuntu server
   B. Install the samba service on the Windows 10 workstations
   C. Install Windows File and Print Sharing on the Ubuntu server
   D. Install samba service on the Ubuntu server

9. Which command allows an administrator to download and install new application packages on a Red Hat Linux workstation?

   A. grep
   B. ps
   C. yum
   D. dig

10. The Human Resources manager is searching the HR folder for a file called Employee-Details. Once found, they need to search the file for information regarding Joe Smith. What TWO commands were used to generate the following output?

    ```
    -rw-r--r-- 1 mark HumanResources 263 Jan  9 18:24 Employee-Details
    Joe Smith   6 Beacon Drive, Edinburgh EH1 4DL    0131 789765
    ```

    A. ls -l Employee-Details
    B. dir /L Employee-Details
    C. cat "Joe Smith" Employee-Details
    D. grep "Joe Smith" Employee-Details

11. A technician is troubleshooting a networking issue on an Ubuntu Linux workstation. The technician issues commands in the terminal window, resulting in the following output:

    ```
    eth0: <BROADCAST,MULTICAST,UP,LOWER_UP> mtu 1500 qdisc mq state
    UP group default qlen 1000
    link/ether 00:15:5d:30:49:57 brd ff:ff:ff:ff:ff:ff
    inet 172.22.64.215/20 brd 172.22.79.255 scope global eth0
    inet6 fe80::215:5dff:fe30:4957/64 scope link

    ANSWER SECTION:
    www.google.com.         0       IN      A       142.250.114.104
    www.google.com.         0       IN      A       142.250.114.106
    www.google.com.         0       IN      A       142.250.114.99
    www.google.com.         0       IN      A       142.250.114.147
    www.google.com.         0       IN      A       142.250.114.103
    www.google.com.         0       IN      A       142.250.114.105
    ;; Query time: 130 msec
    ```

    What TWO Linux network commands were used to generate the output?

    A. ip address
    B. ipconfig
    C. nslookup
    D. dig
    E. tracert
    F. ping

12. A developer raises a support ticket as they cannot access a file shared from a colleague's Red Hat Linux workstation. What command would be BEST to assign permissions for the file?

    A. grep
    B. chmod
    C. ip address
    D. pwd

2
Security

Introduction

This chapter will test an exam candidate's knowledge of security concepts, procedures, and security best practices. Threats and threat actors are constantly changing, and security professionals must understand how to recognize threats and mitigate them in different ways. Common environments that need to be secured include wireless networks, **small office/home office** (**SOHO**) networks, enterprise networks, and situations where securing remote access is crucial. Mobile devices and support for IoT also present many challenges for security professionals. It is important to understand the threats posed by social engineering, often referred to as hacking humans (where users are targeted). To mitigate these threats, it is important to recognize the correct controls that need to be enabled and to understand the correct response to specific threats.

In order to be successful in the CompTIA A+ Core 2 (220-1102) certification exam, candidates must be familiar with the following objectives:

- 2.1 Summarize various security measures and their purposes
- 2.2 Compare and contrast wireless security protocols and authentication methods
- 2.3 Given a scenario, detect, remove, and prevent malware using the appropriate tools and methods
- 2.4 Explain common social-engineering attacks, threats, and vulnerabilities
- 2.5 Given a scenario, manage and configure basic security settings in the Microsoft Windows OS
- 2.6 Given a scenario, configure a workstation to meet best practices for security
- 2.7 Explain common methods for securing mobile and embedded devices
- 2.8 Given a scenario, use common data destruction and disposal methods
- 2.9 Given a scenario, configure appropriate security settings on small office/home office (SOHO) wireless and wired networks
- 2.10 Given a scenario, install and configure browsers and relevant security settings

The rest of this chapter is committed to practice. For each of the previously defined concepts, you will be given a series of questions designed to test your knowledge of each core 2 objective as defined by the official certification exam guidance for this domain. These questions will test the candidate's knowledge of how to implement security best practices within an organization.

Practice Exam Questions

2.1 Summarize various security measures and their purposes

1. What is the purpose of a motion sensor in a security system?

   A. To detect the presence of unauthorized individuals or objects

   B. To control the temperature of the surrounding environment

   C. To amplify the sound of nearby movements

   D. To adjust the brightness of the lighting system

2. A CISO is proposing to use an app on company-deployed smartphones as a soft token. What is the purpose of a soft token?

   A. Generating secure passwords

   B. Authenticating user identity

   C. Encrypting data

   D. Blocking malicious websites

3. A call center manager is proposing to support an initiative where workers will be able to work from home. The security team is discussing methods that will allow the use of personal equipment and the control and management of employees' personal devices. Which of the following controls allows the team to manage this infrastructure and ensure users are given guidance to support this initiative? (Choose two.)

   A. Fingerprint scanner

   B. Multifactor authentication (MFA)

   C. BYOD policy

   D. Equipment locks

   E. MDM policy

   F. Time-based login policies

4. A chief information security manager (CISO) is reviewing the security controls that will best prevent a user from gaining unauthorized physical access to the server room. What two controls would best address this requirement?

   A. Access control vestibule
   B. Alarm
   C. Video surveillance
   D. Bollards
   E. Motion sensors
   F. Door locks

5. A cloud service provider (CSP) has recently added a number of security controls in response to a recent security audit. These controls have required the installation of perimeter fencing and security gates and additional guards to be employed to secure all external entry points. The audit also highlighted the lack of detective controls, within the CSP data center, in the event the perimeter security is breached. What detective controls would BEST address this requirement? (Choose two.)

   A. Access control vestibule
   B. Badge reader
   C. Video surveillance
   D. Equipment locks
   E. Motion sensors
   F. Door locks

6. A security team must design controls to ensure the business will be compliant with stringent requirements regarding safeguarding customer payment card details. Servers hosting customer card payment details will be physically secured in a server room. Access to the server room needs to be controlled using two-factor authentication (2FA). Currently, administrators access the server room using a fingerprint reader. What could be used in addition to fingerprints to support two-factor access control?

   A. Smart cards
   B. Retina scanner
   C. Palmprint scanner
   D. Motion detector

7. A security team is evaluating additional security controls to ensure physical equipment, including storage devices, cannot be removed by authorized members of staff from the internal data center. What control would allow security guards to be alerted if there is an attempt to remove equipment from the data center?

    A. Access control vestibule
    B. Video surveillance
    C. Equipment locks
    D. Lighting
    E. Magnetometers

8. A network administrator onboards a new user who has joined the sales team as a junior sales executive. They have created a unique account for the user and added the user to a security group with limited access rights. What best describes why this process would be adopted?

    A. To adhere to the principle of least privilege
    B. To enforce access control lists (ACLs)
    C. To ensure the user is using multifactor authentication (MFA)
    D. To support the use of organizational units

9. When a user logs in to the Windows domain, an automated process is run that assigns the user a default storage location on a Windows server. The user is able to access this network link through the explorer interface. What describes this feature and how the system automates the creation of the link? (Choose two.)

    A. Use of a login script
    B. Management of security groups
    C. Multifactor authentication
    D. Use of home folders
    E. Organizational units

10. When a user needs to access company assets from a laptop computer, they must have access to an app on their mobile phone. The app provides a time-based one-time password (TOTP) that must be provided along with a log-in ID and password. What best describes the technology used? (Choose two.)

    A. Principle of least privilege
    B. Multifactor authentication (MFA)
    C. Short Message Service (SMS)
    D. Voice call verification
    E. Use of an authenticator application

11. When a user authenticates their Active Directory account from any workstation, they can access all their common folders (Desktop, Documents, Pictures, and more). The folders contain all the up-to-date content that they saved. What two Windows features allow for centralized storage of user data and transparent network access to this data?

    A. Login script
    B. Group Policy settings
    C. Organizational units
    D. Home folder
    E. Folder redirection

12. A bank needs to ensure customers can provide an additional authentication factor when authorizing payments during online banking. The bank intends to support this using a second out-of-band mobile phone authentication. What 2FA methods require the user to have access to a mobile phone? (Choose two.)

    A. Email verification link
    B. Short Message Service (SMS)
    C. Voice call verification
    D. Use of a hard token

13. Which of the following is true about Active Directory security groups?

    A. Security groups are used to assign permissions to shared resources
    B. Security groups are used to organize user accounts
    C. Security groups are used for email distribution lists
    D. Security groups are used to control network connectivity

14. An administrator is creating an Active Directory (AD) organizational unit (OU) for the new research department. What is the primary purpose of an OU in Active Directory?

    A. It determines the physical location of a user or computer object
    B. It defines the security policies for a domain
    C. It groups related objects for easier administration
    D. It provides the domain name resolution services

2.2 Compare and contrast wireless security protocols and authentication methods

1. A security consultant is advising a small business on the subject of securing the Wi-Fi network when giving access to customers. The small business only has access to a wireless router provided by the internet service provider (ISP). The business intends to print a code on the bottom of till receipts to allow customers to access the Wi-Fi. Which wireless standard offers the highest levels of security when a customer needs to access the Wi-Fi using a supplied passcode/passkey?

    A. Wi-Fi Protected Access 2 (WPA2)
    B. Wi-Fi Protected Access 3 (WPA3)
    C. Temporal Key Integrity Protocol (TKIP)
    D. Advanced Encryption Standard (AES)

2. A security team is planning for the deployment of Wi-Fi for internal business units. It is anticipated that over 50% of the workforce will need secure access to Wi-Fi. Management is insisting that all users should use unique domain credentials to authenticate onto the network. What service can be deployed to ensure user authentication requests are securely passed back to the Active Directory?

    A. WPS
    B. WEP Open
    C. RADIUS
    D. WPA-PSK

3. A technician is configuring a wireless LAN and must ensure that the configuration of the Wi-Fi router supports the latest encryption standards. What configuration choice would BEST protect confidential data sent over Wi-Fi?

   A. WEP
   B. WPA2-TKIP
   C. WPA2-AES
   D. WPA Open

2.3 Given a scenario, detect, remove, and prevent malware using the appropriate tools and methods

1. What do boot sector viruses target?

   A. Files stored on external hard drives
   B. The master boot record or boot sector of a computer
   C. Network routers and switches
   D. User passwords and login credentials

2. What is the primary purpose of a keylogger?

   A. To mine cryptocurrencies
   B. To delete files and disrupt system operations
   C. To track user activities and collect sensitive information
   D. To capture and record keystrokes on a computer

3. What are the typical signs that a ransomware attack is taking place?

   A. An attacker is exploiting software vulnerabilities
   B. An attacker is tracking user activities and collecting sensitive information
   C. An attacker is encrypting files and demanding a ransom for their release
   D. An attacker is hijacking a computer's boot process

4. Technicians are investigating an issue with a sales department laptop computer. Windows Defender Security features are turned off and when the technicians attempt to re-enable the features, the settings are reversed. What type of malware may be the cause of the issue?

   A. Trojan
   B. Rootkit
   C. Virus
   D. Spyware
   E. Ransomware

5. Security staff are preparing a set of automated actions to assist the service desk when dealing with malware incidents. They propose to create a number of playbooks to assist the team. One scenario requires the entire hard drive to be erased and the OS to be re-installed. What malware type would require this action?

   A. Trojan
   B. Rootkit
   C. Virus
   D. Spyware

6. A user calls the service desk, complaining that after opening a file sent by a co-worker, they can no longer access any local folders. In addition, they see pop-up messages displaying a telephone number and requests to make payments to fix the problem. What has likely caused this issue on the user's computer?

   A. Trojan
   B. Rootkit
   C. Virus
   D. Spyware
   E. Ransomware

7. After installing a number of technical preventative controls on the company network, in order to reduce malware incidents, there has been a 90% reduction in infected systems. The controls consist of spam filters, content inspection, and endpoint detection and response (EDR). In addition to these technical controls, what would be most effective in further reducing malware incidents?

   A. User education regarding rootkits
   B. User education regarding viruses
   C. User education regarding common threats
   D. User education regarding spyware

8. A user calls the service desk after receiving a number of messages in the Windows 10 action center. The messages appear to be non-malicious and are being generated by the web browser. What action would be the BEST to remediate this issue?

   A. Disable the web browser

   B. Perform a full anti-virus scan

   C. Block all outgoing traffic on ports 80 and 443

   D. Delete and re-install the OS

9. A recent spate of spam emails has targeted the finance team. The emails appear to originate from genuine suppliers and often contain links to reset login details. What course of action will BEST help to reduce these incidents?

   A. Software firewalls

   B. Anti-phishing training

   C. User education regarding common threats

   D. OS re-installation

10. After installing a new video driver from an unofficial third-party internet site, a user's workstation is exhibiting strange behavior. The workstation is running slowly, and the user reports no other changes have been made apart from the updated driver. What action will allow a technician to BEST determine whether the driver is the cause of the behavior?

    A. Reboot the workstation into recovery mode, select Troubleshoot\Advanced options\Startup settings, and choose to enable Safe Mode

    B. Perform a full anti-virus scan

    C. Ensure anti-malware is updated

    D. Configure Windows Firewall to block all outgoing connections

11. A company has recently seen a high number of user accounts compromised. The accounts belong to the engineering team, which hot desks using a limited number of engineering workstations. Despite the user passwords being reset, the problem persists. What is the MOST likely reason for the accounts being compromised?

    A. Remote access trojan

    B. Rootkit replacing key OS files

    C. Hardware keyloggers on the engineering workstations

    D. Cryptominers stealing user credentials

12. A number of users recently returned from a marketing event with digital promotional materials provided on USB media. The service desk received a number of calls from the users complaining that applications are slow to load and their workstations are unacceptably slow. After investigation, it appears that CPU/GPU activity is running at 100%. What type of malware is MOST likely affecting the users?

    A. Spyware
    B. Cryptominers
    C. Keyloggers
    D. Boot sector virus

2.4 Explain common social-engineering attacks, threats, and vulnerabilities

1. A chief information officer (CIO) receives an email from the chief executive officer (CEO) requesting confidential information to be supplied. The email appears to originate from a personal email address that the CIO does not recognize. What type of attack is this likely to be?

    A. Phishing
    B. Dumpster diving
    C. Shoulder surfing
    D. Whaling

2. A user is picking up printed documents from the centralized office printer. Despite the large number of other users in the crowded print room, after a wait in line, the user is able to successfully type in their password to pull down the print job. Later, the user is warned of a suspicious login using the same credentials. What social engineering event likely took place?

    A. Phishing
    B. Vishing
    C. Shoulder surfing
    D. Whaling

3. A team of contractors arrives on site, wearing shirts and jackets with the logo of a well-known support contractor. The contractors say they are responding to error messages that have been received from the bank's critical servers in the data center. There is no record of a support call being generated. What is the likely vector of attack?

   A. Tailgating
   B. Impersonation
   C. Dumpster diving
   D. Evil twin

4. A user raises a support ticket complaining about slow Wi-Fi speeds, local mapped drives, and printers not being available. On several occasions, the user has been asked for credentials when connected to internet sites. The user suspects that their online accounts may have been compromised. What is the likely threat vector?

   A. Tailgating
   B. Impersonation
   C. Dumpster diving
   D. Evil twin

5. A courier wearing a high-visibility jacket carrying a parcel follows an employee into an unmanned reception area. Later, it is discovered that laptop computers and a tablet have been reported as missing or stolen. What was the likely cause of this security breach?

   A. Tailgating
   B. Impersonation
   C. Dumpster diving
   D. Evil twin

6. An online retailer receives multiple complaints that customers cannot access the site. Upon investigation, engineers discover thousands of remote connections to the site's web servers. The connections do not appear to be genuine customers logging in to the site. What is the likely threat?

   A. Distributed denial of service (DDoS)
   B. Denial of service (DoS)
   C. Zero-day attack
   D. Spoofing

7. A user is attempting to log in to their online banking site, but the web browser reports an error regarding the website certificate. The URL in the browser does not appear to be the normal URL that the user was expecting. What type of attack is likely occurring?

    A. On-path attack
    B. Insider threat
    C. Structured Query Language (SQL) injection
    D. Cross-site scripting (XSS)

8. A security engineer is investigating logs on the customer-facing web application server. One of the entries is causing the engineer concern. The following string is logged:

    ```
    <script>alert('http://malwaresite.com/javascriptcookiestealer.com')</script>
    ```

    What type of attack has likely occurred?

    A. Spoofing
    B. Structured Query Language (SQL) injection
    C. Cross-site scripting (XSS)
    D. Zero-day attack

9. An attacker is able to target a vulnerability present on a web server where there is no available patch or update. What type of threat does this describe?

    A. Insider threat
    B. Structured Query Language (SQL) injection
    C. Cross-site scripting (XSS)
    D. Zero-day attack

10. An attacker is able to log on to a website, despite the fact that the attacker has not been assigned valid credentials. The logs indicate that the attacker was able to access the site using the first account stored in a table on the database server. The following log entry was recorded around the time of the incident:

    ```
    SELECT * FROM Users WHERE Username=foo' OR '1' = '1' AND Password='pass' OR '1' = '1'
    ```

    What type of attack has occurred?

    A. Brute-force attack
    B. Dictionary attack
    C. Structured Query Language (SQL) injection
    D. Cross-site scripting (XSS)

2.5 Given a scenario, manage and configure basic security settings in the Microsoft Windows OS

1. An administrator is tasked with configuring permissions for the marketing folder on a user's Windows 10 laptop. The permissions should allow the marketing team to have read permissions on the folder. What should the administrator configure to allow marketing users network access to the folder?

    A. Set NTFS permissions to read for the marketing group
    B. Choose to share the folder and give the marketing group read network access
    C. Select the folder attributes and ensure read-only is checked
    D. Set NTFS permissions to modify for the marketing group

2. A help desk receives a call from a home user who would like to synchronize their preferences, themes, and browser shortcuts when signing in to different Windows devices. Currently, the user has a unique local account configured on each device. The user would also prefer to have a single account for all devices. What feature would satisfy the user's request?

    A. Have the user create a Microsoft account and enable this on each device
    B. Create a local account on the current device and copy the account to all devices
    C. Have the user sign on with the default guest account on each device
    D. Have the user sign in to the Edge browser and enable synchronization options

3. A standard user is assigned a second privileged account that can be used to reset other users' passwords when requested. The user has access to the Active Directory Users and Computers (ADUC) console. What would be the recommended best security practice when considering the use of the two accounts? (Choose two.)

    A. Always sign in to the workstation using a standard user account
    B. Use the run as administrator option when using the privileged account
    C. Always sign in to the workstation using the privileged user account
    D. Use the run as standard user option when using the privileged account

4. A user has requested to store sensitive information on a removable USB drive. Company policy states that all removable storage must support data encryption and all data must be encrypted at rest. What Windows feature can be used to meet the company policy?

    A. Pretty Good Privacy (PGP)
    B. BitLocker to Go
    C. Extensible File Allocation Table (exFAT) filesystem
    D. User Account Control (UAC)

5. A finance manager has raised a support ticket. They would like to protect sensitive files stored on Windows 10 workstations. The files contain customer details and are stored in a single folder. The files must be encrypted to meet security best practices. What can a support technician configure to protect the folder?

   A. Enable Encrypting File System (EFS) for the folder
   B. Enable BitLocker Drive Encryption for the folder
   C. Enable BitLocker to Go on the folder
   D. Ensure NTFS permissions are set to read for the finance tea

6. A technician is attempting to manually set an IP address on a server's network interface card. They are prompted with a security dialog box, asking whether they approve of the application making changes to the computer. What has likely required this extra verification?

   A. Windows Defender anti-virus
   B. User Account Control (UAC)
   C. Multifactor authentication (MFA)
   D. Windows Defender Firewall

7. A technician has quarantined a user's Windows 10 laptop after an unknown process was found running on the system. The process is identified as malicious and is documented on many anti-virus vendor sites. The user has been using the laptop on a network with no internet access for 2 months. What should the technician do next?

   A. Update Windows Defender definition files and run a full anti-virus scan
   B. Manually remove the malicious file and return the laptop to the user
   C. Use a system restore to revert to the last restore point
   D. Wipe the system and perform a fresh Windows installation

8. A recently installed database application has been configured and tested on a departmental server. The departmental users cannot connect to the application across the network. A technician performs a port scan on the server and observes the following output:

   ```
   Nmap scan report for 192.168.0.22
   Host is up (0.000086s latency).
   Not shown: 994 closed ports
   PORT      STATE     SERVICE
   135/tcp   open      msrpc
   139/tcp   open      netbios-ssn
   445/tcp   open      microsoft-ds
   514/tcp   open      shell
   3306/tcp  filtered  mysql
   ```

What should the technician do next to allow users to access the database application?

A. Deactivate the Windows Defender firewall on the server

B. Activate the Windows Defender firewall on the users' workstations

C. Add a firewall rule to allow inbound traffic to port 3306 on the server

D. Re-install the database application on the server and perform a system restart

2.6 Given a scenario, configure a workstation to meet best practices for security

1. A senior manager who is attending a conference needs to ensure that confidential data stored on a laptop computer is secured when the laptop is shut down. What will best secure the data at rest?

   A. BitLocker full disk encryption

   B. Use Pretty Good Privacy (PGP) to encrypt the system files

   C. Restrict login times

   D. Use timeout/screen lock

2. An administrator must ensure that user accounts are added to groups, giving only the necessary privileges needed to carry out assigned tasks. What best practice will ensure that users do not become over-privileged?

   A. Ensure all users are members of the Power Users group only

   B. Implement least privilege policies

   C. Ensure guest accounts are disabled

   D. Rename the default administrator account

3. Which of the following is NOT a recommended practice for creating a strong password?

   A. Using a combination of uppercase and lowercase letters

   B. Including personal information such as your name or birthdate

   C. Incorporating special characters and numbers

   D. Making it at least eight characters long

4. A technician has disabled support for Wake-on-LAN (WoL) network support. This is a requirement for all company laptop computers. The technician is concerned that users will simply turn this feature back on. What is the most effective way to block this action?

   A. Enable Unified Extensible Firmware Interface (UEFI) passwords
   B. Ensure user passwords have complexity requirements set
   C. Ensure user passwords have expiration requirements set
   D. Ensure user passwords have length requirements

5. A CISO is preparing guidance for company employees on the use of password managers. What is the purpose of a password manager?

   A. To generate secure passwords
   B. To store and organize passwords
   C. To encrypt your passwords
   D. All of the above

6. An administrator must ensure that contract personnel employed in the payroll team will only be able to log in to the network when other members of staff are present. What would be the most effective way to ensure this is enforced?

   A. Restrict user permissions outside of core business hour
   B. Restrict login times for contractors to core business hours
   C. Disable guest accounts on all contractors' workstations
   D. Ensure contractors' accounts are locked out after three failed attempts

7. During a security awareness briefing, users are given examples of password attacks. Which of the following is a common method for "brute-forcing" passwords?

   A. Guessing common passwords or phrases
   B. Exploiting software vulnerabilities
   C. Intercepting network traffic
   D. Repeatedly trying different combinations of characters

8. An administrator is concerned that an attacker can gain access to a user's account by using a dictionary attack at the login prompt. What security setting would be the most effective?

    A. Enforce a minimum password length of 10 characters
    B. Restrict login times for contractors to core business hours
    C. Disable guest accounts on all workstations
    D. Ensure accounts are locked out after three failed attempts

9. A senior manager raises a support ticket after encountering a problem during an important presentation. The manager inserted a memory card, to access the presentation material, and a movie file began to play. What can a support technician do to resolve the ticket?

    A. Configure autoplay settings for memory cards
    B. Block access to external media
    C. Configure autoplay settings for removable drives
    D. Ensure Windows Movie Player is blocked from playing

10. Which of the following is the best practice for maintaining password security?

    A. Sharing passwords with trusted family members or friends
    B. Using the same password across multiple accounts
    C. Changing passwords frequently
    D. Writing down passwords on a piece of paper and keeping it in a visible place

11. A CISO must ensure the company is compliant with recommended best security practices. The CISO has noticed that on occasion, users' laptops are displaying personally identifiable information (PII) and intellectual property (IP) when users are not at their desks. What would be the most effective control to secure the workstations?

    A. Use a timeout to automatically enable screen locks
    B. Have all users read and sign an acceptable use policy (AUP)
    C. Have all users lock their laptops in a secure location whenever they leave their desks
    D. Use cable locks to secure the laptops to desks

12. A service desk operator takes a call from a user who suspects that their password has been compromised. What would be the operator's best recommended action for the user?

    A. Continue using the same password but monitor account activity closely

    B. Immediately change the password for the affected account

    C. Delete the account and create a new one

    D. Do nothing and hope for the best

2.7 Explain common methods for securing mobile and embedded devices

1. An administrator is following best practices by ensuring that company-issued mobile devices have preventative controls enabled to ensure the privacy of stored data, in the event of the loss or theft of the devices. What two settings will be most effective?

    A. Restrictive firewall settings

    B. Always-on VPN connection

    C. Screen lock with a password with a minimum of 10 characters

    D. BYOD acceptable use policy

    E. Full device encryption (FDE)

2. Which of the following statements accurately describes a security concern specific to bring your own device (BYOD)?

    A. BYOD devices have limited compatibility with corporate applications

    B. COBO devices may compromise employee privacy and personal data

    C. BYOD increases the risk of unauthorized data access through lost or stolen devices

    D. COBO devices are more susceptible to phishing attacks and social engineering

3. Which network location type in Windows Defender Firewall offers the highest level of security?

    A. Home

    B. Public

    C. Domain

    D. Work

4. An international bank issues smartphones to some employees and allows the use of personal devices for other staff members. It is important that audio and video recordings can be restricted when devices are taken into restricted areas. What would allow mobile devices to be managed in this way? (Choose two.)

   A. MDM
   B. BYOD
   C. Geofencing
   D. Screen locks
   E. Device encryption

5. An organization needs to store data on a mobile device that will include PII and proprietary information. The organization has already implemented FDE and screen locks. In order to add another layer of security, there is a requirement for users to authenticate using biometrics. Which of the following could be used to satisfy the organizational requirements? (Choose two.)

   A. Facial recognition
   B. PIN codes
   C. Fingerprint
   D. Pattern
   E. Swipe

6. What is a major security concern when considering the deployment of IoT devices, when used in building automation systems?

   A. Zigbee protocol
   B. Resilient mesh networks
   C. Location services
   D. Default accounts

2.8 Given a scenario, use common data destruction and disposal methods

1. A CISO is developing a company policy to ensure the correct procedures are followed when data is removed from storage. To ensure that there are no data remnants on magnetic media, what data destruction will be BEST?

    A. Erasing
    B. Standard formatting
    C. Degaussing
    D. Wiping

2. A technician has been tasked with rendering hard disk drives unusable as they have been used to store company intellectual property (IP). It is important the drives cannot be reused and must contain no data remnants. The technician has no access to specialist equipment. What would the best solution be?

    A. Shredding
    B. Standard formatting
    C. Degaussing
    D. Drilling

3. A government agency is working with a third-party data destruction specialist. It is important that the agency has a full audit trail for all data that is in use and for data that is to be removed. What documentation should the vendor provide to the government agency?

    A. Certification of destruction
    B. Non-disclosure agreement (NDA)
    C. Certification of incinerating
    D. Service-level agreement

4. A manager must ensure that paper-based documentation is rendered unreadable. The documents contain data classified as secret. What two methods, when used together, would ensure classified documents are rendered unreadable?

    A. Shredding
    B. Degaussing
    C. Incinerating
    D. Erasing

2.9 Given a scenario, configure appropriate security settings on small office/home office (SOHO) wireless and wired networks

1. A network technician is following a checklist that involves updating firmware on all company SOHO routers. What is the purpose of firmware updates on a SOHO router?

    A. To improve router performance and stability

    B. To add new features and functionalities

    C. To fix security vulnerabilities and bugs

    D. All of the above

2. A technician is helping a user to configure their home router. The wireless router is new and has not been configured. In the first instance, the technician wants to configure the network interface with the correct IP address supplied by the internet service provider (ISP). What configuration option should they choose?

    A. Create Dynamic Host Configuration Protocol (DHCP) reservations

    B. Configure the static wide-area network (WAN) IP

    C. Enable Universal Plug and Play (UPnP)

    D. Configure a screened subnet

3. A home user is having difficulty connecting their PlayStation gaming system to the internet gaming service. The user thinks that the router may be blocking the gaming system from accessing the internet service. What feature would allow the user to access the internet gaming service?

    A. Disable content filtering on the router

    B. Disable Dynamic Host Configuration Protocol (DHCP) on the router

    C. Enable Universal Plug and Play (UPnP) on the router

    D. Deploy a screened subnet

4. A small print shop wants to host an FTP server to allow customers to upload documents that can then be printed as part of the service. The intention is to use a computer that has access to the internet. The print shop has a SOHO wireless router only. What feature will allow this service to be securely hosted? (Choose two.)

    A. Configure IP filtering to protect the customer-facing FTP server

    B. Configure a screened subnet to place the customer-facing computer

    C. Configure firmware updates on the router

    D. Configure port forwarding to route traffic from the internet to the FTP server

5. A technician is helping a user to configure their Wi-Fi home router. The wireless router is new and has not been configured. The technician wants to secure the device against the threat of unauthorized connections. What two settings would be most effective? (Choose two.)

   A. Disabling the SSID broadcast
   B. Enabling a screened subnet
   C. Enabling guest access
   D. Changing default passwords

6. A sales outlet in a shopping mall is experiencing latency on the wireless network. Staff are complaining that when they are demonstrating features on phones and tablets, the devices appear very slow to display pages. A technician notices that there are many other wireless networks in close proximity. What may offer a solution for a better-quality wireless signal?

   A. Disabling SSID broadcast
   B. Encryption settings
   C. Disabling guest access
   D. Changing channels

7. A network technician is assisting a coffee shop with establishing a wireless network for customers to use. The shop intends to print a passkey onto sales receipts so that customers can access free Wi-Fi. The technician is asked to secure the network so that only legitimate customers can securely use the network. What security setting would be best for these requirements?

   A. Enable WPA3-SAE
   B. Enable WEP-PSK
   C. Enable WPA2-TKIP
   D. Enable WPA2-AES

2.10 Given a scenario, install and configure browsers and relevant security settings

1. A technician is advising a customer who requires assistance with the installation of a web browser. For ease of use, the user would prefer to download and install a browser that did not come installed with the default OS. What two pieces of advice can the technician offer the user to ensure a safe installation?

    A. Make sure to download the browser from trusted sources
    B. After download, check that the file size is identical to the file size on the vendor site
    C. Make sure to download a browser with a password manager
    D. After download, check that the hash value is identical to the value published on the vendor site

2. A company would like to allow users to view websites that are not automatically translated into the user's native language. Presently, users are complaining that they need to copy and paste the content into the word processing application to perform translation. What can the company do to best help the users?

    A. Add a language translator as a browser extension
    B. Install a new browser that supports language translation
    C. Ensure the browser supports HTML5
    D. Add support for additional languages to the Windows settings menu

3. A support desk operator has been assigned a support ticket raised by a user who complains that web pages take too long to load and seem to display a lot of advertising content within the pages. What will be the best solution to speed up the user's browser when displaying web pages?

    A. Enable a pop-up blocker
    B. Clear the browsing data cache
    C. Enable private-browsing mode
    D. Enable an ad blocker

4. A customer asks a support technician how can they be sure that the banking website can be trusted. They have been told that fake sites can be made to resemble genuine sites. What ensures that a website can be trusted?

    A. The site will display a padlock when connecting using HTTPS
    B. Ensure there is a trusted certificate when connecting using HTTP
    C. The site will display a security rating when connecting using HTTPS
    D. Ensure to always connect using private-browsing mode

3
Software Troubleshooting

Introduction

In order to successfully pass the A+ certification exam, the candidate must understand the best practice approach used to perform effective software troubleshooting.

When troubleshooting desktop environments, a solid understanding of the Windows OS is a key requirement. A technician must be able to interpret system messages and respond to common errors and events using the correct techniques. Desktop computers are still a mainstay of the modern office environment, and the correct troubleshooting methods should be observed when supporting users on these platforms.

A technician must understand the correct proactive approach to ensure systems are kept optimized and malware free. This includes the timely deployment of OS patches and OS updates.

A thorough understanding of supporting software applications on mobile OSs is also very important.

In order to be successful on the CompTIA A+ Core 2 (220-1102) certification exam, candidates must ensure they are familiar with the following objectives:

- 3.1 Given a scenario, troubleshoot common Windows OS problems
- 3.2 Given a scenario, troubleshoot common personal computer (PC) security issues
- 3.3 Given a scenario, use best practice procedures for malware removal
- 3.4 Given a scenario, troubleshoot common mobile OS and application issues
- 3.5 Given a scenario, troubleshoot common mobile OS and application security issues

The rest of this chapter is committed to practice. For each of the previously defined concepts, you will be given a series of questions designed to test your knowledge of each core two objective as defined by the official certification exam guidance for this domain. These questions will assess the candidate's knowledge of how to support and troubleshoot software applications.

Practice Exam Questions

3.1 Given a scenario, troubleshoot common Windows OS problems

1. Which of the following is a common cause of a blue screen of death (BSOD) error in Windows?

    A. Outdated device drivers

    B. Overclocked CPU

    C. Insufficient disk space

    D. Incorrect BIOS settings

2. Which of the following actions can help resolve a blue screen of death (BSOD) error caused by faulty RAM?

    A. Cleaning the computer's cooling fans

    B. Updating the anti-virus software

    C. Replacing the RAM modules

    D. Re-installing the operating system

3. What is the purpose of the STOP error code displayed on a blue screen of death (BSOD)?

    A. To indicate the severity of the error

    B. To identify the specific cause of the error

    C. To inform the user about available system updates

    D. To provide instructions for recovering data

4. A user raises a support ticket as their Windows computer consistently shuts down after a few minutes of use, and there is no error message displayed. Which of the following is the MOST probable cause of this issue?

    A. Power supply failure

    B. Overheating

    C. Virus or malware infection

    D. Faulty motherboard

5. A user calls the service desk as they have an error that states a Windows service is not starting. Which of the following is the most likely reason for a Windows service not starting?

   A. Insufficient disk space
   B. Outdated device drivers
   C. Incorrect service configuration
   D. Incompatible software installation

6. A technician is responding to a user support ticket. The user is experiencing error messages relating to low memory availability. Which of the following actions can help resolve low-memory warnings in Windows? (Choose two.)

   A. Closing unnecessary applications
   B. Deleting temporary files
   C. Adding more RAM to the system
   D. Upgrading the processor

7. Which of the following warnings is most likely to indicate system instability on a Windows computer?

   A. "The system has detected a critical error and will shut down in 1 minute."
   B. "Your anti-virus software has expired. Please renew your subscription."
   C. "A new update is available for your web browser. Click here to install."
   D. "Low disk space. Free up some space to optimize system performance."

8. A technician is troubleshooting a Windows desktop computer, which displays the error message "No OS found" during startup. What is the most likely cause?

   A. The Windows operating system is missing or corrupted
   B. The hard drive is not properly connected or has failed
   C. The computer's BIOS settings are incorrect
   D. The computer is infected with a virus

9. A user reports slow profile load times when logging in to a Windows computer. Which of the following could be the cause?

   A. Insufficient system resources
   B. Corrupted user profile
   C. Network connectivity issues
   D. Outdated device drivers

10. Which of the following factors can contribute to time drift issues in Windows?

    A. Incorrect time zone settings
    B. Malware infection
    C. Hardware clock malfunction
    D. Power outage

11. Which of the following methods should be used to restart a service using the Windows Services management console?

    A. Right-clicking the service and selecting "Stop" and then "Start"
    B. Right-clicking the service and selecting "Restart"
    C. Double-clicking the service and selecting "Restart" from the toolbar
    D. Right-clicking the service and selecting "Pause" and then "Resume"

12. Which of the following statements is true regarding the impact of a reboot on an unresponsive application?

    A. Rebooting the system resets all running applications to the default configuration settings
    B. Rebooting the system has no effect on unresponsive applications
    C. Rebooting the system may force the closure of the unresponsive application
    D. Rebooting the system automatically repairs any issues with unresponsive applications

13. If an application crashes immediately upon launch, what should be checked first?

    A. System requirements of the application
    B. Available disk space on the computer
    C. Anti-virus software settings
    D. Compatibility mode settings

14. After a recent operating system update, a user's computer fails to boot and displays a "boot device not found" error message. Which of the following is the most likely cause of the failure?

    A. Corrupted boot loader
    B. Overheating CPU
    C. Insufficient hard drive space
    D. Incorrect BIOS settings

15. A user's computer is frequently experiencing blue screen of death (BSOD) errors after installing a new anti-virus software. Which of the following actions should be taken to troubleshoot the issue?

    A. Uninstall the anti-virus software
    B. Upgrade the computer's RAM
    C. Re-install the operating system
    D. Replace the graphics card

16. A user's computer is repeatedly prompted to install the latest operating system update but encounters errors during the installation process. Which of the following steps can be taken to address the OS update failures?

    A. Clear temporary files and retry the update
    B. Install a different web browser
    C. Upgrade the computer's power supply
    D. Increase the screen resolution

17. Which of the following is important to perform if a technician needs to roll back unsuccessful updates?

    A. Re-install the latest updates
    B. Disable automatic updates
    C. Create a system restore point
    D. Increase system resources

18. What troubleshooting step should a technician take when a Windows computer fails to boot and displays a blue screen of death (BSOD)?

    A. Restart the computer and try again
    B. Use System Restore to roll back to a previous working state
    C. Re-install all third-party applications
    D. Update the computer's BIOS

19. When should a computer technician consider running a Windows System File Checker?

    A. When encountering hardware driver issues
    B. After installing new software updates
    C. When experiencing frequent application crashes
    D. Before performing disk defragmentation

20. What command is used to initiate a Windows System File Checker from Command Prompt?

    A. sfc /scanfile
    B. sfc /verifyonly
    C. sfc /scannow
    D. sfc /restorehealth

21. When might a technician consider using Windows reimaging as a troubleshooting step?

    A. When a specific software application is not launching properly
    B. When the computer's internet connection is unstable
    C. When the computer experiences frequent crashes and blue screen errors
    D. When the computer's display resolution needs adjustment

3.2 Given a scenario, troubleshoot common personal computer (PC) security issues

1. A user is unable to access the network from their personal computer (PC). Which of the following steps should a service desk technician take to troubleshoot this issue?

    A. Check the physical network connections and cables
    B. Update the anti-virus software
    C. Re-install the operating system (OS)
    D. Increase the PC's RAM

2. A user frequently receives desktop alerts warning about potential security threats, but these alerts are false positives. Which of the following steps should the technician take to address this issue?

    A. Update the anti-virus software
    B. Adjust the settings of the firewall
    C. Run a full system scan using an anti-virus program
    D. Exclude the false positive files from anti-virus scans

3. A user reports that their personal files have been altered or are missing/renamed on their PC. Which of the following security issues is most likely responsible for this?

    A. Phishing attack
    B. Ransomware infection
    C. Rootkit installation
    D. Unauthorized access by a network intruder

4. A user raises a service ticket as they are experiencing unwanted notifications within the operating system (OS) of their PC. Which of the following steps should a technician take to troubleshoot this issue?

   A. Disable startup programs
   B. Update the BIOS
   C. Re-install the OS
   D. Clean the registry using a registry cleaner tool

5. A user is encountering failures when attempting to install updates for their operating system (OS) on their PC. Which of the following steps should the technician take to resolve this issue?

   A. Disable the anti-virus software temporarily
   B. Restart the PC and try installing the updates again
   C. Re-install the OS from scratch
   D. Clear the browser cache and try again

6. Which of the following browser-related symptoms is typically associated with adware or malware infections?

   A. Random/frequent popups
   B. Certificate warnings
   C. Redirection
   D. Slow internet speed

7. What is the most likely cause of receiving repeated certificate warnings when accessing secure websites?

   A. Outdated browser
   B. Firewall blocking secure connections
   C. Expired security certificate
   D. DNS cache poisoning

8. Which browser-related symptom is commonly associated with browser hijacking?

   A. Random/frequent popups
   B. Certificate warnings
   C. Redirection
   D. Slow internet speed

3.3 Given a scenario, use best practice procedures for malware removal

1. A user's computer is exhibiting slow performance, frequent pop-up advertisements, and unexpected system restarts. Upon investigation, you suspect the presence of malware. What is the best practice procedure to remove the malware from the computer?

   A. Disconnect the computer from the network, perform a full system scan using updated anti-malware software, and remove any detected malware
   B. Manually delete suspicious files and folders from the computer, then restart it to check for any further issues
   C. Re-install the operating system to ensure the complete removal of all malware
   D. Ignore the issue as it may be a temporary glitch in the system

2. Which of the following is the recommended practice for updating anti-malware software?

   A. Disable automatic updates to prevent interruption during important tasks
   B. Update the software manually only when prompted by the operating system
   C. Configure the software to update automatically and regularly
   D. Uninstall and re-install the software to ensure the latest version is installed

3. Why is it important to investigate and verify malware symptoms before proceeding with the removal process?

   A. It helps to determine the cost of the malware removal process
   B. It allows for more accurate identification and selection of appropriate removal techniques.
   C. It helps in estimating the time required to remove the malware
   D. It ensures the end user is educated about the potential risks of malware

4. A technician must follow best practice procedures to BEST prevent future malware infections. Which best practice should be followed?

   A. Regularly update anti-virus software
   B. Disable the system's user account control (UAC) feature
   C. Share user credentials with trusted colleagues
   D. Enable all browser extensions and plugins by default

5. Why is it necessary to quarantine infected systems during the malware removal process?

    A. To prevent the malware from spreading to other systems
    B. To disable System Restore in Windows
    C. To create a restore point for future use
    D. To schedule scans and run updates

6. What is the purpose of disabling System Restore in Windows during malware removal?

    A. To prevent the malware from spreading to other systems
    B. To remove any infected restore points
    C. To ensure the malware cannot re-infect the system after removal
    D. To speed up the malware removal process

7. What happens when System Restore is disabled during malware removal?

    A. The malware is immediately deleted from the system
    B. All existing restore points are deleted
    C. The malware is isolated and prevented from executing
    D. The system becomes immune to further malware infections

8. Why is it important to educate the end user as part of the malware removal process?

    A. To shift the responsibility of malware removal to the end user
    B. To enhance the end user's technical skills
    C. To minimize the risk of re-infection and prevent future malware incidents
    D. To create a sense of panic and urgency among end users

9. Which of the following is a potential benefit of educating the end user about malware removal?

    A. Decreased user productivity
    B. Increased reliance on IT support
    C. Improved incident response time
    D. Increased likelihood of data breaches

10. What is one potential consequence of neglecting to educate the end user about malware removal?

    A. Increased IT budget allocation
    B. Decreased system performance
    C. Higher incidence of successful malware attacks
    D. Decreased network bandwidth

3.4 Given a scenario, troubleshoot common mobile OS and application issues

1. Sara's smartphone battery drains quickly even though she does not use it extensively. Which of the following could be a possible cause of the issue?

    A. Background app refresh
    B. Low screen brightness
    C. Mobile data usage
    D. Overcharging the device

2. David is preparing to use AirDrop to wirelessly share files, photos, and more between Apple devices. Which of the following statements accurately describes AirDrop?

    A. AirDrop only works when both devices are connected to the same Wi-Fi network
    B. AirDrop can only be used to transfer files between iPhones
    C. AirDrop requires Bluetooth and Wi-Fi to be enabled on both devices
    D. AirDrop can transfer files between Apple devices and non-Apple devices

3. A user's smartphone suddenly becomes unresponsive and does not respond to touch inputs. Which of the following troubleshooting steps should be attempted first?

    A. Perform a soft reset on the device
    B. Clear the cache of all installed applications
    C. Re-install the mobile operating system
    D. Remove the battery and reinsert it

4. Which of the following is a common symptom of a malware-infected mobile device?

    A. Frequent battery drain
    B. Improved device performance
    C. Enhanced battery life
    D. App icons rearranging automatically

5. Which of the following technologies enables contactless data exchange between two devices in close proximity?

    A. Near-field communication (NFC)
    B. Bluetooth
    C. Wi-Fi
    D. GPS

6. A user reports that the screen of their mobile device does not autorotate. Which of the following troubleshooting steps should be performed first to resolve the issue?

    A. Restart the device
    B. Check the screen rotation settings
    C. Update the mobile operating system
    D. Perform a factory reset

7. A user reports that their mobile device randomly reboots while they are using an application. Which of the following troubleshooting steps should be performed first to address this issue?

    A. Clear the cache and data of the application
    B. Update the operating system to the latest version
    C. Re-install the application
    D. Factory reset the mobile device

8. A user reports that their mobile device is running out of storage space and is unable to install new applications. Which of the following actions would be the MOST appropriate troubleshooting step to resolve the issue?

    A. Clear the device cache
    B. Uninstall unnecessary applications
    C. Perform a factory reset
    D. Upgrade the device's operating system

9. A user's mobile device battery drains quickly, even when not in use. Which of the following actions should be taken to troubleshoot this issue? (Choose two.)

    A. Enable battery optimization settings
    B. Close background applications
    C. Replace the device battery
    D. Disable push email notifications

10. A user reports that their mobile device's touchscreen is unresponsive. Which of the following troubleshooting steps should be performed FIRST to address the issue?

    A. Restart the device
    B. Calibrate the touchscreen
    C. Update the device's firmware
    D. Clean the touchscreen

11. A mobile device user complains about frequent app crashes. Which of the following actions should be taken to troubleshoot this problem?

    A. Clear the app cache
    B. Uninstall and re-install the app
    C. Update the device's operating system
    D. Restart the device

12. A mobile device user is experiencing slow performance when launching apps and navigating the interface. Which of the following steps should be taken to troubleshoot this problem?

    A. Clear app cache and data
    B. Perform a factory reset
    C. Install a performance optimization app
    D. Upgrade the device's memory (RAM)

13. A mobile device user reports that their device frequently loses Wi-Fi connectivity. Which of the following steps should be taken to troubleshoot this issue? (Choose two.)

    A. Forget and reconnect to the Wi-Fi network
    B. Reset the device's network settings
    C. Replace the device's Wi-Fi antenna
    D. Update the device's firmware

14. A user's mobile device frequently displays the message "Insufficient storage available." Which of the following troubleshooting steps would BEST resolve this issue?

    A. Clear the app cache
    B. Move apps and data to an external storage device
    C. Delete unnecessary files and applications
    D. Upgrade the device's storage capacity

15. A mobile device user complains about frequent device reboots and freezes. Which of the following actions should be taken to troubleshoot this problem? (Choose two.)

    A. Update the device's firmware
    B. Perform a factory reset
    C. Replace the device's battery
    D. Disable unnecessary background processes

3.5 Given a scenario, troubleshoot common mobile OS and application security issues

1. Which of the following best describes an APK file?

    A. A file format used to store music files on mobile devices
    B. An executable file containing an Android application
    C. A compressed file format used to store images on iOS devices
    D. A system file responsible for managing network connections

2. What does enabling developer mode on a mobile device allow you to do?

    A. Access advanced system settings and debugging features
    B. Install applications from unofficial sources
    C. Extend battery life by optimizing system performance
    D. Increase the device's screen resolution

3. What is the primary purpose of rooting an Android device?

    A. To remove malicious applications
    B. To enhance device security
    C. To gain administrative access and control over the operating system
    D. To extend battery life and improve performance

4. What is the term used to describe the process of bypassing software restrictions on an iOS device?

    A. Jailbreaking
    B. Bootlegging
    C. Application spoofing
    D. Malicious application

5. Which of the following terms refers to a pirated or unauthorized copy of a mobile application?

   A. APK file
   B. Developer mode
   C. Bootleg application
   D. Root access

6. Which of the following symptoms is commonly associated with a mobile device experiencing high network traffic?

   A. Sluggish response time
   B. Limited internet connectivity
   C. High number of ads
   D. Fake security warnings

7. Which symptom is commonly observed when a mobile device reaches its data usage limit?

   A. No internet connectivity
   B. Unexpected application behavior
   C. Leaked personal files/data
   D. Sluggish response time

8. Which of the following is a common symptom of a compromised mobile operating system or application?

   A. Slow device performance and frequent crashes
   B. Improved battery life and faster processing speed
   C. Enhanced security features and increased app compatibility
   D. Smooth user interface and seamless multitasking

9. Which of the following can suggest a security issue with mobile applications?

   A. Excessive battery usage
   B. Regular software updates
   C. Limited app permissions
   D. Encrypted data storage

10. Which of the following is a common symptom of a mobile OS vulnerability?

    A. Unexpected app crashes

    B. Enhanced device performance

    C. Improved battery life

    D. Seamless network connectivity

11. Which of the following is a common security issue with mobile devices?

    A. Weak network signal strength

    B. Strong device encryption

    C. Regular backups of data

    D. Unauthorized app installations

12. Which of the following is a common symptom of a mobile application security breach?

    A. Unwanted pop-up advertisements

    B. Enhanced app functionality

    C. Increased device storage capacity

    D. Improved user experience

13. Which of the following is a common indication of a security issue associated with mobile operating systems?

    A. Excessive RAM utilization

    B. Prompt security updates

    C. Secure boot process

    D. Encrypted user data

14. Which of the following is a common symptom of a mobile application vulnerability?

    A. Application crashes upon launch

    B. Faster battery charging

    C. Enhanced network connectivity

    D. Increased app compatibility

15. Which of the following is a common security issue with mobile operating systems?

    A. Frequent app updates

    B. Encrypted device backups

    C. Outdated software versions

    D. Optimized power-saving features

16. Which of the following is a common symptom of a compromised mobile application?

    A. Unexpected data usage

    B. Improved device performance

    C. Enhanced battery longevity

    D. Seamless app integration

4

Operational Procedures

Introduction

As a support technician, you play a crucial role in ensuring the smooth operation of computer systems and providing efficient technical support to end users. This chapter focuses on operational procedures. A vital aspect of your role involves following established protocols and best practices to maintain a productive and secure computing environment.

In this chapter, you will face questions on the key objectives outlined in CompTIA A+ Core 2 (220-1102) domain 4: Operational Procedures. These objectives are designed to equip you with the necessary knowledge and skills to perform your duties effectively and contribute to the overall success of your organization.

By mastering these operational procedures, you will enhance your effectiveness as a helpdesk technician and improve user satisfaction.

In order to be successful on the CompTIA A+ Core 2 (220-1102) certification exam, candidates must ensure they are familiar with the following objectives:

- 4.1 Given a scenario, implement best practices associated with documentation and support systems information management
- 4.2 Explain basic change-management best practices
- 4.3 Given a scenario, implement workstation backup and recovery methods
- 4.4 Given a scenario, use common safety procedures
- 4.5 Summarize environmental impacts and local environmental controls
- 4.6 Explain the importance of prohibited content/activity and privacy, licensing, and policy concepts
- 4.7 Given a scenario, use proper communication techniques and professionalism
- 4.8 Identify the basics of scripting
- 4.9 Given a scenario, use remote access technologies

Operational Procedures

The rest of this chapter is dedicated to practice. For each of the concepts defined above, you will be given a series of questions designed to test your knowledge of each core objective as defined by the official certification exam guidance for this domain. These questions will assess the candidate's knowledge of how to implement operational procedures.

Practice Exam Questions

4.1 Given a scenario, implement best practices associated with documentation and support systems information management

1. A company is implementing regulatory compliance requirements for its documentation and support systems. It wants to ensure that users are informed about the organization's policies and procedures before accessing the system. Which of the following best practices should it implement?

   A. Password complexity rules

   B. Network segmentation

   C. Splash screens

   D. Incident reports

2. A helpdesk team is responsible for documenting and reporting any incidents that occur during their support activities. Which of the following documents should they use to record detailed information about each incident?

   A. Knowledge base articles

   B. Splash screens

   C. Incident reports

   D. Service-level agreements

3. Which of the following is an example of a best practice for complying with regulatory requirements related to incident reporting?

   A. Implementing splash screens on all company devices

   B. Conducting regular vulnerability assessments

   C. Encrypting sensitive customer data during transit

   D. Training employees on data handling and privacy policies

4. Which of the following is an example of documentation that should be included in a support system information management plan?

   A. Network diagrams
   B. Software licenses
   C. Customer contact information
   D. User passwords

5. In the context of support system information management, which of the following is the purpose of a knowledge base?

   A. To store customer feedback
   B. To track hardware inventory
   C. To centralize troubleshooting guides
   D. To schedule technician appointments

6. When documenting a support request, which of the following details should be included?

   A. Customer's favorite color
   B. Date and time of the request
   C. Technician's lunch preferences
   D. Weather conditions in the area

7. Which of the following is the best practice for managing support system documentation?

   A. Storing documents in multiple physical locations
   B. Sharing sensitive information via email
   C. Regularly updating and reviewing documentation
   D. Printing documentation only when necessary

8. Which of the following is an example of a ticketing system used in support systems?

   A. Microsoft Office Suite
   B. ServiceNow
   C. Adobe Photoshop
   D. Google Chrome

9. What is the primary purpose of a service level agreement (SLA) in support system documentation?

    A. To outline the technician's work schedule
    B. To establish pricing for support services
    C. To define response and resolution times
    D. To determine the customer's preferred contact method

10. Which of the following should be included in a support system knowledge base article?

    A. Sales promotional material
    B. Personal opinions of support technicians
    C. Tested solutions to known issues
    D. Company's financial reports

11. Which of the following is a common method of organizing and categorizing support system documentation?

    A. Alphabetical order
    B. Reverse chronological order
    C. Color-coded labels
    D. Random arrangement

12. Which of the following is an example of a customer relationship management (CRM) system used in support systems?

    A. Salesforce
    B. Dropbox
    C. Microsoft Word
    D. Spotify

13. In support system documentation, what is the purpose of creating an inventory list?

    A. To track technician attendance records
    B. To monitor customer satisfaction ratings
    C. To keep an inventory of spare parts and equipment
    D. To schedule routine maintenance tasks

14. Which of the following statements best describes an acceptable use policy (AUP) in relation to documentation and support systems information management?

    A. An AUP outlines the procedures for creating backups of critical data
    B. An AUP establishes guidelines for the appropriate use of computer systems and networks
    C. An AUP specifies the steps to troubleshoot and resolve hardware-related issues
    D. An AUP defines the process for documenting software license agreements

4.2 Explain basic change-management best practices

1. A company is updating operational procedures and will adopt change management. Which of the following best describes a basic change-management best practice?

    A. Implementing changes without proper planning
    B. Communicating changes only after they have been implemented
    C. Documenting changes thoroughly
    D. Ignoring user feedback

2. Which of the following is a key element of change management?

    A. Minimizing user involvement
    B. Avoiding communication with stakeholders
    C. Assessing and managing risks
    D. Rushing the implementation process

3. Which of the following is a recommended practice for managing user resistance during change implementation?

    A. Ignoring user concerns
    B. Providing clear communication and training
    C. Limiting user access to system documentation
    D. Implementing changes abruptly without prior notice

4. Which of the following best describes the purpose of a change advisory board (CAB)?

    A. Approving all changes without review
    B. Monitoring the progress of change implementation
    C. Evaluating and prioritizing proposed changes
    D. Limiting user involvement in the change process

5. Which of the following is a common risk associated with change management?

    A. Improved system performance
    B. Increased user satisfaction
    C. Temporary service disruptions
    D. Enhanced security measures

6. Which of the following is an example of a change management best practice for software deployments?

    A. Skipping the testing phase
    B. Performing regular backups
    C. Implementing changes during peak hours
    D. Avoiding user communication

7. Which of the following is an example of a change management best practice for hardware replacements?

    A. Ignoring user feedback
    B. Conducting a thorough inventory assessment
    C. Implementing changes without testing
    D. Excluding stakeholders from the process

8. Which of the following best describes the purpose of a rollback plan in change management?

    A. Preventing any changes from being implemented
    B. Documenting the reasons for change implementation
    C. Identifying potential issues and their resolutions
    D. Excluding user feedback during the change process

9. Which of the following is a recommended practice for managing change-related risks?

    A. Avoiding risk assessment altogether
    B. Implementing changes without backup plans
    C. Conducting regular risk assessments
    D. Ignoring risk mitigation strategies

10. Which of the following is a key consideration when communicating changes to users during change management?

    A. Providing vague and general information
    B. Overemphasizing the negative aspects of the changes
    C. Tailoring the message to the target audience
    D. Delaying communication until after the changes are implemented

4.3 Given a scenario, implement workstation backup and recovery methods

1. Which workstation backup method involves creating a copy of all user data and settings at a specific point in time?

    A. Full backup
    B. Differential backup
    C. Incremental backup
    D. Selective backup

2. Which workstation recovery method involves using a backup of the entire workstation's hard drive to restore the system to its previous state?

    A. Bare-metal recovery
    B. Cloud-based recovery
    C. File-level recovery
    D. Incremental recovery

3. Which backup storage medium provides the fastest transfer rates but is also the most expensive option for workstation backup?

    A. Tape drive
    B. External hard drive
    C. Network-attached storage (NAS)
    D. Cloud storage

4. Which workstation backup method only backs up data that has changed since the last backup, regardless of whether it was a full or incremental backup?

   A. Differential backup
   B. Incremental backup
   C. Synthetic backup
   D. Continuous backup

5. Which backup rotation scheme involves using a set of backup media and cycling through them on a daily basis, overwriting the oldest backup when the set is full?

   A. Grandfather-father-son
   B. Tower of Hanoi
   C. Back up to disk
   D. Back up to tape

6. Which workstation backup method provides the fastest recovery time when compared to other backup methods?

   A. Incremental backup
   B. Differential backup
   C. Snapshot backup
   D. Full backup

7. Which backup method ensures data redundancy by creating multiple copies of backups on different backup media?

   A. Mirroring
   B. Replication
   C. Archiving
   D. Versioning

8. Which backup method provides the highest level of data protection by storing multiple copies of backups across different geographical locations?

   A. Cloud-based backup
   B. Tape backup
   C. Disk-to-disk backup
   D. Offsite backup

9. Which workstation backup method captures an exact copy of the workstation's operating system, applications, and data, allowing for quick restoration to a functional state?

    A. Image backup
    B. File-level backup
    C. Incremental backup
    D. Differential backup

10. Which workstation backup method involves automatically backing up data in real time as changes occur, ensuring minimal data loss in the event of a failure?

    A. Continuous backup
    B. Synchronization backup
    C. Manual backup
    D. Snapshot backup

4.4 Given a scenario, use common safety procedures

1. Which of the following is a common safety procedure when working on computer hardware?

    A. Wear an ESD wrist strap
    B. Disconnect the power supply without turning it off
    C. Handle circuit boards with bare hands
    D. Stand on a wet surface

2. When working on computer equipment, which of the following safety precautions should be taken?

    A. Use compressed air to clean debris from fans and heatsinks
    B. Use a magnetized screwdriver to secure components
    C. Store liquids near the computer to easily access them
    D. Place the computer on an unstable surface

3. Which of the following safety measures should be followed when handling computer cables?

    A. Pull the cable from a distance to disconnect it
    B. Bend the cable sharply to fit it in tight spaces
    C. Secure cables using cable ties or clips
    D. Leave cables loose and tangled

4. What safety precaution should be taken before opening a computer case?

   A. Ensure the computer is turned off and unplugged
   B. Wear gloves to protect against static electricity
   C. Use a metal tool to open the case
   D. Keep the case on a soft, cushioned surface

5. What should be done to prevent injuries while working with computer hardware?

   A. Follow ergonomic practices
   B. Wear heavy jewelry and accessories
   C. Use damaged tools if no others are available
   D. Skip breaks and work for long periods without rest

6. Which safety measure should be taken when cleaning the inside of a computer?

   A. Use an antistatic vacuum cleaner
   B. Spray cleaning solution directly onto components
   C. Clean the computer while it is still powered on
   D. Use a dry cloth to wipe the motherboard

7. Which safety precaution should be taken when disposing of old computer equipment?

   A. Recycle the equipment according to local regulations
   B. Disassemble the equipment without protective gear
   C. Throw the equipment in regular household waste
   D. Store the equipment in a humid environment

8. Which of the following safety precautions should be followed when working with high-voltage equipment?

   A. Wear insulated gloves and safety glasses
   B. Work alone to minimize distractions
   C. Use a metal ladder when working at heights
   D. Use equipment with damaged cords

9. What should be done if a chemical spill occurs in the vicinity of computer equipment?

    A. Shut down the equipment immediately
    B. Use a vacuum cleaner to remove the spill
    C. Follow proper procedures for chemical cleanup
    D. Ignore the spill and continue working

10. What safety measures should be taken when installing or replacing computer hardware components?

    A. Use proper lifting techniques for heavy components
    B. Use excessive force when inserting connectors
    C. Install components in an unventilated area
    D. Install components without grounding yourself

4.5 Summarize environmental impacts and local environmental controls

1. Which of the following describes the purpose of material safety data sheets (MSDSs) in relation to handling and disposal of hazardous materials?

    A. To provide guidelines for safe transportation of hazardous materials
    B. To document the potential hazards and precautions for using a specific material
    C. To outline the proper procedures for recycling electronic waste
    D. To certify the quality and durability of protective equipment

2. What is the primary purpose of reviewing material safety data sheets (MSDSs) before handling or disposing of hazardous materials?

    A. To assess the financial cost associated with the materials
    B. To determine the expiration date of the materials
    C. To understand the potential health and safety risks
    D. To identify potential sources of the materials

3. Proper battery disposal is essential to protect the environment and prevent hazardous materials from contaminating landfills. Which of the following statements accurately describes the correct way to dispose of used batteries?

    A. Place used batteries in the regular trash bin
    B. Take the batteries to a nearby electronics store for disposal
    C. Recycle used batteries at designated recycling centers or facilities
    D. Bury the batteries in the backyard to decompose naturally

4. When disposing of toner cartridges from printers and copiers, what is the recommended method to ensure proper disposal?

    A. Place the toner cartridges in any nearby recycling bin for regular waste collection
    B. Throw the toner cartridges in the trash as they are not considered hazardous waste
    C. Return the used toner cartridges to the manufacturer or a designated recycling program
    D. Burn the toner cartridges to reduce waste volume before disposing of them

5. When disposing of other electronic devices and assets, which of the following methods should you avoid to ensure data security and prevent environmental damage? (Choose all that apply.)

    A. Selling the devices to an unknown individual or entity
    B. Donating the devices to a local charity or non-profit organization
    C. Erasing all the data from the devices before recycling or disposal
    D. Disassembling the devices and disposing of their parts separately

6. What environmental factors should be considered to maintain optimal equipment performance and longevity?

    A. Temperature, humidity, and proper ventilation
    B. Noise level, cable management, and power supply
    C. Lighting conditions, firewall settings, and antivirus software
    D. Backup systems, network security, and data encryption

7. What device is designed to protect electronic equipment from power surges, under-voltage events, and power failures?

    A. Uninterruptible Power Supply (UPS)
    B. Power over Ethernet (PoE)
    C. Network-Attached Storage (NAS)
    D. Wireless Access Point (WAP)

8. Which device is used to suppress power surges and voltage spikes?

    A. Surge protector
    B. Uninterruptible Power Supply (UPS)
    C. Power inverter
    D. Power strip

9. What is the purpose of using a battery backup system?

    A. To provide backup power during outages
    B. To increase network bandwidth
    C. To protect against electromagnetic interference
    D. To prevent power surges

10. What is a recommended practice for location/equipment placement to ensure optimal computer performance?

    A. Placing the computer on an uneven surface
    B. Locating the computer near direct sunlight
    C. Positioning the computer away from electrical interference
    D. Stacking multiple computers on top of each other

11. A technician must choose the best method suitable for dust cleanup in a computer system. Which of these is the recommended solution?

    A. Blowing compressed air directly into the components
    B. Using a dry cloth to wipe the components
    C. Applying water or liquid cleaning agents on the components
    D. Utilizing a vacuum designed for electronics

4.6 Explain the importance of prohibited content/activity and privacy, licensing, and policy concepts

1. Which concept ensures the integrity and preservation of data during an incident response in relation to prohibited content/activity?

    A. Chain of custody
    B. Incident escalation
    C. Password recovery
    D. Data compression

2. When encountering prohibited content/activity during an incident response, which action should be taken?

    A. Inform management or law enforcement, if necessary
    B. Continue the investigation without involving anyone else
    C. Delete the prohibited content/activity immediately
    D. Perform a system reboot

3. What is the purpose of making a copy of a drive during an incident response?

    A. To preserve data integrity and evidence
    B. To speed up the incident resolution process
    C. To minimize the impact on system performance
    D. To reduce the risk of future incidents

4. Which concept involves documenting the handling and transfer of evidence during an incident response?

    A. Chain of custody
    B. Incident containment
    C. Data classification
    D. System hardening

5. What is the purpose of documenting an incident during an incident response?

    A. To provide a reference for future incidents
    B. To inform management of ongoing activities
    C. To facilitate collaboration with other teams
    D. To create a detailed record for analysis and accountability

6. Which concept defines the terms and conditions under which software can be used by an individual or organization?

    A. Privacy policy
    B. Open source license
    C. End-user license agreement (EULA)
    D. Digital rights management (DRM)

7. What distinguishes a personal use license from a corporate use license?

    A. Personal use licenses require individual registration, while corporate use licenses allow multiple users
    B. Personal use licenses have shorter validity periods compared to corporate use licenses
    C. Personal use licenses have fewer restrictions on usage compared to corporate use licenses
    D. Personal use licenses are free, while corporate use licenses require a fee

8. Which licensing concept ensures that users comply with the terms of the software license and prevents unauthorized copying or distribution?

    A. Open source license
    B. Valid license
    C. Non-expired license
    D. Digital rights management (DRM)

9. What is the purpose of licensing/digital rights management (DRM)/the end-user license agreement (EULA) in relation to prohibited content/activity?

    A. They facilitate the sharing of prohibited content/activity
    B. They prevent the use of prohibited content/activity
    C. They monitor and report the use of prohibited content/activity
    D. They establish penalties for the use of prohibited content/activity

10. Which type of license allows users to view, modify, and distribute the source code of software?

    A. Privacy policy
    B. Open source license
    C. End-user license agreement (EULA)
    D. Digital rights management (DRM)

11. Which of the following best describes regulated data in the context of privacy and policy concepts?

    A. Data that is subject to government regulations and restrictions

    B. Data that is freely accessible to the public

    C. Data that is stored without any encryption or security measures

    D. Data that is shared among employees within an organization

12. Which type of data is considered as personally identifiable information (PII)?

    A. Social media posts and comments

    B. Names and addresses of individuals

    C. Publicly available company information

    D. Non-sensitive email communication

13. Which of the following describes a key concern when handling credit card transactions?

    A. Ensuring data availability

    B. Securing cardholder data

    C. Maintaining accurate financial records

    D. Maximizing transaction speed

14. Which of the following is an example of personal government-issued information?

    A. Social media account usernames

    B. Driver's license number

    C. Wi-Fi network passwords

    D. Home address

15. Which of the following best describes data retention requirements?

    A. The amount of time it takes to process data

    B. The policies and procedures for storing and managing data

    C. The frequency at which data is backed up

    D. The speed of data transmission over a network

4.7 Given a scenario, use proper communication techniques and professionalism

1. When service desk personnel are communicating with customers, which communication technique demonstrates professionalism and empathy?

    A. Interrupting the customer to provide quick solutions

    B. Using technical jargon to establish expertise

    C. Active listening and paraphrasing the customer's concerns

    D. Offering discounts or freebies to resolve the issue

2. Which of the following is an example of non-verbal communication that reflects professionalism?

    A. Maintaining eye contact and nodding in agreement

    B. Checking personal emails on a mobile device

    C. Speaking softly to avoid disrupting others

    D. Using slang terms and informal language

3. In a business email, which of the following is the most appropriate way to address the recipient?

    A. Hey [Recipient's First Name],

    B. Dear [Recipient's First Name],

    C. To whom it may concern,

    D. Hi there,

4. Which of the following communication methods is most suitable for conveying complex technical information to a non-technical audience?

    A. Using technical terms and acronyms extensively

    B. Providing detailed written documentation only

    C. Utilizing visual aids, diagrams, and illustrations

    D. Speaking rapidly to ensure all information is covered

5. Which of the following is an example of appropriate use of professional language in customer communication?

    A. "Your computer is totally messed up"

    B. "Your device is experiencing some technical difficulties"

    C. "Your machine is acting weird"

    D. "Your PC is broken"

6. When speaking with a customer, which of the following is a professional way to handle a disagreement or conflict?

    A. Raising your voice to assert dominance
    B. Blaming the customer for the issue
    C. Offering alternative solutions and compromises
    D. Ignoring the customer's concerns

7. Which of the following is an example of appropriate professional behavior when interacting with colleagues?

    A. Gossiping about other team members
    B. Taking credit for others' work
    C. Actively listening and respecting others' opinions
    D. Criticizing colleagues in public forums

8. Which of the following communication methods is best suited for delivering sensitive or confidential information?

    A. Public announcement during a team meeting
    B. Sending a mass email to all employees
    C. Holding individual face-to-face meetings
    D. Posting the information on a public bulletin board

9. Which of the following is an example of maintaining professionalism in a virtual meeting?

    A. Eating a meal while on camera
    B. Keeping the microphone on mute when not speaking
    C. Using informal language and abbreviations in chat messages
    D. Sharing irrelevant personal anecdotes

10. When communicating with customers, which of the following is a professional approach to managing their expectations?

    A. Overpromising to ensure customer satisfaction
    B. Setting realistic expectations and providing updates
    C. Ignoring customer requests to avoid conflicts
    D. Redirecting customers to a different support channel

11. Which of the following actions should a technician take to deal appropriately with a customer's confidential and private materials stored on a desktop computer?

    A. Regularly share the customer's data with colleagues for collaborative purposes
    B. Encrypt the customer's sensitive files and folders using strong encryption algorithms
    C. Upload the customer's confidential data to a cloud storage service for backup
    D. Dispose of the customer's computer without securely wiping the hard drive

12. When dealing with a customer's confidential materials on a printer, which of the following steps should a technician take to maintain security?

    A. Share the printer's access credentials with other technicians for easier troubleshooting
    B. Disable logging features on the printer to prevent potential privacy breaches
    C. Implement access controls on the printer to restrict unauthorized usage
    D. Print the customer's confidential documents in a public area for quick access

13. A technician is helping a customer secure their desktop computer. The technician must implement best practices to protect the customer's confidential materials. Which offers the best solution?

    A. Create a shared user account with unrestricted access for the customer and their colleagues
    B. Regularly perform data backups without verifying the integrity and confidentiality of the backup media
    C. Implement strong password policies and enable full disk encryption for the customer's desktop
    D. Store the customer's confidential files in publicly accessible folders for easier collaboration

4.8 Identify the basics of scripting

1. A developer must identify the scripting language used by the web development community. Which scripting language will be the best choice?

    A. Python
    B. Bash
    C. JavaScript
    D. PowerShell

2. Which scripting language is commonly used for task automation in Windows environments?

    A. Python
    B. Bash
    C. JavaScript
    D. PowerShell

3. Which scripting language is commonly used for system administration tasks in Unix-like operating systems?

    A. Python
    B. Bash
    C. JavaScript
    D. PowerShell

4. Which scripting language is known for its versatility and can be used for a wide range of tasks, including web development, automation, and data analysis?

    A. Python
    B. Bash
    C. JavaScript
    D. PowerShell

5. Which scripting language is commonly used for client-side scripting in web browsers?

    A. Python
    B. Bash
    C. JavaScript
    D. PowerShell

6. What are some potential risks associated with using scripts that need to be considered to avoid unintentionally introducing malware, inadvertently changing system settings, and causing browser or system crashes due to mishandling of resources?

    A. Inadequate error handling
    B. Insufficient debugging tools
    C. Lack of version control
    D. Incompatible scripting languages

7. Which precaution should be taken to prevent unintentionally introducing malware when using scripts?

   A. Regularly update antivirus software
   B. Implement input validation and sanitization
   C. Disable the firewall temporarily
   D. Increase user privileges

8. What can cause browser or system crashes due to mishandling of resources when using scripts?

   A. Excessive memory usage
   B. Frequent disk read/write operations
   C. Incompatible browser extensions
   D. Network connectivity issues

9. Which of the following actions poses a risk of unintentionally introducing malware into a system when using scripts?

   A. Using reputable script repositories
   B. Regularly updating the script interpreter
   C. Downloading scripts from untrusted sources
   D. Running scripts in a sandbox environment

10. What can be a consequence of inadvertently changing system settings when executing scripts on a computer?

    A. Improved system performance
    B. Enhanced user experience
    C. Increased security measures
    D. System instability or malfunction

11. To prevent browser or system crashes due to mishandling of resources in scripts, what should be done?

    A. Increase script execution speed
    B. Avoid error handling in scripts
    C. Optimize resource usage in scripts
    D. Disable browser extensions

4.9 Given a scenario, use remote access technologies

1. A technician needs to troubleshoot a user's computer remotely. The user is running a Windows operating system and is connected to the same network as the technician. Which remote access technology should the technician use in this scenario?

    A. Microsoft Remote Assistance (MSRA)

    B. Virtual Network Computing (VNC)

    C. Remote Desktop Protocol (RDP)

    D. Secure Shell (SSH)

2. In a scenario where an IT technician needs to remotely monitor and manage multiple devices in a network, which remote access technology would be most suitable?

    A. Virtual private network (VPN)

    B. Remote Desktop Protocol (RDP)

    C. Telnet

    D. Remote monitoring and management (RMM)

3. Which remote access technology allows users to access their office computer from a remote location?

    A. Virtual private network (VPN)

    B. Remote Desktop Protocol (RDP)

    C. Telnet

    D. Secure Shell (SSH)

4. In a scenario where a user needs to remotely access a Windows server, which remote access technology would be most suitable?

    A. Remote Desktop Protocol (RDP)

    B. File Transfer Protocol (FTP)

    C. Telnet

    D. Secure Shell (SSH)

5. A user wants to remotely connect to a Linux server using a command-line interface. Which remote access technology would be most appropriate?

   A. Telnet
   B. Remote Desktop Protocol (RDP)
   C. Secure Shell (SSH)
   D. Virtual private network (VPN)

6. In a scenario where a user wants to remotely access their home network from a remote network, which remote access technology would be the most appropriate?

   A. Virtual private network (VPN)
   B. Remote Desktop Protocol (RDP)
   C. Telnet
   D. Secure Shell (SSH)

7. Which remote access technology commonly uses port 3389 by default?

   A. Remote Desktop Protocol (RDP)
   B. File Transfer Protocol (FTP)
   C. Telnet
   D. Secure Shell (SSH)

8. In a scenario where a user wants to remotely access a Mac computer from another Mac, which built-in remote access technology can be used?

   A. Apple Remote Desktop
   B. Virtual Network Computing (VNC)
   C. Remote Desktop Protocol (RDP)
   D. Secure Shell (SSH)

9. Which remote access technology allows users to access their office network resources securely over the internet?

   A. Virtual private network (VPN)
   B. Remote Desktop Protocol (RDP)
   C. Telnet
   D. Secure Shell (SSH)

Mock Exam

The final chapter is intended to provide the candidate with a realistic mock exam comprising 93 questions. The official CompTIA A+ Core 2 (220-1102) certification exam allows for 90 minutes to complete all questions. This mock exam is intended to cover all the following CompTIA certification objectives:

- Install, configure, and maintain computer equipment, mobile devices, and software for end users
- Service components based on customer requirements
- Understand networking basics and apply basic cybersecurity methods to mitigate threats
- Properly and safely diagnose, resolve, and document common hardware and software issues
- Apply troubleshooting skills and provide customer support using appropriate communication skills
- Understand the basics of scripting, cloud technologies, virtualization, and multi-OS deployments in corporate environments

To get an accurate measurement of your knowledge, it is recommended that you give yourself 90 minutes to complete all 90 questions (or break it down into blocks of 30 questions per 30 minutes).

Mock Exam Questions

1. You are troubleshooting a smartphone that is exhibiting unusual behavior, such as slow performance, excessive data usage, and unexpected pop-up ads. You suspect it may be infected with malware. What is the most appropriate first step to take in addressing this issue?

    A. Perform a factory reset on the smartphone
    B. Download a popular antivirus app and run a full scan
    C. Disconnect the smartphone from the internet
    D. Update the smartphone's operating system and all apps

2. Management within a banking organization is reviewing change management documentation. The team needs to understand the correct steps used within the process. When a change has been approved, what is the next step?

   A. End user acceptance
   B. Conduct risk analysis
   C. Communicate the change to stakeholders
   D. Perform sandbox testing

3. A user reports encountering sporadic, seemingly non-malicious advertisement notifications within the Windows 10 Action Center. These notifications suggest that the advertisements originate from a web browser. What is the MOST effective solution for a technician to implement?

   A. Deactivate the browser's ability to send notifications to the Action Center
   B. Perform a comprehensive antivirus scan on the computer
   C. Turn off all notifications within the Action Center
   D. Transfer specific site notifications from the Allowed category to Block

4. What action should the systems administrator take to minimize the number of help desk tickets submitted, as reported by the manager regarding staff members frequently forgetting passwords for their mobile devices and applications?

   A. Enable multifactor authentication
   B. Raise the failed login threshold
   C. Eliminate complex password requirements
   D. Implement a single sign-on system with biometrics

5. A service desk technician is responding to a service ticket that appears to indicate the presence of a rootkit. In order to resolve the suspected rootkit installation, which of the following options would be the MOST effective?

   A. Updating applications
   B. Utilizing anti-malware software
   C. Reinstalling the operating system
   D. Restoring files

6. A technician is asked to re-deploy unused wireless access points for the new warehouse. The devices have been in storage since 2015. The technician must ensure they are configured with the most secure wireless network settings. Bearing in mind the age of the equipment, which configuration will provide the technician with the most secure implementation?

   A. WPA3 with AES-128

   B. WPA2 with AES

   C. WPA3 with AES-256

   D. WPA2 with TKIP

7. A call center technician receives a call from a home user seeking guidance on updating Windows. They would like to ensure that they are running the latest Windows edition when it is made available to customers. What is the appropriate course of action for the technician to take?

   A. Suggest that the user consider using a different system if they are unable to complete updates

   B. Instruct the user to send their password via text to the technician

   C. Guide the user to click on the Search field, type "Check for Updates," and then press the Enter key

   D. Suggest the user waits for an upcoming, automatic patch

8. When a customer contacts a technician to report an issue, what practice should the technician employ to ensure the service ticket is correctly associated with the user?

   A. Verify the customer's identity then issue a unique ticket

   B. Assign a random ticket number to maintain customer privacy

   C. Use the technician's personal identification as the ticket reference

   D. Create a generic ticket without associating it with any user

9. The service desk for a large financial institution has raised support tickets after several members of staff returned to the workplace, after months of working remotely from home. When the users attempt to connect to the wired network, they encounter login errors. What is the most likely cause of the login issue for the users, considering that the network uses 802.1X with EAP-TLS for wired network authentication?

   A. The OS may need the latest security updates

   B. An important service has not started

   C. Application crash

   D. The client certificates may have expired

10. A user wants to exclude certain folders from the Windows search feature to improve search results. Which of the following steps should they follow?

    A. Disable Windows Search Service in Services.msc
    B. Add the folders to the "Excluded Folders" list in the Windows search settings
    C. Delete the folders from the hard drive
    D. Reinstall the Windows operating system

11. When the "cat ssh_config" command is executed on a Linux terminal, which of the following outcomes should be anticipated?

    A. The original "ssh_config" file will be replaced with a new blank document
    B. The contents of the "ssh_config" file will be displayed
    C. The lines of text in the "ssh_config" file will be sorted in alphabetical order
    D. The contents of the "ssh_config" file will be copied to another file named " ssh_config"

12. In order to preserve evidence for potential litigation, what is the MOST likely action an incident handler will take?

    A. Apply encryption to the files
    B. Create duplicates of any affected hard drives
    C. Reach out to the cyber insurance company
    D. Notify law enforcement authorities

13. Important business data must be backed up to meet industry regulations, a technician is seeking the most suitable backup method. The requirement is to regularly modify only a few files while considering limited storage space. Which backup methods should the technician choose?

    A. Full backups
    B. Incremental backups
    C. Cloud-based backups
    D. Tape rotation

14. Why would a support technician set their mobile to silent before visiting a customer?

    A. To avoid disrupting the customer's environment
    B. To conserve battery life during the visit
    C. To prevent incoming calls from being recorded
    D. To enable location tracking for service records

15. A technician must identify a solution to copy a large number of files, which may take several hours. In the past, they have experienced interrupted connections and network disruptions. If the network connection between the source and destination machines is unstable or experiences a temporary interruption, what will allow the file copying process to recover?

    A. System File Checker (sfc)
    B. Check Disk (chkdsk)
    C. Git Clone (git clone)
    D. Robocopy

16. A technician, working for a large regional bank, is configuring a new tape backup system. After installing the system in the server room, which backup types will need to be completed FIRST?

    A. Copy backup
    B. Mirror backup
    C. Differential backup
    D. Full backup

17. A user is experiencing frequent popups on their web browser. What will offer the BEST solution to remediate this problem? (Choose two.)

    A. Install a reputable ad blocker extension
    B. Update the browser to the latest version
    C. Disable the computer's firewall
    D. Ignore the popups; they are harmless
    E. Download and run a registry cleaner tool
    F. Reset the computer to factory settings

18. When installing new software on a macOS computer, which of the following file extensions is most commonly used by technicians?

    A. .pkg
    B. .bat
    C. .msi
    D. .dmg

19. A user reports that their smartphone is overheating when not being used, and newly launched applications frequently crash. Which actions will BEST resolve these issues with minimal impact on the user? (Choose two.)

    A. Clear the app cache and data, update the apps, and ensure proper ventilation
    B. Perform a factory reset and install a third-party cooling app
    C. Disable automatic updates and limit app background processes
    D. Buy a new smartphone with better hardware capabilities
    E. Ignore the issues, as they are common with older smartphones
    F. Close down unneeded applications

20. A user's desktop computer was automatically rebooted overnight, and now the system will no longer run some of the Windows applications. What is the recommended action to fix the problem?

    A. Perform a System Restore to a previous working state
    B. Reinstall Windows
    C. Delete the affected applications and reinstall them
    D. Ignore the issue; it will resolve itself eventually

21. What option from the list below can be utilized to establish secure physical access to a data center?

    A. Perimeter barrier
    B. Intrusion detection system
    C. Proximity card reader
    D. Surveillance camera

22. A user notifies a technician about a sluggish computer performance. Which of the following tools can assist the technician in identifying the underlying cause of the issue?

    A. System Optimizer
    B. Performance Monitor
    C. Registry Editor
    D. Task Scheduler

23. An open source software build is downloaded from the GitHub repository. Prior to installing the software image, a technician encounters the following string:

    A. 7d3bb8e188cd9154e99b7ea8db38a24181efb2d1

    B. Which option MOST accurately describes the intended use of this string?

    C. Checksum for verification of download integrity

    D. Encryption key

    E. Product license key

    F. Network port number

24. A user has installed unapproved utilities and applications on a mobile phone. The company has recently deployed MDM tools and would like to prevent users from sideloading unapproved applications. What two MDM policies will prevent future users from sideloading unapproved applications?

    A. App whitelisting

    B. Enforce application store restrictions

    C. Enable USB debugging control

    D. Implement full device encryption

    E. Enable remote wipe

    F. Implement geofencing

25. A technician is experiencing problems while trying to add a sales manager's personal laptop to the company's Active Directory domain. What is the most probable reason why a technician is unable to join a Windows 10 laptop computer to an Active Directory domain?

    A. The computer processor is an AMD version

    B. The laptop is equipped with Windows 10 Home edition

    C. The laptop does not have a touchscreen

    D. The laptop is connected to a docking station

26. An engineering firm is considering implementing the latest version of its computer-aided design (CAD) software, which includes a feature requiring backups of all CAD files to be stored externally in the software vendor's data center. Which of the following is MOST likely to raise concerns for the IT manager?

    A. Comprehensive compatibility testing with all system types and accessories must be conducted for the updated software
    B. Adequate budget allocation for additional staff hours during the installation of updates needs to be ensured
    C. Network utilization is expected to significantly increase due to the larger size of CAD files being backed up
    D. The local hard drives may become overloaded due to the size of the update and installation files

27. A company employee receives a phone call from an individual falsely claiming to represent a mortgage company. Which of the following best describes this incident?

    A. Social engineering
    B. Phishing
    C. Impersonation
    D. Identity theft

28. Following an overnight network breach, security logs reveal that a dictionary attack successfully breached a single user's account after 400 attempts. Which of the following measures would be the MOST effective in mitigating this specific threat?

    A. Two-factor authentication
    B. Intrusion detection system
    C. Password complexity requirements
    D. Network segmentation
    E. Account lockout

29. A payroll manager has created a file on a shared drive and wants to protect it from accidental deletion by other team members. Which of the following applications should the technician recommend to assist the manager in hiding the file?

    A. Disk Cleanup
    B. Task Scheduler
    C. File Properties
    D. Control Panel

30. After dedicating several hours to troubleshooting a computer problem for the company's Chief Executive Officer (CEO), the technician is now pressed for time to resolve the issue promptly. What should the technician do as the next step?

    A. Engage in further research to address the problem

    B. Restart the diagnostic process from the beginning

    C. Notify the CEO that the repair may take a few weeks

    D. Escalate the support ticket to higher-level technicians

31. While configuring a Small Office/Home Office (SOHO) device, a technician needs to ensure that the server maintains a consistent IP address at all times, following the company's policy against static IP addresses. Which of the following options should the technician choose to achieve this requirement?

    A. IP address reservation via DHCP

    B. Network address translation (NAT)

    C. Dynamic Name System (DNS) record

    D. Virtual private network (VPN) configuration

32. A research scientist needs access to a specialist application that is only supported on a Linux OS. The scientist currently only has access to a Windows OS. The scientist needs to work in a remote laboratory with no access to external networks during the day. What offers the BEST solution for the scientist to access the specialist application?

    A. Pay for a remote desktop utilizing a Linux OS

    B. Install the Linux application within the supported Windows Linux subsystem

    C. Install Linux as the primary OS and purchase a second computer to handle the Windows application

    D. Enable the Windows Hyper-V client and install the Linux OS and the Linux application

33. Several desktop computers are to be upgraded in order to support a new software installation. The system upgrades will involve replacing the processor and increasing the memory in the desktop computers. Which of the following should be done to ensure no damage occurs during this upgrade process?

    A. Ground yourself by using an anti-static wrist strap before handling any components

    B. Upgrade the processor first, then add the memory modules afterward

    C. Keep the computers powered on while making the upgrades

    D. Skip the anti-static precautions as they are not necessary for desktop upgrades

34. A customer calls the service desk as they would like to activate speech recognition on their Windows 10 Home PC. Which Windows Settings tool should the user utilize to enable this feature?

    A. Regional Settings
    B. Accessibility
    C. Appearance
    D. Privacy

35. A recent security audit within a company has identified the widespread use of several unauthorized software applications on employee's work desktops, employees are engaged in social media activities using these installed applications. These activities are against the company's policies. In light of this violation, which of the following should be modified to reflect this new requirement?

    A. EMM
    B. SLA
    C. DLP
    D. AUP

36. A departmental manager is proposing to upgrade the design team's workstations with 32 GB of RAM. The plan is also to upgrade the OS from 32-bit to 64-bit. What will be the major benefit of the move to a 64-bit OS?

    A. A 64-bit OS can utilize more RAM efficiently, allowing applications to access larger amounts of memory
    B. A 64-bit OS provides faster processing speeds than a 32-bit OS
    C. A 64-bit OS improves graphics performance and rendering capabilities
    D. A 64-bit OS enhances network connectivity and data transfer rates

37. What is the most probable cause of an issue where a user cannot log in to the domain with a desktop PC, while a laptop PC on the same network functions properly, and a technician is unable to access the secure intranet site for troubleshooting tools?

    A. Network connectivity issues
    B. Incorrect domain credentials
    C. Browser compatibility problems
    D. Firewall restrictions

38. A network technician is deploying a new desktop computer into a SOHO environment. The computer must be configured so that the user can share folders with other Windows users on the network. Which of the following configurations should the technician implement to accomplish this objective?

    A. Set the network configuration to private
    B. Establish a proxy server connection
    C. Assign the user with network administrator privileges
    D. Create a shortcut to the shared drive's public documents

39. In order to resize a partition on the internal storage drive of a computer running macOS, which tool should a technician utilize for this task?

    A. Activity Monitor
    B. Disk Utility
    C. Time Machine
    D. Terminal

40. A development company has a high staff turnover. They would like to identify the most efficient way to use Microsoft Windows 10 features to install a fresh Windows OS when a laptop is re-purposed for a new member of staff. Which of the following is the most suitable?

    A. Manually reinstall Windows 10 from installation media
    B. Use Windows 10's Reset This PC feature
    C. Clone the laptop's hard drive
    D. Use Windows 10 System Restore

41. While using in-flight Wi-Fi on an iPhone to watch a movie, an executive received unexpected pictures without any prior contact history. To effectively address this issue, which of the following actions should the executive take?

    A. Configure AirDrop to exclusively accept transfers from known contacts
    B. Disable all wireless systems entirely throughout the flight
    C. Cease using iMessage and opt for secure communication applications
    D. Restrict messages and calls to saved contacts only

42. A high-street jewelry store needs to improve its physical security measures after a spate of ram-raids have hit similar businesses. To improve building security and prevent vehicles from driving into the premises while not impacting pedestrian access, which of the following options is MOST effective?

    A. Security personnel
    B. Protective barriers
    C. Motion detection systems
    D. Controlled entryway

43. A small retail store has recently set up a wireless network, but they are encountering interference from other wireless networks within proximity of the store. Which of the following actions would be MOST effective in resolving the interference with the LEAST disruption?

    A. Choosing a wireless frequency that is not currently being used
    B. Replacing the wireless equipment with Ethernet cables and switches
    C. Regular power cycling of the equipment
    D. Renaming the access point

44. Given the Chief Financial Officer's concerns about maintaining access to sensitive, legacy, unmaintained personally identifiable information (PII) on a workstation in the event of a ransomware outbreak, and considering the regulatory requirement to retain this data for an extended period, which of the following backup methods would be the MOST suitable?

    A. Daily, incremental backup that is securely stored on an external hard drive
    B. Regular snapshots taken and stored on a network-attached storage (NAS) device
    C. A complete backup of the data that is transferred to an offline, encrypted tape storage
    D. Weekly, differential backups that are securely transmitted to an offsite backup service

45. When a doctor needs to briefly leave their workstation, which of the following methods is the most effective for quickly securing the workstation?

    A. Implementing a key combination to lock the computer upon departure
    B. Verifying the absence of unauthorized individuals in the vicinity
    C. Setting up a screensaver to automatically lock the computer after approximately 30 minutes of inactivity
    D. Powering off the monitor to prevent unauthorized access to displayed information

46. Which of the following options would a technician utilize to enable automatic application boot-up upon logging into a conference room computer? (Choose two.)

    A. Windows Explorer
    B. Startup Folder
    C. System Overview
    D. Programs and Features
    E. Task Scheduler
    F. Device Manager

47. A systems administrator needs to reset a user's password due to the user forgetting it. After creating the new password, the systems administrator wants to implement additional security measures to protect the user's account. Which of the following actions should the systems administrator take?

    A. Enable password change requirement at the next login
    B. Prohibit the user from changing the password
    C. Deactivate the user's account
    D. Set a password with no expiration date

48. A home user downloaded free software from an online gaming site. While installing the downloaded software, the user was prompted to read through a long document with legal phrases and terminology. In order to complete the download, the user was prompted to agree to the terms of use set out within the document. What is being presented to the user in this scenario?

    A. Service level agreement (SLA)
    B. Non-disclosure agreement (NDA)
    C. End user license agreement (EULA)
    D. Memorandum of understanding (MOU)

49. After a regulatory audit, an administrator is tasked with adding more security to the authentication process. The audit recommends deploying multi-factor authentication (MFA). Which method would best address this requirement?

    A. Voice recognition and facial recognition
    B. Username and password
    C. One-time password (OTP) and fingerprint scan
    D. Password and PIN

50. When configuring a new laptop for an employee who frequently travels, which security practice would be most effective in ensuring data protection?

   A. Implementing PIN-based login for authentication
   B. Enforcing quarterly password changes for enhanced security
   C. Enabling hard drive encryption to safeguard sensitive information
   D. Utilizing a physical laptop lock for theft prevention

51. A university professor who is unable to connect to the staff network submits a help desk ticket. The assigned help desk technician inquires about whether any recent changes have been made. The professor reports that due to the college vacation, there is a large amount of construction activity in the surrounding offices. The help desk technician proceeds to ping the user's desktop, which does not respond. Which of the following is the MOST likely cause of this issue?

   A. The DHCP server is offline
   B. The firewall is blocking network access
   C. The user's account is locked
   D. The network cable has become disconnected

52. A sales manager has been unable to access a website and has submitted a help desk ticket. The website that is causing the problem for the manager has been verified to be online. Which of the following troubleshooting steps will MOST likely resolve the issue?

   A. Deleting the browser history
   B. Clearing the DNS cache
   C. Flushing the ARP cache
   D. Enabling JavaScript in the browser

53. Which method should the support technician choose to perform a local Windows 8.1 to Windows 10 upgrade, migrating files and user preferences while ensuring that each system is upgraded individually?

   A. Master image
   B. Fresh install
   C. In-place upgrade
   D. Windows Deployment Services (WDS)

54. A recent security audit highlighted a high risk of data loss from lost or stolen laptops. To mitigate this risk for Windows laptop users while minimizing the impact on user experience, which of the following measures would be the most effective?

    A. Implementing full disk encryption
    B. Enforcing regular laptop backups
    C. Implementing biometric authentication
    D. Enforcing mandatory laptop tracking software

55. A technician has been tasked with configuring a new wireless router for the payroll office. They must ensure optimal security is configured. Which of the following security measures should the technician implement to achieve the highest level of wireless network protection?

    A. Wi-Fi Protected Setup (WPS)
    B. Temporal Key Integrity Protocol (TKIP)
    C. Wi-Fi Protected Access 3 (WPA3)
    D. Wired Equivalent Privacy (WEP)
    E. Media Access Control (MAC) filtering

56. A support technician installed an antivirus application on a user's home computer. The user later reports that the computer has been running slowly, with the hard drive activity light constantly solid. What should be the FIRST step to address this issue?

    A. Check Services in Control Panel to identify any overutilization of system resources
    B. Monitor performance using Performance Monitor to analyze resource utilization
    C. Run System File Checker to verify the integrity of Windows files for any modifications
    D. Review Event Viewer logs to identify any errors or issues

57. A customer services representative asks a professional to fix a laptop problem. The representative complains that the browser redirects to several pages and programs open without being activated. Which of the following is the MOST LIKELY cause?

    A. Keylogger
    B. Cryptominers
    C. Virus
    D. Malware

58. A technician is dealing with frequent micro power outages in their area of operation. These outages are typically brief, with the longest occurrence lasting up to five minutes. Which of the following options should the technician employ to effectively address this issue and minimize its impact?

    A. Surge suppressor
    B. Battery backup
    C. CMOS battery
    D. Generator backup
    E. Uninterruptible power supply (UPS)

59. A marketing team leader is helping a new starter get acquainted with their iMac desktop computer. Which graphical user interface (GUI) and file manager is typically set as the default in macOS for managing files and folders?

    A. Disk Utility
    B. Finder
    C. Dock
    D. FileVault

60. A publishing company supports a mixed desktop environment, containing many older versions of the Microsoft Windows OS. In order to ensure the compatibility of removable media, which of the following filesystem formats would be the BEST choice?

    A. APFS
    B. ext4
    C. CDFS
    D. FAT32

61. After performing a System Restore on a Windows workstation that was affected by malware, the technician notices that the malware is still detected. Which of the following BEST explains why the system still has malware?

    A. The antivirus protection and host firewall were disabled by a system patch
    B. The system updates did not include the latest anti-malware definitions
    C. The malware compromised the System Restore process
    D. The malware was installed before the creation of the System Restore point

62. While working at a local office, a technician discovers that multiple copies of home edition software are installed on computers. Which of the following is the MOST likely violation in this scenario?

    A. End user license agreement (EULA)
    B. Personally identifiable information (PII)
    C. Digital rights management (DRM)
    D. Open source agreement

63. When preserving data from a hard drive for forensic analysis, which two options should be given the MOST consideration?

    A. Licensing agreements
    B. Chain of custody
    C. Incident management documentation
    D. Data integrity
    E. Material safety data sheet
    F. Retention requirements

64. When a technician needs to remotely connect to a Linux desktop for troubleshooting assistance, which of the following tools is the most likely choice, considering the requirement for a tool natively designed for Linux?

    A. SSH
    B. VNC
    C. Remote Desktop Protocol (RDP)
    D. TeamViewer

65. During a hotel stay, a guest wants to connect to the hotel Wi-Fi network but notices that several SSIDs have extremely similar names. What social engineering attack is most likely being attempted in this scenario?

    A. Evil twin
    B. Impersonation
    C. Insider threat
    D. Whaling

66. After installing Windows 10 on a workstation, a technician notices that the system is only utilizing 3.5 GB of the installed 8 GB RAM. What is the MOST probable reason for this discrepancy?

   A. The system is missing critical updates
   B. The system is operating on a 32-bit operating system
   C. The system's RAM modules are malfunctioning
   D. The system requires updates to its BIOS

67. A computer on a corporate network has been infected with malware. What is the most effective method for restoring the computer to operational status?

   A. Scanning the system with a Linux live disk, flashing the BIOS, and then returning the computer to service
   B. Flashing the BIOS, reformatting the drive, and then reinstalling the OS
   C. Degaussing the hard drive, flashing the BIOS, and then reinstalling the OS
   D. Reinstalling the OS, flashing the BIOS, and then scanning with on-premises antivirus

68. A user reports that all the desktop icons on their newly issued PC have become unusually large after a recent software patch deployment. Which of the following actions would be the most effective in resolving this issue?

   A. Rolling back video card drivers
   B. Restoring the PC to factory settings
   C. Repairing the Windows profile
   D. Reinstalling the Windows OS

69. A bank must implement operational controls after recommendations were made by a third-party audit. The bank must implement change management best practices for all its information systems. The implementation team must understand what term is used to describe the range or boundaries of a change. Which of the following is the correct term?

   A. Impact
   B. Purpose
   C. Analysis
   D. Scope

70. A user encounters connection issues when attempting to use a third-party USB adapter. Which of the following tools should a technician employ to address this problem?

    A. taskschd.msc
    B. eventvwr.msc
    C. devmgmt.msc
    D. diskmgmt.msc

71. Upon investigating, a technician uncovers that user input has been surreptitiously captured by a malicious actor. Considering the circumstances, which of the following malware types is the MOST probable cause for this occurrence?

    A. Cryptominers
    B. Rootkit
    C. Spear phishing
    D. Keylogger

72. An asset disposal company needs to ensure potential customers that sensitive data will be rendered uncoverable when it is sent for destruction. When it comes to the physical destruction of SSDs containing sensitive information, which method is considered the most effective?

    A. Overwriting
    B. Formatting
    C. Physical destruction
    D. Deleting

73. A software development company would like to support a hybrid OS environment. How can they easily access shared filesystems and printers between Windows and Linux systems?

    A. yum
    B. CIFS
    C. Samba
    D. chmod

74. A pharmaceutical company needs to ensure all new employees are correctly onboarded, which of the following documents must be signed by the employee before being granted login access to the network?

    A. MSDS
    B. EULA
    C. UAC
    D. AUP

75. Following a failed update, an application is no longer launching and displays the error message "Application needs to be repaired." To address this concern in Windows 10, which of the following utilities should a technician utilize?

    A. Device Manager
    B. Administrator Tools
    C. Programs and Features
    D. Recovery

76. Which protocol can a technician utilize to establish a secure tunnel that conceals IP addresses and ensures enhanced security for network traffic?

    A. DNS
    B. IPS
    C. VPN
    D. SSH

77. While troubleshooting an issue with a computer that contains sensitive information, a technician determines that the computer needs to be taken off-site for repair. What should the technician do NEXT?

    A. Remove the hard disk drive (HDD) and then send the computer for repair
    B. Check corporate policies for guidance
    C. Delete the sensitive information before the computer leaves the buildin
    D. Get authorization from the manager

78. When creating a comprehensive inventory of a company's IT hardware, which documentation management method should a technician employ?

    A. Checklist for new user setup
    B. User information
    C. Asset tags and IDs
    D. Procurement life cycle

79. A user receives a call from someone who claims to be from the user's bank and requests information to ensure the user's account is safe. Which of the following social engineering attacks is the user experiencing?

    A. Phishing
    B. Smishing
    C. Whaling
    D. Vishing

80. In order to manually set an IP address on a computer running macOS, which of the following commands should a technician use?

    A. ipconfig
    B. ifconfig
    C. arpa
    D. ping

81. What is the term used to indicate that a vendor no longer supports a product, including the discontinuation of patches and updates?

    A. AUP
    B. EULA
    C. EOL
    D. UAC

82. A large online retailer must support wireless networks in all of its main warehouse facilities, where there is a mixture of older wireless access points using WPA2 and newer equipment supporting WPA3. Which of the following is an advantage of continuing to support WPA2 instead of WPA3?

   A. A higher level of security
   B. Greater backward compatibility
   C. Improved resistance to brute-force attacks
   D. Support for larger device networks

83. You are troubleshooting a Windows 10 computer that is experiencing slow performance. Task Manager shows high disk usage, but no specific application is consuming a significant amount of resources. Which of the following steps should you take first?

   A. Run a full antivirus scan
   B. Update the graphics card driver
   C. Increase the virtual memory (pagefile) siz
   D. Clear the browser cache.

84. You are setting up a new wireless network for a small office. Which wireless encryption method provides the highest level of security?

   A. Wired Equivalent Privacy (WEP)
   B. Wi-Fi Protected Access (WPA)
   C. Wi-Fi Protected Access 2 (WPA2)
   D. Wi-Fi Protected Setup (WPS)

85. A customer's computer is displaying a "No bootable device found" error during startup. Which of the following should you check first?

   A. Boot sequence in BIOS
   B. RAM modules
   C. Graphics card drivers
   D. Internet connectivity

86. A user's smartphone is not connecting to the company's Wi-Fi network. Other devices are connecting without issues. What should you check first?

   A. Bluetooth settings
   B. Network password
   C. Cellular data usage
   D. App updates

87. You are setting up a new email account for a user in Microsoft Outlook. Which protocol should you use if you want the email to be accessible from multiple devices and keep emails synchronized across them?

   A. Post Office Protocol 3 (POP3)
   B. Simple Mail Transfer Protocol (SMTP)
   C. Internet Message Access Protocol (IMAP)
   D. Hypertext Transfer Protocol (HTTP)

88. You receive a report from a mobile device user complaining about sluggish response time and an unusually high number of ads appearing while using various applications on their Android device. What is the most likely security issue causing these symptoms?

   A. Developer mode enabled
   B. Bootleg/malicious application
   C. Limited internet connectivity
   D. Unexpected application behavior

89. A user's Android device suddenly displays fake security warnings, even when not using any particular application. What security issue is most likely causing this problem?

   A. Android package (APK) source
   B. Data-usage limit notification
   C. Root access/jailbreak
   D. Application spoofing

90. A mobile device user reports that they are unable to connect to the internet, even though they have a stable Wi-Fi connection. What could be the security concern causing this issue?

    A. Developer mode enabled
    B. Limited internet connectivity
    C. High network traffic
    D. Leaked personal files/data

91. A user's Android device frequently displays unexpected application behavior, such as apps crashing or freezing. What is the most likely security issue?

    A. High network traffic
    B. No internet connectivity
    C. Security concerns related to the Android package (APK) source
    D. Root access/jailbreak

92. A mobile device user keeps receiving fake security warnings and notices a high number of ads, even when not using any applications. What is the most likely security issue?

    A. Limited internet connectivity
    B. Unexpected application behavior
    C. Developer mode enabled
    D. Bootleg/malicious application

93. A user's mobile device constantly exceeds its data usage limit, despite not using data-intensive applications. What is the most likely security issue?

    A. High network traffic
    B. Data-usage limit notification
    C. Root access/jailbreak
    D. Application spoofing

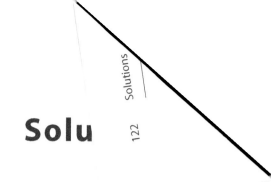

Chapter 1: Operating Systems

1.1 Identify basic features of Microsoft Windows editions

1. **Answer: D**

    Explanation: BitLocker Drive Encryption requires an additional BitLocker password before the Windows OS is launched. If this is successfully entered, then the user will be presented with the regular login prompt next.

    Incorrect: A BIOS password requires a special key sequence, such as Ctrl + D, the purpose of which is to prevent a user from entering the BIOS/UEFI at startup. Windows Privacy and Security does not ask for a prompt before the OS launches. Windows Accessibility is typically used for the configuration of Windows settings to help users with audio or visual impairments.

2. **Answer: A, D**

    Explanation: Windows 10 Home is intended for personal use and does not offer support features for enterprise/business users. ChromeOS is a simple-to-use OS and does not allow domain join.

    Incorrect: All Windows Pro and Enterprise editions DO support domain join functionality.

3. **Answer: A, D**

    Explanation: Windows 10 Pro and Enterprise editions are intended for business use and support additional functionality, including security features. They therefore support BitLocker.

    Incorrect: Older versions of Windows require Enterprise (or Windows 7 Ultimate) licenses to access advanced security features. Windows Home editions do not have access to BitLocker. macOS offers File Vault as an alternative to Windows BitLocker.

4. **Answer: A**

    Explanation: Assuming there are no compatibility issues, an in-place upgrade will require the least administrative effort to migrate all user settings and applications.

    Incorrect: A fresh installation will not migrate the settings and applications. The user settings would need to be backed up separately, and applications would need to be reinstalled.

5. **Answer: B**

   Explanation: As the manager is using a personal computer, it is highly likely that the system was purchased from a retail store, where the default Windows OS edition will be Home. BitLocker Drive Encryption requires at least Windows Professional.

   Incorrect: Having only 2GB of memory would not prevent BitLocker from being enabled. The size of the hard drive would only be an issue if there is not sufficient space to create a small unencrypted partition (100MB). BitLocker is supported on 32-bit and 64-bit editions of Windows.

6. **Answer: A**

   Explanation: The Remote Desktop Protocol (RDP) establishes a connection that allows a remote user to take control of another console/desktop, logging any existing users off the device.

   Incorrect: Virtual Network Computing (VNC) and Remote Assistance (RA) allow remote sharing of a desktop, meaning that the user would be able to view the session. Secure File Transfer Protocol (SFTP) only allows the transfer of files, not any configuration changes.

7. **Answer: C**

   Explanation: A limitation of installing a 32-bit Operating System (OS) is that 4GB of RAM is the maximum available to the system, even if the underlying hardware is 64-bit.

   Incorrect: There are some restrictions on the maximum amount of memory even if a 64-bit OS is installed. 64-bit Windows Pro and Enterprise support 2TB of RAM, while the 64-bit edition of Home supports 128GB.

8. **Answer: D**

   Explanation: BitLocker To Go can be used on a supported Windows OS to encrypt removable media.

   Incorrect: BitLocker can be used to encrypt fixed drives on supported Windows OSs but cannot be used to encrypt optical media.

9. **Answer: C**

   Explanation: An in-place upgrade is intended to migrate user settings and installed applications.

   Incorrect: A network installation deploys from a server-based image (i.e., image deployment) and will perform the equivalent of a clean install. A clean install will install a fresh version of Windows, overwriting all the user settings.

10. **Answer: B**

    Explanation: Windows Home editions are intended for the consumer market and do not have the same tools and utilities as those offered in the Pro/Enterprise versions. RDP is only offered as a host service on Home editions. This means you can connect to a Pro or Enterprise desktop, but they cannot connect to your desktop.

    Incorrect: RDP service memory dependency is the same as the OS, so 2GB RAM is acceptable. RDP is offered on both 32-bit and 64-bit platforms. Using Windows Pro would not in itself be the reason for a failed RDP connection.

1.2 Given a scenario, use the appropriate Microsoft command-line tool

1. **Answer: B**

    Explanation: ipconfig /all will give comprehensive configuration details for the workstation network interface/s, showing the IP address, subnet mask, DHCP server, DNS settings, and more.

    Incorrect: ping is a useful utility but, in this case, will only ping the loopback address (127.0.0.1), giving no configuration information. netstat will show network connections and listening ports. It can also be used to display Ethernet statistics but will not show network card configuration settings. hostname is a command that will show only the workstation name.

2. **Answer: A**

    Explanation: robocopy (robust copy) is designed to mirror large amounts of data. It supports the copying of additional attributes, including hidden files, and maintains folder permissions. It has been included in the Windows OS since Vista.

    Incorrect: The copy command is not designed as a bulk copying tool; it does not retain permissions. xcopy does not support hidden files or maintain folder permissions. The cp command is a Linux command (although it would meet the criteria requested).

3. **Answer: D, E**

    Explanation: nslookup (Name Server Lookup) is used to send a query to a DNS server (i.e., Name Server). The output in the question is from nslookup www.google.com. tracert is the Windows trace route command. It displays the "hops" as packets are forwarded to the destination system. It is useful to identify bottlenecks where traffic is slowed down.

    Incorrect: ping is useful to perform connectivity tests but does not display the hops. ipconfig is used to show network card configuration settings. netstat is used to display the network connections and listening ports of the local computer. nbstat (NetBIOS statistics) is used to show NetBIOS-related information.

4. **Answer: C**

   Explanation: RDP and Group Policy Editor (gpedit.msc) are both features that are only included in the Pro and Enterprise versions of Windows.

   Incorrect: The computer is not running Linux as the technician would have discovered this when installing third-party tools. Windows 10 Enterprise would have allowed for the functionality that the technician required. It is unlikely that a corrupt registry would have caused these two very specific problems without impacting other services on the user's computer.

5. **Answer: A**

   Explanation: ping will allow a support technician to establish where the connectivity fails. The ping command can be used to test gateway access and remote (internet) connectivity.

   Incorrect: msconfig will display the configuration used during the boot process. nbtstat will not allow a technician to test connectivity on the network. nslookup will be useful if the technician is troubleshooting name resolution but would typically be used after ping.

6. **Answer: C**

   Explanation: nslookup can resolve names to IP addresses (that is, forward lookups) and IP addresses to names (reverse lookups). DNS servers need to be configured with Pointer Records (PTR) and reverse lookup zones to support reverse lookups.

   Incorrect: gpresult allows a technician to troubleshoot Group Policy settings on the local machine. ipconfig is used to display local network configuration settings (it does not display remote workstation configuration settings). net user is a Windows command that's used to manage local user accounts.

7. **Answer: A**

   Explanation: USB access must be stopped quickly on multiple workstations. A domain-based group policy would be the most effective way to push out this security setting. For an immediate update, the support team can run invoke-gpupdate remotely or use the Group Policy Management Console (GPMC) to update multiple workstations at the same time with minimal disruption.

   Incorrect: Local security policy changes would be time-consuming to implement. A login script would impact the users as they would all need to log out of their workstations and log back in for a login script to be effective. Acceptable Use Policy (AUP) is a policy describing expected behavior while using an organization's information system and does not guarantee users will comply with that expected behavior.

8. **Answer: C**

   Explanation: gpresult will process and output the current group policy settings, and the level of detail can be determined by a command switch. /Z is super-verbose output (that is, the most detailed).

   Incorrect: ipconfig /all will not display group policy settings. netstat /e will display only Ethernet statistics for a local network interface. nslookup will use DNS to resolve registered names to Internet Protocol (IP) addresses.

9. **Answer: A**

   Explanation: netstat -p TCP (-p for protocol) allows the display of current TCP or UDP connections. In this case, the desired output is TCP connections. Note that switches can be combined. If the required output was connections and listening ports, netstat -a -p tcp could be used.

   Incorrect: net use would not support this function as it is used to manage local user accounts. nslookup is not used to display connections and listening ports but rather for DNS lookups. netstat -p UDP would only display UDP ports (NOT TCP ports).

10. **Answer: B**

    Explanation: gpresult will display the current group policy that has been deployed to the workstation.

    Incorrect: nbtstat displays NetBIOS statistics (not group policy). nslookup is used to query a DNS server. gpupdate will process any new and existing group policy but will not display the resultant settings. tasklist is a Windows command roughly equivalent to the GUI Task Manager process tab.

11. **Answer: A**

    Explanation: net use allows temporary access to a shared folder (or, in this case, a persistent drive mapping to a shared folder). It is important to choose the correct syntax. The allocated drive letter p: must be defined before the \\server1\public location.

    Incorrect: tracert is not used to map drives. The syntax for the command is also incorrect. net use \\P will not work as the syntax is wrong.

12. **Answer: B**

    Explanation: SFC is the built-in Windows "system file" checker. It runs as a background process, but it can also be run on demand. /SCANNOW scans for the integrity of all protected system files and repairs files with errors when possible. As the malware in this instance has targeted Windows operating system files, this is the best tool.

    Incorrect: chkdsk is a tool that's used to repair disk errors, such as corrupt areas on the disk. diskpart is a command-line tool for managing disk volumes. It can create and format disks.

13. **Answer: C**

    Explanation: There are three group policy tools in this question, so it is important to read this question carefully, as the goal is for a technician to verify the group policy locally. gpresult is run at the command prompt of a workstation to display applied group policy settings.

    Incorrect: The Group Policy Management Console (gpmc.msc) is typically run remotely by administrators to manage and report group policy objects. gpupdate could be used to apply new settings but does not report. msconfig is used to troubleshoot the boot process. shutdown -r (restart) will not report on group policy settings, although it could be used as a troubleshooting step, as some settings may require a reboot.

1.3 Given a scenario, use features and tools of the Microsoft Windows 10 operating system (OS)

1. **Answer: A**

    Explanation: Task Manager's Processes tab will display all running applications, background processes, and Windows processes. The unwanted application or process can be terminated using the End task option.

    Incorrect: The task cannot be ended from either the Startup or Performance tabs of Task Manager. Directly editing the registry should never be the first choice for ending a task as it may have unpredictable outcomes.

2. **Answer: D**

    Explanation: The reason for the blue screen error will be logged in one of the event viewer logs, and if it was a hardware driver issue, it will be found in the Windows System log.

    Incorrect: SFC can be used to ensure Windows system files are validated but will not display the event details. msconfig can be used to troubleshoot the boot process and could be configured to boot into safe mode if there is an unstable driver. regedit is the registry editor, which is not useful in this case. msinfo32 (system information) can be useful as a support tool for gathering configuration information but will not store details about the blue screen event.

3. **Answer: A**

    Explanation: Task Scheduler (taskschd.msc) is the tool for configuring background tasks. Any settings that have been changed can be seen here.

    Incorrect: Device Manager (devmgmt.msc) will allow a technician to troubleshoot hardware. Task Scheduler (taskschd.msc) and Performance Monitor (perfmon.msc) can be useful for identifying performance bottlenecks. Certificate Manager (certmgr.msc) is used to manage local user and computer certificates as well as trusted certificate authorities.

4. **Answer: C**

   Explanation: Performance Monitor can be configured to run a schedule, capturing detailed performance data during specific times of the day.

   Incorrect: Computer Management allows a technician to use multiple administrative tools on a local or remote workstation (user and group management services). Event Viewer logs can be useful to identify faulting applications or drivers. Task Manager shows events in real time and would require the support technician to interactively monitor the computer (it is not as convenient as Performance Monitor).

5. **Answer: A**

   Explanation: System Information (msinfo32.exe) will display a comprehensive inventory of hardware, software, drivers, and so on.

   Incorrect: Resource Monitor (resmon.exe) shows system and network performance data in real time. System Configuration (msconfig.exe) allows configuration of the boot process. Registry Editor (regedit.exe) will not be the easiest tool with which to find this information.

6. **Answer: C, E**

   Explanation: Disk Cleanup will identify files that are not needed and can be removed, and by defragmenting the hard drive, the technician will optimize the file fragments for large files. The defrag will actually move data so that large files occupy sequential clusters on the drive surface (which is not necessary for SSD drives).

   Incorrect: Booting the computer in safe mode is not necessary as the system is not unstable, just underperforming. Rebooting the computer may be necessary when configuration changes or new drivers require it. There is no reason to install any device drivers as there are no reported issues with hardware drivers.

7. **Answer: B**

   Explanation: Disk Management will allow a disk to be extended if there is unused free space.

   Incorrect: Diskpart would allow the disk to be extended; however, it runs at the command prompt and, thus, is not graphical. Device Manager displays information about controllers and disk drives but does not allow the disk to be resized. Disk Cleanup would not allow the disk partition to be re-sized.

8. **Answer: E**

    Explanation: The recommended tool to identify poorly performing start-up applications and disable them is to use the Task Manager.

    Incorrect: Using the System Configuration | Startup options to disable startup applications is only supported on older versions of Windows. Directly editing registry keys is not usually the best approach, and in this case, you would not know which startup apps to disable. Manually disabling all startup tasks currently listed as enabled and rebooting to check for issue resolution at startup is not necessary, as the startup impact is measured by Windows and is better addressed by following the steps in answer E.

9. **Answer: C**

    Explanation: The Task Manager's Performance tab will give the technician real-time information on the system's all-around performance and enable the technician to identify obvious bottlenecks.

    Incorrect: Task Scheduler will allow heavy load tasks to be rescheduled but won't show performance data. Windows Memory Diagnostic is a tool that performs a health check on physical memory (for example, to determine whether there are any cells on a RAM module that are corrupt). Disk Defragmenter could be run in response to high disk latency, but it will not show actual disk performance information.

10. **Answer: A**

    Explanation: certmgr.msc can be used to manage certificates for the computer, user, and system accounts. The Trusted Root Certificate Authorities store is populated with trusted root certificate authorities. This list can be modified manually or centrally using group policy.

    Incorrect: Removing the certificates from the store using regedit.msc is not a good choice, as this may lead to unpredictable results. Device Manager (devmgmt.msc) does not allow the management of certificates on the laptop. A certificate revocation list (CRL) is used by a certificate authority to publish certificates that they have issued but that are now compromised/untrusted, and this is not appropriate in this case.

1.4 Given a scenario, use the appropriate Microsoft Windows 10 Control Panel utility

1. **Answer: C**

    Explanation: Device Manager must be used to disable a hardware device.

    Incorrect: Devices and Printers allows for the installation and management of printers but does not offer the option to disable them. Sync Center allows for the management of offline files. Power Options does not offer any options to control printers.

2. **Answer: A**

   Explanation: It is likely that the file type has been associated with the wrong application and this is what is causing an error. The default settings would open the JPEG in the Photos app. This can be corrected using the Control Panel | Default Programs option.

   Incorrect: Display settings do not offer the option to change file associations. Device Manager does not contain the option to change file associations. Internet Options contains web browser settings only.

3. **Answer: B**

   Explanation: By configuring the Connections tab, we can ensure all web browser traffic is forwarded to the proxy server.

   Incorrect: Network and Sharing Centre | Change Adapter Settings does not allow for proxy configuration. Windows Defender Firewall cannot be used to configure proxy settings. Device Manager is used to troubleshoot problems with hardware.

4. **Answer: C**

   Explanation: Ease of Access Center allows the system to be optimized for a variety of different disabilities. For example, the system can be optimized for users who cannot use a mouse or keyboard, as well as for visually impaired users.

   Incorrect: Device Manager allows the configuration of extra hardware for users with disabilities, but not the optimization of the interface for the user. System and Programs and Features would each allow the installation of new software, not the optimization of default system features.

5. **Answer: B**

   Explanation: If a device is not working after installing device drivers, the first place to look is Device Manager, which offers important information to aid in troubleshooting.

   Incorrect: The Services console and Event Viewer's System logs (which will report a failed driver) would be useful to troubleshoot background services that may have failed, but Device Manager offers more information. Programs and Features is useful if a problematic application needs to be repaired.

6. **Answer: D**

   Explanation: Internet Options allows browser settings to be adjusted or reset to their defaults.

   Incorrect: System offers no browser-related settings. Programs and Features allows the browser to be uninstalled or repaired, but not for settings to be changed. Network and Sharing Center allows for troubleshooting network adapters and connections.

7. **Answer: A**

   Explanation: Network and Sharing Center allows an IP address to be manually set.

   Incorrect: Sync Center is used primarily to manage the synchronization of offline files. User Account Control is used to manage security prompts when configuration changes are attempted. Credential Manager is used to store accounts and passwords that allow the signed-in user to access third-party sites without being prompted for additional credentials.

8. **Answer: D**

   Explanation: This setting can be accessed using the Mail option in the Control Panel.

   Incorrect: Internet Options configures browser settings, Windows Defender Firewall allows for the configuration of network access through ports and protocols, and User Accounts is where the local user account database can be managed.

9. **Answer: A**

   Explanation: When the lid is shut, the Do nothing option will ensure the system does not enable any power-saving settings preventing the function of external peripherals.

   Incorrect: Sleep, Hibernate, and Shut down each enable a power saving setting that will power the screen off.

10. **Answer: B**

    Explanation: Control Panel | Sound allows the user to view settings to change their preference for the hardware used for audio output, as there will now be two choices (the original and new hardware).

    Incorrect: Device Manager | Audio inputs and outputs is where drivers are updated and devices disabled. Devices and Printers allows new devices to be detected or removed (but not the choice of preferred audio playback device). Speech Recognition is not a setting that allows for the default playback device to be selected.

1.5 Given a scenario, use the appropriate Windows settings

1. **Answer: A**

   Explanation: Selecting Settings | Time & Language allows the current language keyboard to be selected. If this is not done, then a user in the United States, for example, would press Shift + 2 and expect to see the @ symbol. But if the keyboard language was set to U.K., the character displayed would be ".

   Incorrect: Settings | Accessibility is primarily used to configure settings for users with a disability. Settings | Personalization is used to manage a user's Windows environment, which includes options such as theme and default colors. Settings | Apps controls Windows applications.

2. **Answer: C**

   Explanation: Settings | System allows the configuration of multiple monitors through the Display settings.

   Incorrect: The other choices do not give access to the multiple display configuration settings.

3. **Answer: C**

   Explanation: It is possible to access Storage settings from Settings | System. The disk space used is displayed along with options to free up disk space.

   Incorrect: The other options here do not give access to Storage settings to review storage usage.

4. **Answer: A**

   Explanation: The screensaver settings can be configured from the Settings | Personalization | Lock screen options.

   Incorrect: All the other choices are either non-existent paths or do not offer the option to set a screen lock timeout.

5. **Answer: C**

   Explanation: In an organization where group policy is centrally managed, the BitLocker settings will be configured by the organization. To access the controls directly, you would need to enter Settings, then Privacy & security. Note that additional operating system and hardware support is required to successfully enable BitLocker (OS version needs to be a minimum of Windows Professional and TPM hardware support is needed).

   Incorrect: None of the other choices offer the option to enable BitLocker Drive Encryption.

6. **Answer: D**

   Explanation: A proxy server enables an organization to protect client browser sessions by restricting access to unsafe sites based on URI/URLs and employing content filtering.

   Incorrect: None of the other choices offer the option to select a proxy server.

7. **Answer: D**

   Explanation: To access mailbox configuration options from the Settings menu, Accounts must be selected. Settings | Accounts allows a user to customize their preferences for a number of options (including email).

   Incorrect: None of the other choices give access to email options.

8. **Answer: A**

   Explanation: A company can use the same features to provide visual and audio feedback during a gaming session that a user would use to record and share their own gaming sessions. These are accessed through Settings | Gaming | Captures.

   Incorrect: This feature must be accessed through gaming controls. The other options will not provide access to the required settings.

1.6 Given a scenario, configure Microsoft Windows networking features on a client/desktop

1. **Answer: C**

   Explanation: A domain-joined computer will allow the enterprise to centrally manage settings through tools such as Group Policy. There are a number of ways to add a computer to the domain, including the PowerShell Add-Computer command. To access the function through the settings menu, you must first select the System feature.

   Incorrect: While there are other ways to add a computer to a domain (for example, PowerShell), the other menu options presented do not allow this action.

2. **Answer: B, D**

   Explanation: If a DHCP server cannot be located when a host computer requests an IP address, then an APIPA address will be locally assigned to the interface. The same behavior will occur if a lease expires on a previously assigned IP address.

   Incorrect: 169.254.23.66 is not a private IP address. A private IP address is from a range reserved for internal use. Private ranges include 10.0.0.0, 172.16.0.0-172.31.0.0, and 192.168.0.0. IPv6 does not assign APIPA addresses. Instead, a locally assigned (that is, default) address is a link-local address in a 32-character hexadecimal format and always begins with FE80. Active Directory and DNS services are not responsible for allocating IP addresses.

3. **Answer: B**

   Explanation: Windows Defender Firewall does not allow Windows file and print traffic while the firewall profile is set to Public (this is intended to add security when not using a trusted network).

   Incorrect: The private network profile will allow file and print traffic. The user has been assigned the requisite privileges so this should not be a problem. Other network services are working so there cannot be a problem with the network card.

4. **Answer: A**

   Explanation: Windows Defender Firewall can be configured to block unwanted incoming and outgoing connections. This is the most effective way to prevent the use of a P2P file-sharing application.

   Incorrect: Windows Virus & threat protection will protect a Windows operating system from malware. There are legitimate P2P file-sharing applications that will be considered malware. Windows Secure Boot is designed to ensure a private key cannot be tampered with. Windows BitLocker Drive Encryption offers protection from unauthorized access to Windows hard disk drives.

5. **Answer: C**

   Explanation: Only Administrator accounts can modify Windows Defender Firewall settings.

   Incorrect: Power Users is a group that is provided for backward compatibility and allows the same privileges as a Standard user. Guest Account has the least privileges of all accounts, and Standard users do not have privileges to change system configuration settings.

6. **Answer: C**

   Explanation: The current IP address of 169.154.44.89 is an Automatic Private IP Address (APIPA), which is self-assigned by the client computer. This happens if the DHCP service is unable to respond to a client request. It is likely that there was a temporary service disruption. ipconfig /renew will indicate whether the DHCP service is available or if the issue needs to be escalated.

   Incorrect: ipconfig /all shows the current network configuration. ipconfig /flushdns is used to resolve DNS-related problems. ipconfig /flushdhcp is a non-existent option.

7. **Answer: B, C**

   Explanation: In order to restrict data usage on a network interface, a limit must be set and the Metered Connection setting must be configured.

   Incorrect: System | Storage settings allows you to optimize the use of locally available storage devices, not network traffic. Advanced Network Settings | Advanced Sharing enables the configuration of network profiles used by Windows Defender Firewall. Network Interface | Flight Mode – On will disable Wi-Fi and Bluetooth.

8. **Answer: B**

   Explanation: The configuration will need to include an IP address or hostname as the printer is connected directly to the network switch.

   Incorrect: Selecting a shared printer by name would only work if the printer was already installed and shared by an existing computer on the network. The other options would not give the desired result as the printer is not wireless or connected via USB.

1.7 Given a scenario, apply application installation and configuration concepts

1. **Answer: C**

   Explanation: The x86 architecture describes a processor that has 32 registers. This architecture means that a maximum of 4GB of RAM can be accessed by the system. To access any additional RAM purchased would require the system to be upgraded to an x64-bit architecture.

   Incorrect: Installing Ubuntu Linux will not affect the amount of memory that can be accessed. Installing a larger hard drive will not help, and the addition of more RAM on the existing x86 architecture will not be effective.

2. **Answer: B**

   Explanation: While the exact requirements of the CAD application are unknown and the base hardware seems reasonably sufficient, the exception to this is the graphics card. CAD applications place heavy demands on the graphics hardware and will benefit from dedicated hardware comprising a multi-core Graphics Processing Unit (GPU) and dedicated video RAM.

   Incorrect: As the existing hardware is of a high standard, there is no obvious requirement to upgrade anything but the integrated graphics.

3. **Answer: C**

   Explanation: 32-bit applications are able to run on 64-bit Windows using a compatibility setting provided by the Windows on Windows (WOW) architecture. They will run in a similar fashion as they would on a native 32-bit host, with the same memory restrictions (4 GB RAM at most).

   Incorrect: Apart from the memory restrictions, all other functionalities will still be supported, including multi-tasking and multi-threading.

4. **Answer: B**

   Explanation: In some cases, an application makes a call to the operating system to get the current version and checks to see if that matches its requirements. Often, the application fails simply because the value is not the same as its requirements when the application is told that the OS is Windows 10, but it expected Windows 8. A quick fix is to try and trick the application into believing it is running on Windows 8 by selecting that as the compatibility setting.

   Incorrect: Updating the application to the latest version may be a long-term option, but it doesn't offer a quick fix. Safe mode is used to troubleshoot faulting drivers and services but is unlikely to offer a solution to the technician's current problem.

5. **Answer: B**

   Explanation: A hardware token can store a unique key that is used to authorize the launch of the CAD software. Where the value of a single license may run into several thousand dollars, this is an effective way to ensure the software is not fraudulently used.

   Incorrect: None of the other options fully protect the developers from unscrupulous users.

1.8 Explain common OS types and their purposes

1. **Answer: A**

   Explanation: The technician must find a filesystem compatible with both operating systems. FAT32 is compatible with many common operating systems, including Linux, macOS, and Windows.

   Incorrect: ext4 is used on Linux. NTFS and exFAT do not have the same wide support as FAT32 and may not be readable by some Linux operating systems.

2. **Answer: A**

   Explanation: An End of Life (EOL) operating system no longer receives updates or security patches from the vendor.

   Incorrect: The issue is not an incompatible operating system as it still works on the hardware platform. The issue raised here is more about security and reliability issues; the fact that it is a 32-bit OS is not significant. A vendor may offer extended support for important customers (usually requiring the customer to pay for this extended support). In this instance, extended support is not being offered.

3. **Answer: C**

   Explanation: ChromeOS is a lightweight OS based on the popular Chrome browser.

   Incorrect: There are many examples of versions of minimalist OSs, such as Windows IoT and Linux Lite, while Apple is rumored to be testing a Lite version of macOS for iPads. None of these are based on a browser-based interface, however.

4. **Answer: C**

   Explanation: Windows offers the best solution to standardize all servers, workstations, and mobile devices across a single vendor OS. Windows Server offers centralized datacenter services, Windows 11 Enterprise can be used for managed desktops, and Windows Mobile can be employed for handheld devices.

   Incorrect: Linux is used to deliver datacenter services and is a very capable server-based platform. There are also user-friendly desktop editions such as Ubuntu/Red Hat, but these editions are not supported on smartphones or tablets. iOS is the Apple operating system used on the iPhone and iPad. ChromeOS is desktop only.

5. **Answer: D**

   Explanation: Linux operating systems use the Extended Filesystem (ext), the first edition of which was created around 1992 and supported storage limits of 2GB. ext2 was followed by ext3 in 2001, which supported a maximum partition size of 16TB. ext4 was introduced around 2008 and supports a maximum partition size of 1EB (1,000,000 TB). The ext4 filesystem also supports online defragmentation, which is important to maintain efficient file access.

   Incorrect: FAT32 is not used as a core filesystem on Linux. It is intended for removable media and has a maximum volume size of 32GB. ext3 will not support online defragmentation or the volume size required. NTFS is a Windows filesystem.

6. **Answer: C**

   Explanation: Android is an open source (that is, royalty free) operating system developed by Google. It was initially released in 2008 and, in 2023, is currently on version 13 (codename Tiramisu). Android OS is based on a Linux kernel and supports many of the security features used in mainstream Linux distributions.

   Incorrect: iOS is a proprietary Apple-based mobile operating system originally used exclusively on Apple hardware, specifically the code base for iPhones, iPods, and iPads. SUSE Linux is not used on mobile devices or smartphones; it is primarily deployed on datacenter servers. Windows Mobile uses a modified version of the Windows desktop OS.

1.9 Given a scenario, perform OS installations and upgrades in a diverse OS environment

1. **Answer: D**

   Explanation: Pre-Boot Execution Environment (PXE) allows a computer to boot from the Network Interface Card (NIC) and access services on the network. In this case, the technician could use the media to create a Windows Deployment Server and perform the upgrades from a central location.

   Incorrect: Booting from a Solid State Drive (SSD) does not meet the requirements of installing over the network. Optical drives and flash drives can be used to install a single image but do not solve the problem of upgrading multiple computers across the network.

2. **Answer: D**

   Explanation: An unattended installation allows a central deployment image to be made available alongside an automated setup file (or unattended script). Once the installation is started, the technician can leave it to complete on its own.

   Incorrect: A remote network installation does not meet the requirements for an automated installation. A repair installation allows for a faulting computer to be reimaged back to a standard build configuration. A clean installation does not describe an automated process.

3. **Answer: C**

   Explanation: The GUID Partition Table (GPT) disk format allows partition sizes of up to 18 EB (that is, 18.8 million TB). A GPT drive can also contain as many as 128 separate partitions.

   Incorrect: ext4 is not supported on Windows; it is used on Linux filesystems. Master Boot Record (MBR) partitions are limited to a maximum size of 2TB and support a maximum of four partitions per disk. Apple File System (APFS) is not supported natively on Windows computers.

4. **Answer: D**

   Explanation: An in-place upgrade will allow the customer to keep all supported applications and retain their settings. It is important to check that in-place upgrades are supported for the version of Windows they are currently using.

   Incorrect: A clean install will not retain applications or settings. A repair installation will reset the image back to default for the current build of Windows on the customer's system and is intended as a troubleshooting option. An unattended install does not necessarily mean that an upgrade will be selected.

5. **Answer: C**

   Explanation: Windows 10 was the first Windows operating system to support feature upgrades (Windows 11 also supports feature upgrades). Typically released every six months, feature upgrades include additional features and functionality. In previous releases of Windows, new features and functionality were delivered with service packs or interim releases, such as the upgrade of Windows 8.0 to 8.1.

   Incorrect: Windows 7 and Windows 8.1 do not support feature upgrades.

6. **Answer: C**

   Explanation: An image deployment allows for a customized build of the operating system (along with any required applications) to be created. The image can be hosted on a Windows Deployment Server, and all new installations will use the standard centralized image.

   Incorrect: An upgrade will retain current applications and settings (some existing desktop computers may have different applications installed and be configured differently). Clean installations do not always ensure the same settings will be applied. A repair installation is used to set a Windows computer back up on a standard image as a troubleshooting step.

7. **Answer: B**

    Explanation: When installing images from a central server across the network, it is expected that the overall traffic on the network segment will increase. It is important that any unacceptable load on the network is identified.

    Incorrect: The impact on users will only be a concern if the network is overwhelmed with additional traffic. DHCP will need to provide IP addresses to 30 workstations at a time (during the build), so this should not add any great burden to the DHCP server. The impact on production workstations will only be a negative concern if the network is experiencing unacceptable volumes of additional traffic during the build process.

8. **Answer: B, C**

    Explanation: Unified Extensible Firmware Interface (UEFI) replaces the original Binary Input Output System (BIOS) seen in computer systems since the original 1980s PC systems. UEFI is needed to support GPT disks. Windows 11 installation requires the presence of a Trusted Platform Module (TPM) to support some of the security features now standard in the operating system.

    Incorrect: Windows 11 requires 4GB RAM and a 1GHz 64-bit processor in addition to TPM 2.0 and UEFI support.

9. **Answer: B**

    Explanation: A repair installation allows for boot issues, such as missing or corrupt startup files, to be fixed. The technician will be presented with the Advanced Options menu if Windows cannot boot and the Automatic Repair function has failed. This menu provides options including System Restore, System Image Recovery (if you have a backup), or to run a Startup Repair.

    Incorrect: Unattended, image deployment, and remote installations are not intended as troubleshooting steps.

10. **Answer: B**

    Explanation: The Windows PC Health Check App is a free Microsoft download and allows a Windows computer to be assessed prior to an upgrade. Following this assessment, the app will provide you with a list of system requirements for the given upgrade and state whether or not these are met by the system in question.

    Incorrect: While the other options do provide useful information for technicians, they do not present an easy-to-read upgrade report.

1.10 Identify common features and tools of the macOS/desktop OS

1. **Answer: C**

   Explanation: The standard file extensions for a Mac installation file is DMG (from **D**isk i**M**a**G**e) and replaces the much older IMG file format.

   Incorrect: MSI and EXE file formats are used by Windows computers. APK files are Android Package files and are used to deploy applications on devices running the Android operating system.

2. **Answer: B**

   Explanation: The Mac Finder application allows the user to view files on all supported media.

   Incorrect: Keychain is used to support single sign-on (SSO) and allows transparent authentication across multiple sites. Mission Control is used to switch between different workspaces on a Mac. Explorer is a Windows feature.

3. **Answer: B**

   Explanation: The Mac feature used to back up and restore data files is Time Machine.

   Incorrect: File History and Windows Backup are features supported only on Windows operating systems. Mission Control is not used to back up or restore files.

4. **Answer: A**

   Explanation: The Force Quit menu allows unresponsive applications to be terminated.

   Incorrect: Task Manager, Task List, and Control Panel are all features available only on Windows computers.

5. **Answer: C**

   Explanation: FileVault allows a Mac hard drive to be encrypted using 128-bit or 256-bit Advanced Encryption Standard (AES). Once the feature has been enabled, the user must supply their password before the system can boot up. If no password is provided, then the disk will remain encrypted.

   Incorrect: iCloud is used to synchronize data from Apple devices to cloud-based storage. Keychain is used to manage multiple identities when accessing different sites. BitLocker is a disk encryption technology used on Windows operating systems.

6. **Answer: C**

   Explanation: The Mac operating system (beginning with Mac OS X in 1996) was developed as a custom operating system based on Berkeley Software Distribution (BSD) Unix.

   Incorrect: macOS is not based on Linux, Android, or ChromeOS.

7. **Answer: C**

    Explanation: The Keychain feature allows a user to store passwords and account information that can then be used to reduce the number of passwords that a user would otherwise need to remember.

    Incorrect: Mission Control is used to switch between applications and desktops. Spotlight is used for system-wide searches (such as searching for an application, email, or files) on a macOS machine. Dock is used to quickly navigate to applications and features.

8. **Answer: A**

    Explanation: The easiest way for this task to be accomplished is to locate the application and delete the application folder.

    Incorrect: None of the other options will give the desired result.

9. **Answer: A**

    Explanation: In the event that a Mac computer fails to boot, it is likely that one or more critical files on the hard disk are missing or damaged. To access the Recovery menu, Command + R must be pressed during the boot process. The recovery options can then be accessed to attempt to fix the error.

    Incorrect: Do not attempt to reinstall the operating system until all other options have been attempted. Important data files could be lost if they have not been backed up. The Recovery menu cannot be accessed by booting the computer from a DVD, not to mention that most modern Macs do not include a DVD drive. Safe mode is a feature of the Windows operating system.

10. **Answer: A**

    Explanation: To permanently delete the files and free up disk space, the Trash application should be emptied.

    Incorrect: Recycle Bin and Disk Cleaner are Windows features. Separating a disk into separate partitions with Disk Utility will not increase the available disk space.

11. **Answer: B**

    Explanation: The Dock is normally displayed at the bottom of the screen and is a convenient place through which to access features, applications, folders, and files. The Dock will display recently used applications by default but can be customized by dragging an item onto the Dock to create a persistent link.

    Incorrect: Mission Control allows users to switch between different workspaces. The Start menu is a Microsoft Windows feature. Toolbars are used to access features within an application.

12. **Answer: B**

    Explanation: System Preferences allows the configuration and customization of all common configuration preferences.

    Incorrect: Mission Control allows users to switch between different workspaces. Dock offers easy access to applications and files. Disk Utility is a system tool that handles disk-specific tasks on Mac computers.

13. **Answer: A, C**

    Explanation: To avoid an overly cluttered desktop due to a large number of running applications, it is possible for a Mac user to create additional desktops. These desktops are known as spaces. The user can switch between them either by using Control + right or left arrow keys or by adding and/or selecting another desktop in Mission Control.

    Incorrect: Desktops (or spaces) cannot be accessed directly from the Dock. Command + spacebar is used to call up the Spotlight search function.

1.11 Identify common features and tools of the Linux client/desktop OS.

1. **Answer: B, C**

    Explanation: To list files in a directory, the ls (list) command with the -l switch (for long listing) would be used to show all permissions for the contents of the directory. To show all possible options for the ls command, ls --help would be used. sudo + chown would allow the ownership of the Employee-Reports file to be changed from sales group ownership to the HumanResources group. Looking at the other permissions that have been allocated, it seems likely that the sales group has incorrectly been given group ownership of the file.

    Incorrect: dir is a Windows command and would show the same output. sudo + chown would allow the ownership of a file to be changed. sudo + chmod would reset permissions on a file or directory. pwd (present working directory) will show the directory where commands are currently being processed. sudo + mv will move a file to a different location.

2. **Answer: D**

    Explanation: Using the sudo command, a user can access the privileges of the superuser account. They will be prompted to type their own user password. It is also possible to switch user to an account that's alive with the su command. For more information on both these commands, use the given command along with --help switch.

    Incorrect: pwd displays the present working directory. grep is used to search for text strings. Samba is an interoperability suite that allows Windows platforms to access shared files from a Linux computer.

3. **Answer: C**

    Explanation: The Linux top command shows real-time active processes. PID is the Process ID number, USER is the owner of the task, PR and NI show the priority of the task, and VIRT and RES show memory usage. Other important values are %CPU, which shows CPU usage, and %MEM, which shows the memory being used per process.

    Incorrect: nano is a text editor on Linux systems. dig is used to send DNS queries to a Name Server. ps is used to list running processes on a Linux system but does not display the details of resources being used to the same extent as the top command.

4. **Answer: D**

    Explanation: The rm command (also known as the remove command) is used to delete files and directories from a Linux system. The command supports additional switches, such as -r (recursive), that allow for directories to be deleted along with files. Type rm --help to see all options.

    Incorrect: chmod allows for permissions on files and directories to be changed. man is used to display the manual for a command (for example man rm will display verbose information for the remove command). df is the disk-free command and displays filesystem information.

5. **Answer: C**

    Explanation: The output from df shows the developer how much unused space remains on the storage location (hard disk).

    Incorrect: ps and top display the running processes. ip is used to configure settings for network interfaces.

6. **Answer: B**

    Explanation: SSH (secure shell) will allow the technician to access a remote terminal session using a secure link. SSH uses symmetric encryption to protect the confidentiality of any data transferred.

    Incorrect: RDP is used on the Windows operating system to access the desktop of a Windows host. telnet is not secure; a malicious user may be able to intercept the network traffic and access details of the data. The cp command can be used to copy files between different Linux hosts but is not secure.

7. **Answer: C**

    Explanation: The man command displays help in the form of a manual, usually offering much more detail than the corresponding --help command when typed after the CLI command.

    Incorrect: The other explanations are false.

8. **Answer: D**

    Explanation: Installing the samba service on the Linux Ubuntu server will allow Windows computers to use native services and applications to access files and printers on the Linux server in the same way that they connect to other Windows computers. Windows uses a Microsoft protocol called Server Message Block (SMB), also known as Common Internet File System (CIFS) to access shared content across a network. samba supports the same protocols.

    Incorrect: telnet is used to access the CLI of a remote system but does not allow files to be transferred between systems. Windows 10 workstations do not run the samba service, as they already support the network protocols needed to create a persistent connection to shared resources using a mapped drive. Windows File and Print Sharing is native to Windows operating systems and cannot be installed on Linux systems.

9. **Answer: C**

    Explanation: A package management system allows for the installation, update, and removal of software packages. There are two common package management systems supported on Linux operating systems. Red Hat Linux supports yum. To install a package called application1, the following command could be used: sudo yum install application1. Ubuntu Linux uses a packager named apt.

    Incorrect: The remaining CLI tools are not used to install applications.

10. **Answer: A, D**

    Explanation: The first command, ls -l, will display the "long" listing for the Employee-Details file. The grep command searches for patterns in any line of text. Therefore, the second command will display any lines that have the pattern Joe Smith within the Employee-Details file.

    Incorrect: dir /L is a Windows command (although many Linux distributions do support a number of native Windows commands). /L is not supported when run from a Linux CLI. The Linux cat (concatenate) command cannot be used to search for a pattern of characters but could be used to display the contents of the Employee-Details file.

11. **Answer: A, D**

    Explanation: The Linux ip (Internet Protocol) command queries a network object. ip route will show the computer's default gateway, and in this case, ip address will show the configuration settings for all network interfaces.

    The second command, dig (Domain Internet Groper), is used to retrieve records from DNS servers. dig www.google.com was used to display the records for IP addresses registered against the domain name www.google.com.

    Incorrect: ipconfig, nslookup, and tracert are networking commands supported only on Windows operating systems (not Linux). ping is used to test connectivity between hosts on a network.

12. **Answer: B**

    Explanation: The chmod (change and modify) command allows the permissions to be reset.

    Incorrect: grep is used to search for patterns in lines of text. ip address displays the network configuration. pwd displays the current directory where commands are being run.

Chapter 2: Security

2.1 Summarize various security measures and their purposes

1. **Answer: A**

    Explanation: Motion sensors are primarily designed to detect any movement within their range. They are commonly used in security systems to identify the presence of unauthorized individuals or objects, trigger an alarm, or activate other security measures.

    Incorrect: Option B describes HVAC systems. Option C describes audio detection. Option D describes a photosensor.

2. **Answer: B**

    Explanation: Soft tokens are software-based security tokens that generate one-time passwords (OTPs) to authenticate the user's identity during the login process. They are commonly used in logical security systems to provide an additional layer of security. Soft tokens generate unique passwords that are valid for a short period of time, ensuring that only authorized users can access sensitive information or perform specific actions.

    Incorrect: Option A, generating secure passwords, is incorrect because soft tokens are not primarily used for password generation. They are focused on the authentication aspect rather than password creation. Option C, encrypting data, is incorrect because soft tokens do not directly handle data encryption. Their primary function is to authenticate the user's identity, not to encrypt data. Option D, blocking malicious websites, is incorrect because soft tokens are not designed to block or prevent access to websites. They are specifically used for user authentication and cannot block malicious websites.

3. **Answer: C, E**

    Explanation: A BYOD policy allows for standards and guidelines to be addressed for the use of personal equipment to access business systems. Mobile device management (MDM) allows the team to manage and configure a wide range of mobile devices.

    Incorrect: Options A, B, and F are designed to enhance security during the authentication process. Option D is designed to physically secure hardware.

4. **Answer: A, F**

   Explanation: Physical controls are designed to prevent unauthorized access to facilities and information systems. An access control vestibule forces a user to enter a small space (designed for only one person), with interlocking doors to enforce security. The user must provide authentication before being allowed access through the second door. Door locks prevent unauthorized users from gaining access.

   Incorrect: Alarms, video surveillance, and motion sensors would allow intrusion to be detected but would not prevent unauthorized access to the server room. Bollards would help prevent intrusion using motor vehicles to ram or crash through perimeter fencing or guard posts.

5. **Answer: C, E**

   Explanation: Detective controls would allow the security staff to be aware of breaches that evaded the physical security controls. This is referred to as defense in depth. Video surveillance and motion sensors would allow a security team to detect unauthorized intrusion.

   Incorrect: Access control vestibule, badge reader, equipment locks, and door locks are all considered preventative controls.

6. **Answer: A**

   Explanation: To support two-factor authentication (2FA), you cannot choose another factor from the same group. A smart card is a physical device; it is something you have.

   Incorrect: Retina scanners and palmprint scanners are both considered biometrics, or something you are. They are in the same category as a fingerprint reader. A motion detector is not a method of authentication.

7. **Answer: E**

   Explanation: Magnetometers are devices that can detect concealed metallic objects. This technology can be deployed at access points to the data center. Equipment can also be tagged in order to sound an alert on the magnetometer.

   Incorrect: An access control vestibule is designed to ensure only authorized personnel have access to a facility. In this case, we need additional controls. Video surveillance may not identify equipment that could be concealed (under a jacket or other clothing). Lighting is used to ensure video surveillance is effective. Equipment locks would be a good choice, but in this case, the requirement is for detective control (alerts).

8. **Answer: A**

    Explanation: Adding a user to a group with security restrictions would adhere to the principle of least privilege.

    Incorrect: ACLs are used to ensure access is only given to the correct user or group. When combined with security groups, it will ensure only the correct security group has access to data. Adding a user to a group with restrictions is not part of MFA. An organizational unit (OU) is an administrative control that is useful when applying Group Policy settings to different business units.

9. **Answer: A, D**

    Explanation: Home folders give each user a unique storage location, hosted on a central server. Home folders are assigned using login scripts.

    Incorrect: Option B, management of security groups, is not normally performed when a user logs in to the system. Option C, multifactor authentication, is designed to secure authentication by using two or more factors. Option E, organizational units, is used to manage objects within Active Directory services.

10. **Answer: B, E**

    Explanation: MFA requires the use of two or more authentication factors when logging on to their user account. There are three main groups: something you know, something you have, and someone you are. In this case, the user used something they knew (password) and a hardware token to generate TOTP HMACs (hash-based message authentication code). This would be considered something you have.

    Incorrect: Option A is associated with good account management. Options C and D are valid for MFA but are not being described in this instance.

11. **Answer: B, E**

    Explanation: Group Policy is used to ensure the user settings are updated on any workstation that the user accesses. The specific Group Policy configuration will be found under User Configuration\Administrative Templates\System\Folder Redirection.

    Incorrect: Login scripts are not used to configure folder redirection. Organizational units can be used to target particular users with settings, but do not actually push out configuration settings. A home folder is a default folder assigned to a user through a login script.

12. **Answer: B, C**

    Explanation: Voice call verification requires a user to take a call from a phone (including a mobile), and SMS messages require the user to validate a code sent to their mobile device.

    Incorrect: An email verification link can be received without access to a mobile phone. A hard token refers to a specific security device, such as a USB security key or an RSA key fob.

13. **Answer: A**

    Explanation: Active Directory security groups are primarily used to assign permissions to shared resources such as files, folders, printers, and other network resources. By assigning users or other groups to a security group, you can easily manage access control to various resources within the network. This option is correct because it accurately describes the main purpose of security groups in Active Directory.

    Incorrect: Option B is incorrect because while security groups can help organize user accounts, their primary purpose is to manage access control and permissions. Option C is incorrect because email distribution lists are typically implemented using distribution groups in Active Directory, not security groups. Option D is incorrect because controlling network connectivity is usually achieved through network security mechanisms such as firewalls and network access control lists (ACLs), rather than Active Directory security groups.

14. **Answer: C**

    Explanation: An organizational unit (OU) is a container within an Active Directory domain that can be used to group related objects such as users, computers, and other OUs. The primary purpose of an OU is to organize and manage these objects in a logical hierarchy that reflects the organizational structure. An OU helps in applying group policies, permissions, and administrative tasks to a specific set of objects.

    Incorrect: Option A is incorrect because the physical location is typically determined by attributes such as IP address or network subnet. Option B is incorrect because security policies are defined at the domain or group level, not at the OU level. Option D is incorrect because domain name resolution services are provided by the Domain Name System (DNS), not by OUs.

2.2 Compare and contrast wireless security protocols and authentication methods.

1. **Answer: B**

    Explanation: Wi-Fi Protected Access 3 (WPA3) uses a secure handshaking process called simultaneous authentication of equals (SAE). This replaces the previous method, called preshared key (PSK).

    Incorrect: WPA2 uses an older security standard based on PSK. Temporal Key Integrity Protocol (TKIP) was designed to increase security when using WPA and RC4 encryption. Advanced Encryption Standard (AES) is the default encryption strength used to protect wireless data.

2. **Answer: C**

   Explanation: Remote Authentication Dial-In User Service (RADIUS) is also referred to as an authentication, authorization, and accounting (AAA) service. RADIUS servers allow the Wi-Fi controller to forward authentication requests from client devices. These authentication requests will then be forwarded to directory services.

   Incorrect: WPS allows a device to be paired with a Wi-Fi router without the need to share a key or password. WEP Open does not require an account or password (anyone can connect). WPA-PSK does not use Active Directory accounts.

3. **Answer: C**

   Explanation: WPA2-AES offers the highest levels of security. It uses AES 128-bit encryption.

   Incorrect: Wired Equivalent Privacy (WEP) was used prior to WPA and is no longer used. It is over 20 years old and crucially, it is not secure. WPA2-TKIP uses the older RC4 encryption algorithm. Open Wi-Fi networks do not use encryption.

2.3 Given a scenario, detect, remove, and prevent malware using the appropriate tools and methods.

1. **Answer: B**

   Explanation: Boot sector viruses infect the master boot record (MBR) or the boot sector of a computer system's hard drive. When the infected computer starts up, the virus becomes active and can spread to other parts of the system.

   Incorrect: Option A is not correct as this type of drive is not used to boot the OS. Option C, network routers and switches, is not targeted by boot sector viruses. Option D would more likely be associated with social engineering or password attacks.

2. **Answer: D**

   Explanation: Keyloggers are able to record every keystroke made by a user on a targeted system. Attackers use it to steal login credentials, sensitive information, and payment card numbers.

   Incorrect: Options A, B, and C describe other types of malware or attacks, making them incorrect.

3. **Answer: C**

   Explanation: Ransomware is malware that encrypts a victim's data files, making them inaccessible. This is then followed by a demand for payment in order to receive the decryption key.

   Incorrect: Options A, B, and D describe other types of attacks, making them incorrect.

4. **Answer: B**

   Explanation: A rootkit will replace a privileged OS executable and is then able to block and disrupt OS processes. When a privileged account is used to configure OS functions or services, the rootkit can override these actions.

   Incorrect: Option A, trojan, doesn't typically focus on manipulating or reversing system settings like what's described in the scenario. While option C, viruses, can cause harm to a computer system, including disrupting its normal operation, it doesn't commonly target security settings such as Windows Defender. Viruses tend to focus more on replicating and spreading. While option D, spyware, can disable security features to facilitate its covert activities, the primary goal of spyware is data collection rather than actively manipulating system settings. Option E, ransomware, is more concerned with encrypting files and extorting money from the victim.

5. **Answer: B**

   Explanation: Rootkits are difficult to remove as they will replace key system files and block attempts to remove malicious files. Completely wiping or erasing the hard drive will ensure no malicious files remain.

   Incorrect: Trojans, viruses, and spyware will not need the OS drive to be wiped and re-installed. An effective anti-malware suite should detect and remove these malicious files and processes.

6. **Answer: E**

   Explanation: Ransomware demands a payment be made to access the data. Ransomware typically forces the user or organization to make a payment as important personal or business has been encrypted by the attacker.

   Incorrect: A trojan is installed along with a useful application. It is hidden within the application. A rootkit will replace a privileged OS executable and is then able to block and disrupt OS processes. A virus is malware that is typically introduced by a user clicking on an email attachment. Spyware will run in the background, stealing user information, including passwords.

7. **Answer: C**

   Explanation: As there is no specific malware type mentioned, the best approach is to roll out user awareness training to cover a broad range of threats.

   Incorrect: All other options only cover a specific single threat type.

8. **Answer: B**

   Explanation: As the web browser is the source of the incident and has access to websites, it makes sense to ensure the activity is not malicious. If the activity is harmless, then the anti-virus scan can confirm this.

   Incorrect: Disabling the web browser will be very disruptive and does not resolve the issue. Blocking ports 80 and 443 will be very disruptive as all web traffic is now blocked. Re-installing the OS is very disruptive and should only be used as a last resort.

9. **Answer: B**

   Explanation: Links sent in email messages are phishing attacks. In this case, specific training to counter this type of attack is the best solution.

   Incorrect: A firewall will not block content embedded with an email message. User education regarding common threats will not be as effective as specific training to counter phishing attacks. OS re-installation is not an option as the OS has not been compromised.

10. **Answer: A**

    Explanation: Windows Safe Mode will allow the system to be launched using a minimal set of drivers. If the newly installed video driver is corrupt or malfunctioning, then Safe Mode should launch into a stable desktop environment.

    Incorrect: An anti-virus scan using the latest definition files may reveal whether malicious code is present. However, in this case, there is the possibility that the driver is corrupt or not compatible. Windows Firewall can be used to block both incoming and outgoing network connections, but not verify whether the driver is stable.

11. **Answer: C**

    Explanation: As the compromised accounts are associated with a specific number of workstations, the hardware could have been the vector of attack. As the accounts have had passwords reset, this would not be effective as the keylogger will reveal the new passwords.

    Incorrect: Remote access trojan will allow an attacker to maintain command and control access to workstations and can be used to steal information. A rootkit is designed to intercept calls to system services. Cryptominers use CPU/GPU cycles to mine cryptocurrency.

12. **Answer: B**

    Explanation: Malicious cryptominers may be downloaded using a web browser or as a mobile app. The software will steal the resources of the computer to generate new cryptocurrency. This will target the central processing unit (CPU) and the graphical processing unit (GPU) found on advanced graphics cards.

    Incorrect: Spyware will be used to gather private information from a user or organization. It may slow the computer down but does not target the CPU/GPU specifically. Keyloggers will record all keystrokes entered and store them in a log file. A boot sector virus will replace the OS boot files, launching malware during the boot process.

2.4 Explain common social-engineering attacks, threats, and vulnerabilities

1. **Answer: D**

   Explanation: When a single individual is targeted and that individual has a senior management position, they are considered a big fish. So, whaling is based on phishing, but it is a targeted attack against the big fish (a user in a senior position).

   Incorrect: Phishing is not correct in this case. Option B refers to stealing documents from dumpsters or trash cans that can contain useful intelligence. Option C refers to when somebody tries to catch a user typing a password or PIN code.

2. **Answer: C**

   Explanation: Shoulder surfing is likely to take place in congested spaces when an attacker can be in close proximity to observe a user typing a password.

   Incorrect: Options A and D typically use an email link to coerce a user into sharing confidential data. Option B refers to eliciting information from a voice call.

3. **Answer: B**

   Explanation: As the contractors have turned up unannounced, this could represent a threat. In this case, they are using impersonation by wearing clothing that gives them the appearance of genuine support contractors.

   Incorrect: Option A would be when an unauthorized person is able to follow closely behind a valid user through a physical control, such as a locked door controlled by an RFID badge. Option C refers to stealing documents from dumpsters. Option D refers to the placement of malicious Wi-Fi access points.

4. **Answer: D**

   Explanation: An evil twin refers to a deceptive and malicious wireless network that is designed to resemble a legitimate network. It is essentially a rogue access point that appears to be a trusted Wi-Fi network but is set up by an attacker with the intention of intercepting sensitive information or conducting other malicious activities. As the access point is not connected to a legitimate trusted network, mapped drives, and shared printers will not be accessible.

   Incorrect: Options A, B, and C are other examples of social-engineering attacks.

5. **Answer: A**

   Explanation: Tailgating is when an unauthorized person pretends to be an employee, delivery person, or visitor and attempts to enter a secure area by closely following an authorized employee through a controlled access point, such as a door with an access card or a security checkpoint.

   Incorrect: Options B, C, and D are other types of social engineering.

6. **Answer: A**

   Explanation: In a DDoS attack, the targeted network or system becomes overloaded and is unable to handle legitimate user requests, effectively denying service to legitimate users. DDoS attacks can involve thousands of connections. Botnets can be used to generate massive amounts of traffic.

   Incorrect: Option B does not involve thousands of connections, as a DoS could be created by a single malicious host. Option C refers to a vulnerability for which there is no remediation or patch. Option D involves an attacker spoofing an email address, IP address, or MAC address of another genuine host.

7. **Answer: A**

   Explanation: An on-path attack refers to a type of network attack where an adversary gains control or inserts themselves into the communication path between two networked entities. This enables them to intercept, modify, or block network traffic flowing between these entities, allowing them to eavesdrop on sensitive information, manipulate data, or disrupt communication. This type of attack is also known as man in the middle (MiTM).

   Incorrect: Option B refers to a user who works for the organization that has malicious intent or is poorly trained and so poses a threat. Options C and D are used when an attacker targets a web application server to upload scripts or manipulate the database server (typically in an attempt to gain unauthorized access to the system).

8. **Answer: C**

   Explanation: The main goal of an XSS attack is to manipulate the website's content and interact with the user's session. If the script can be uploaded to the web server, then other users will automatically run the script when they use a browser to visit the site. The malicious payload is identified by the use of arrowhead brackets, <>.

   Incorrect: Option A would involve the use of a spoofed network identity. Option B would use a different syntax, unique to the SQL language. A zero-day attack describes a vulnerability for which no patch is available.

9. **Answer: D**

   Explanation: A zero-day attack is used to describe a vulnerability where there is no patch available.

   Incorrect: Options A, B, and C are described in other questions in this chapter.

10. **Answer: C**

   Explanation: In a SQL injection attack, attackers exploit vulnerabilities in a web application's input fields to manipulate the SQL queries executed by the application's database. In this case, the attacker has entered a malicious input into the login fields that alters the SQL query executed by the application. The condition '1' = '1' is always true, so the attacker is essentially bypassing the authentication process by manipulating the query to return results for any username and password combination.

   Incorrect: Option A, a brute-force attack, involves trying all possible combinations of usernames and passwords until the correct one is found. This log entry doesn't indicate repeated login attempts or trying various combinations. Option B, a dictionary attack, is similar to a brute-force attack but involves trying a list of common passwords or dictionary words. Option D, cross-site scripting (XSS), involves injecting malicious scripts into a web application, which then get executed by other users. It doesn't directly relate to unauthorized login attempts or manipulating database queries as seen in the provided log entry.

2.5 Given a scenario, manage and configure basic security settings in the Microsoft Windows OS

1. **Answer: B**

   Explanation: This will both set the local NTFS permission and also share the folder on the network.

   Incorrect: Option A will not share the folder on the network. Option C, referring to read-only attributes, can be used to prevent a file or folder from being accidentally deleted. Option D would not share the folder on the network and would grant more permissions than required.

2. **Answer: A**

   Explanation: All the required settings will be saved with a Microsoft account that is centrally managed and available. This also supports single sign-on (SSO). The account can be enabled through the Windows settings menu.

   Incorrect: Option B is not possible. Option C is a poor security choice and would still only create local accounts. Option D would only synchronize browser settings and would require that the user create a Microsoft account.

3. **Answer: A, B**

   Explanation: Option A ensures that if the main user account is compromised, then an attacker will have limited privileges. Option B ensures the privileged account is exposed for short periods of time only.

   Incorrect: Option C is not a recommended best practice for the reasons mentioned previously. Option D is not going to work as the standard user will not have the required privileges.

4. **Answer: B**

   Explanation: BitLocker to Go is intended to protect removable media. The USB drive will be encrypted and will require a BitLocker password or smart card to be used to view any content on the drive.

   Incorrect: Option A would require the installation of a third-party security suite, although it would support similar functionality. Option C offers no built-in security features. Option D is designed to prevent unauthorized configuration changes on a Windows device.

5. **Answer: A**

   Explanation: EFS can enable a single file or an entire folder to be encrypted using AES symmetric encryption. The user who encrypts the folder will be the only user who will be able to decrypt the files contained within the folder. Additional users can be added at the owner's discretion.

   Incorrect: Option B is not appropriate as it does not allow a data owner to encrypt individual folders. Option C is used only for removable media. Option D sets permissions but does not encrypt the data.

6. **Answer: B**

   Explanation: UAC is intended to prevent unauthorized configuration changes and will present the user with an option to use an administrator account or approve the action.

   Incorrect: Option A will pop up alert dialogs relating to suspicious files. Option C is not the answer, although an additional authentication factor could be required if a system detects a risky login event. Option D is not the answer as the user is making a configuration change on a network card, not the firewall.

7. **Answer: A**

   Explanation: It is important to ensure all security updates and anti-virus definitions are kept up to date. In this case, the system was not able to be kept up to date, so the best action is to pull down all updates.

   Incorrect: Option B is not the best solution as the system may have more malware that has not been detected. Option C is not recommended when dealing with malware; the opposite is recommended (that you delete all restore points) to avoid re-infecting a system. Option D is only required as a last resort, perhaps when all other avenues of remediation have been attempted.

8. **Answer: C**

   Explanation: When a firewall is blocking inbound connections to a port, then a scanner will show the port as being filtered. At the same time, we can see that the filtered port is associated with a database application (MySQL).

   Incorrect: Option A is not a good choice as it will leave the server unprotected from unwanted connections. Option B will not work as the problem seems to be with the application server. Option D is not an action that will solve the problem, as there is no evidence that the application is the problem.

2.6 Given a scenario, configure a workstation to meet best practices for security

1. **Answer: A**

   Explanation: BitLocker will protect the data at rest. If the laptop is stolen, then the thief would have to know the BitLocker password. If they enter the wrong password, then the system will lock the attacker out.

   Incorrect: Option B would not protect sensitive data, only OS files. Option C would prevent the use of an authorized user account outside of core business hours. Option D would ensure a system is logged out if it is not being actively used.

2. **Answer: B**

   Explanation: The least privilege policy is designed to minimize the potential damage or unauthorized access that can occur when a user's account is compromised or misused. By limiting user privileges, the policy reduces the attack surface and limits the ability of an attacker to move laterally within a system or network.

   Incorrect: Power Users is a group provided for backward compatibility. There are no privileges given to this group. Option C, disabling guest accounts, is a good security best practice but is not exactly what the question is asking for. Option D is a good security best practice as attackers will not know the name of the renamed administrator account.

3. **Answer: B**

   Explanation: Including personal information such as your name or date of birth is not a best practice to create a strong password as personal information can be easily guessed.

   Incorrect: Option A is not the strongest option. A dictionary word could be used with a single capitalized character. However, combined with other password-hardening techniques, it can add to password complexity. Option C, incorporating special characters and numbers, will offer protection from simple password-guessing, dictionary, and rainbow table attacks. Option D, referring to longer passwords, is generally a more secure practice because it increases the number of possible combinations that attackers need to guess. However, longer passwords should also incorporate a mix of character types (letters, numbers, and special characters) for optimal security.

4. **Answer: A**

   Explanation: UEFI includes a graphical user interface (GUI) that can be accessed through a mouse or touch input. This allows for easier configuration and management of system settings, such as boot options and hardware configurations. This replaces the older Binary Input/Output System (BIOS). To prevent a user from tampering with any settings, a password should be set.

   Incorrect: Options B, C, and D refer to the strengthening of passwords that will be used.

5. **Answer: D**

   Explanation: A password manager is a software application or service that helps you securely store and manage your passwords. It provides a convenient way to generate, store, and retrieve complex passwords for different online accounts. The main purpose of a password manager is to improve security by eliminating the need to remember multiple passwords or to use weak and easily guessable passwords. Instead, you only need to remember a single master password or use other authentication methods, such as biometrics (fingerprint or face recognition), to unlock the password manager. A password manager will also protect passwords using encryption.

   Incorrect: None.

6. **Answer: B**

   Explanation: Option B will restrict the ability of the contractors to log on to systems when there are other members of the payroll staff present.

   Incorrect: Option A would allow the contractors to log in at any time. Option C would have no effect as the contractors would have assigned accounts (you would never use the guest account for a privileged role). Option D is a good security best practice but does not address the question.

7. **Answer: D**

   Explanation: A brute-force password attack is a technique used by hackers to gain unauthorized access to a system or account by systematically trying all possible combinations of passwords until the correct one is found. It is a straightforward and exhaustive method where the attacker uses automated tools to generate and try different passwords in rapid succession.

   Incorrect: Option A would use a wordlist or dictionary. Option B does not describe a password attack type. Option C is an example of a network packet sniffer, which can detect passwords sent unencrypted.

8. **Answer: D**

   Explanation: Account lockout will prevent attacks against the interactive login process. Any automated attacks using wordlists or brute force will be highly unlikely to succeed.

   Incorrect: Option A does not prevent a password from being set that would match an entry in a wordlist. Option B, which refers to login hours restrictions, will not mitigate the threat if an attacker launches attacks during permitted hours. Option C will have no impact on other user accounts.

9. **Answer: A**

   Explanation: By configuring autoplay settings for memory cards, the action can be set to do nothing. The card will be recognized but no automated actions will be taken.

   Incorrect: Option B would not help as it would make the presentation material unavailable. Option C refers to the wrong autoplay option as the media is a memory card. Option D may partially solve the problem but is not the best answer.

10. **Answer: C**

    Explanation: By changing your password on a regular basis, you will reduce the risk of someone using stolen credentials to access your accounts, counteracting password-guessing or cracking attacks, and limit the impact of stolen passwords.

    Incorrect: Options A, B, and D are all unsecured ways of managing passwords.

11. **Answer: A**

    Explanation: This would ensure the screens are locked after a period of inactivity (this can be as short as 1 minute).

    Incorrect: Option B is useful to remind users of their responsibilities but is not the most effective control. Option C is impractical. Option D does not solve the problem as the screen will still be visible.

12. **Answer: B**

    Explanation: The password should be changed in the first instance, to protect the account.

    Incorrect: Option A is not good advice, although after changing the password, additional monitoring would be good advice. Option C is not practical as an account may be assigned encryption keys/certificates that cannot now be used. Option D is clearly not a recommended practice.

2.7 Explain common methods for securing mobile and embedded devices

1. **Answer: C, E**

    Explanation: A screen lock will prevent unauthorized access to the mobile device and FDE ensures the data is protected. After a predetermined number of unsuccessful password attempts, the data is rendered unrecoverable.

    Incorrect: Options A and B protect a device when accessing network resources only. Option D is useful but will not have much effect if a device is lost or stolen.

2. **Answer: C**

    Explanation: In a BYOD scenario, if an employee's personal device is lost or stolen, there is an increased risk of unauthorized individuals gaining access to sensitive corporate data stored on the device. Since BYOD devices are not under full control of the organization, it can be more challenging to implement robust security measures such as remote wiping or encryption. This risk highlights the importance of strong security policies and protocols for BYOD, such as password protection, device tracking, and data encryption.

Incorrect: Option A is incorrect because compatibility issues with corporate applications can exist for both BYOD and company-owned business only (COBO), depending on the device and application requirements. Option B is incorrect because employee privacy and personal data compromise can happen in both BYOD and COBO scenarios if not properly managed. Option D is incorrect because phishing attacks and social engineering are not specific to COBO devices but can affect any device, regardless of ownership (including BYOD).

3. **Answer: B**

   Explanation: The Public profile in Windows Firewall is the most restrictive. It is designed for use in public places where you have the least amount of trust in the network environment. It blocks many incoming connections and provides a higher level of security.

   Incorrect: Options A and C are trusted network profiles; they will not block incoming connections as strictly as the public profile. D is not a valid firewall profile.

4. **Answer: A, C**

   Explanation: By deploying mobile device management (MDM), configuration settings can be enforced. Geofencing allows a virtual fence or boundary to be set when the device is geolocated within the fence, and then the settings can be enforced.

   Incorrect: Option B describes using a personal device in a work environment. Options D and E are good choices when the goal is to protect lost or stolen mobile devices, but not for this situation.

5. **Answer: A, C**

   Explanation: Options A and C would satisfy the requirements for biometrics (something you are).

   Incorrect: Options B, D, and E would be something you know.

6. **Answer: D**

   Explanation: IoT devices will connect to wireless networks and will be vulnerable if the default account password is not changed.

   Incorrect: Option A refers to a secure wireless protocol for personal area networks used in home automation. Option B is useful to provide a strong wireless signal. Option C is used to report on the location of a device using IP address or GPS coordinates.

2.8 Given a scenario, use common data destruction and disposal methods

1. **Answer: C**

   Explanation: Degaussing will completely remove all data from magnetic media such as mechanical hard disk drives and backup tapes. It is not possible to reverse this process.

   Incorrect: Option A, erasing, does not remove all data remnants; recovery tools can be used to gain access to deleted or erased data. Option B, standard formatting, marks allocation units on a disk volume as free; data can be recovered from formatted volumes. Option D, wiping, erases the data but it can be recovered using certain software.

2. **Answer: D**

   Explanation: Drilling would be a low-tech solution to achieve physical destruction. Drilling through disk platters will physically destroy the storage media.

   Incorrect: Options A and C require specialist equipment that can be expensive. Option B allows data to be recovered.

3. **Answer: A**

   Explanation: A certification of destruction (CoD) is a document that verifies the complete and secure destruction of sensitive or confidential materials. It is typically issued by a professional shredding or destruction service provider to ensure compliance with legal and regulatory requirements, as well as to provide proof that the materials have been properly disposed of.

   Incorrect: Option B is used to deter unapproved removal or disclosure of sensitive data. Option C is not a certificate type; if an approved service provider incinerated printed materials, they would provide a CoD. Option D would be used to ensure a service provider meets targets using agreed-upon performance metrics.

4. **Answer: A, C**

   Explanation: It is common that regulatory compliance will require highly classified documents to be sanitized using these two methods.

   Incorrect: Options B and D are applicable to electronic storage media.

2.9 Given a scenario, configure appropriate security settings on small office/home office (SOHO) wireless and wired networks.

1. **Answer: D**

    Explanation: Firmware updates on a small office/home office (SOHO) router serve multiple purposes. Firstly, they aim to improve the overall performance and stability of the router, ensuring it runs smoothly and efficiently. Secondly, firmware updates can introduce new features and functionalities, enhancing the router's capabilities. Lastly, and most importantly, firmware updates often address security vulnerabilities and bugs, providing necessary patches to safeguard against potential attacks or unauthorized access. It is crucial to keep the firmware up to date to protect the network and connected devices.

    Incorrect: Options A, B, and C on their own do not answer the question fully.

2. **Answer: B**

    Explanation: A static wide-area network (WAN) IP, also known as a static public IP, is a fixed internet protocol (IP) address assigned to a device or network that is connected to the internet via a wide-area network.

    Incorrect: Option A may be something that could be used on the internal network so that a printer always gets assigned the same address. Option C allows for firewall exceptions to be added for internal devices such as gaming stations. Option D would only be required if there was a requirement for an internet-facing service such as an FTP server.

3. **Answer: C**

    Explanation: UPnP is a protocol that allows devices on a network to discover and communicate with each other without requiring a user to perform manual configuration. This simplifies tasks such as port opening for online gaming and accessing printers, media servers, and smart TVs.

    Incorrect: Option A is used to block web pages and email messages that contain inappropriate content. Option B will not affect the firewall rules in this case. Option D is not needed.

4. **Answer: B**

    Explanation: A screened subnet allows a semi-secure zone where a hardened host server can be placed. The server will be accessed from the internet through the firewall and will also be accessible from the internal network. Port forwarding will ensure the requests sent by external customers to the WAN IP address are routed currently to the FTP server on the screened subnet.

    Incorrect: Option A wouldn't be very useful in this case as we would not have more than one IP address in the screened subnet. Option C is definitely something that would ensure that the router was running the latest firmware but does not offer a solution to this question.

5. **Answer: A, D**

   Explanation: Without broadcasting the MAC address of the router and the assigned wireless network identifier, an attacker will have to use specialist equipment to detect the presence of the network. Manufacturers of network equipment use standard default administrator account names and passwords on products. These should always be changed.

   Incorrect: Option B is not needed as there is no requirement for an internet-facing FTP or WWW server. Option C is not something that is needed in this case and would reduce the security of the router.

6. **Answer: D**

   Explanation: In an area where there may be multiple wireless access points deployed, it is worthwhile investigating whether there are channels that are unused or have less congestion. Wireless controllers using the 2.4 GHz range only have the option for three non-overlapping channels.

   Incorrect: In this case, the other options all focus on security, not the speed or strength of the signal.

7. **Answer: A**

   Explanation: In a small business, such as a coffee shop, it is common to share the passkey with customers to provide access to free Wi-Fi. The most secure way to do this is to use simultaneous authentication of equals (SAE). This uses AES 256-bit encryption and prevents brute-force attacks against the key.

   Incorrect: Option B is not secure as WEP has been discontinued. WPA2 is an old standard and does not support SAE, so options C and D are incorrect.

2.10 Given a scenario, install and configure browsers and relevant security settings

1. **Answer: A, D**

   Explanation: When installing new software, it is recommended to always use a trusted site. If a user wants to download Google Chrome, for example, then it is best to visit the vendor site, not a third-party unknown site. Many software vendors publish the hash, or checksum, for the download file. This can be verified using a hashing utility on the user's workstation.

   Incorrect: Option B is not that important as a malicious download file could still be the same size as the genuine one. Option C describes a useful feature but does not ensure a trusted download and installation of a piece of software.

2. **Answer: A**

   Explanation: Adding a language translator as a browser extension is the most convenient and user-friendly solution for the company to help users translate websites into their native language. Browser extensions, such as Google Translate, allow users to translate web content directly within the browser without the need to copy and paste the content into a separate application.

   Incorrect: Option B, which refers to browser extensions, can provide the same functionality without requiring users to switch to a new browser. While support for HTML5 is important for modern web browsing, option C doesn't directly address the issue of translating websites into the user's native language. Option D, add support for additional languages to the Windows settings menu, is unrelated to the issue of translating websites.

3. **Answer: D**

   Explanation: By enabling an ad blocker, the browser will be able to render and display web pages much quicker.

   Incorrect: Option A is not really effective anymore as advertising content is embedded within pages, although it can block bogus popups that suggest a host system may have multiple malicious files. Options B and C are not designed to block advertising.

4. **Answer: A**

   Explanation: When browsing websites that are secure, the client browser will display a padlock symbol to show the user that the site has a valid certificate.

   Incorrect: Option B is incorrect as a certificate is not used with the HTTP protocol. Option C is not correct as a rating is not used. Option D allows browsing with no history being retained, which is not relevant to the question.

Chapter 3: Software Troubleshooting

3.1 Given a scenario, troubleshoot common Windows OS problems

1. **Answer: A**

   Explanation: Outdated device drivers are a common cause of BSOD errors in Windows. When drivers are not up to date, they can conflict with the OS, leading to system instability and crashes.

   Incorrect: Options B, C, and D can also cause system issues, but outdated device drivers are specifically known to trigger BSOD errors more frequently.

2. **Answer: C**

   Explanation: Faulty RAM can cause BSOD errors, and the most effective solution is to replace the faulty RAM modules.

   Incorrect: Cleaning the computer's cooling fans (option A) may prevent overheating issues but will not directly address RAM-related errors. Updating the anti-virus software (option B) is unrelated to RAM errors. Re-installing the operating system (option D) is a more extensive troubleshooting step and is usually not required for resolving RAM-related BSOD errors.

3. **Answer: B**

   Explanation: The STOP error code displayed on a BSOD is designed to help identify the specific cause of the error. It provides a hexadecimal error code and often includes additional information that assists in troubleshooting and resolving the issue.

   Incorrect: Options A, C, and D do not accurately reflect the purpose of the STOP error code.

4. **Answer: B**

   Explanation: When a computer consistently shuts down after a brief period without displaying an error message, overheating is a common cause. Overheating can be due to a malfunctioning CPU fan, inadequate ventilation, or dust buildup.

   Incorrect: Power supply failure (option A) is less likely to cause consistent shutdowns without any error message. A virus or malware infection (option C) typically manifests as different symptoms, such as popups, system slowdowns, or unexpected behavior, rather than consistent shutdowns. A faulty motherboard (option D) can cause various issues, but it is not the most probable cause in this scenario.

5. **Answer: C**

   Explanation: One of the common reasons for a Windows service not starting is an incorrect service configuration. This can happen if the service is not set to start automatically, or if its dependencies are not properly configured. The service configuration should be checked to ensure that it is set correctly.

Incorrect: While option A, insufficient disk space, can cause various issues on a computer, it is not directly related to a service not starting. If a service requires disk space to function properly, it may encounter problems once it is running, but it is not the primary reason for the service not starting. Option B, outdated device drivers, can lead to issues with hardware components, but they are not typically the cause of a service not starting. Services are software components that are separate from device drivers and their functionality. Option D, incompatible software installation, can cause conflicts and system instability, but it is unlikely to prevent a Windows service from starting. While conflicts between software components can occur, they are not a common cause for a service failing to start.

6. **Answer: A, C**

   Explanation: Option A, closing unnecessary applications, can help free up memory by releasing resources used by those applications. When the system is running low on memory, closing unused or unnecessary programs can alleviate the issue. Option C, adding more RAM to the system, is an effective solution for low-memory warnings. Increasing the physical RAM capacity provides more memory for the system to manage its workload.

   Incorrect: Option B, deleting temporary files, can help free up disk space but does not directly address low-memory warnings. Low-memory warnings are specifically related to insufficient RAM, not disk space. Option D, upgrading the processor, is incorrect because low-memory warnings are not directly related to the processor. Upgrading the processor may improve overall system performance but will not resolve low-memory warnings on its own.

7. **Answer: A**

   Explanation: This warning indicates that the system has encountered a severe issue that could lead to instability and is about to shut down. It is important to investigate and resolve the critical error to ensure the stability of the system.

   Incorrect: Option B, "Your anti-virus software has expired. Please renew your subscription," is not directly related to system instability. While it is important to keep anti-virus software up to date for security purposes, an expired subscription does not necessarily indicate system instability. Option C, "A new update is available for your web browser. Click here to install," is a notification for a web browser update. While it is recommended to keep software up to date for security reasons, a browser update is unlikely to directly indicate system instability. Option D, "Low disk space. Free up some space to optimize system performance," is a warning related to disk space, which can impact system performance. While low disk space may affect system stability in the long term, it is not an immediate indicator of system instability. It is more likely to impact system performance and storage capacity.

8. **Answer: B**

   Explanation: When the computer displays the "No OS found" message, it indicates that the system is unable to locate a valid OS. This can occur if the hard drive is not properly connected or if it has failed. In such cases, the computer cannot access the necessary files to start the OS.

   Incorrect: The other options (A, C, and D) may also cause boot-related issues, but they are less likely to directly result in the "No OS found" error. Option A is incorrect because if the Windows OS is missing or corrupted, it would typically display an error related to the OS, such as "Windows Boot Manager error." Option C is incorrect because incorrect BIOS settings could lead to booting issues, but they usually do not result in the specific error message "No OS found." Option D is incorrect because while viruses can cause various issues, they are less likely to directly result in the "No OS found" error. Viruses typically affect the functionality of the OS rather than completely preventing its detection.

9. **Answer: B**

   Explanation: A corrupted user profile can cause slow profile load times during login. When a user profile is corrupted, Windows may have difficulty loading the necessary settings and preferences, resulting in delays.

   Incorrect: The system resources (option A) are typically not the cause unless the computer is severely underpowered. Network connectivity issues (option C) would generally affect the user's ability to access network resources after login, but they are unlikely to directly impact the profile load times. Outdated device drivers (option D) can cause various issues, but they are not specifically related to slow profile load times.

10. **Answer: C**

    Explanation: Hardware clock malfunctions can lead to time drift problems as the system may not accurately track the passage of time.

    Incorrect: While incorrect time zone settings (option A) can cause time display discrepancies, a malware infection (option B) generally does not directly affect the system clock. Power outages (option D) may temporarily disrupt the system clock, but they are not a common cause of persistent time drift.

11. **Answer: B**

    Explanation: In the Windows Services management console, you can right-click on a service and choose the "Restart" option to restart the service.

    Incorrect: Option A, right clicking the service and selecting "Stop" and then "Start," is incorrect because it stops the service first and then starts it, which is different from a restart. Option C, double-clicking the service and selecting "Restart" from the toolbar, is incorrect because double-clicking a service typically opens the properties window for the service, not the option to restart it. Option D, right clicking the service and selecting "Pause" and then "Resume," is incorrect because it pauses and resumes the service, but it does not perform a restart.

12. **Answer: C**

    Explanation: When a system is rebooted, all running applications are terminated. This includes any unresponsive applications. Rebooting provides a fresh start and can help resolve issues with unresponsive applications.

    Incorrect: Rebooting does not reset configuration settings (option A). Rebooting does not automatically repair any issues (option D). Option B is not true as rebooting does have an effect on unresponsive applications.

13. **Answer: A**

    Explanation: When an application crashes immediately upon launch, it is essential to ensure that the computer meets the minimum system requirements specified by the application. Inadequate system resources can lead to crashes.

    Incorrect: Checking available disk space is important, but it is not the first step in this scenario unless the application explicitly requires a certain amount of free space (option B). Reviewing anti-virus software settings is a good practice, but it is not typically the primary cause of an application crashing immediately upon launch (option C). Compatibility mode settings are relevant if the application worked previously but stopped functioning after changes in the compatibility settings. However, it is not the initial step when the application crashes right at launch (option D).

14. **Answer: A**

    Explanation: The "boot device not found" error message typically indicates a problem with the boot loader, which is responsible for starting the OS. A corrupted boot loader can occur during an update process or due to other factors, preventing the system from booting properly.

    Incorrect: Option B, overheating CPU, can cause system instability and unexpected shutdowns, but it is not directly related to the "boot device not found" error. Option C, insufficient hard drive space, can impact system performance and prevent certain operations, but it is not the primary cause of the boot failure in this scenario. Option D, incorrect BIOS settings, can affect system functionality, but it is unlikely to result in the specific error message mentioned.

15. **Answer: A**

    Explanation: The installation of the new anti-virus software is causing BSOD errors, indicating a compatibility issue. To troubleshoot the problem, it is recommended to uninstall the anti-virus software and check whether the BSOD errors persist. If the errors cease after the uninstallation, alternative anti-virus software can be considered.

    Incorrect: Option B, upgrade the computer's RAM, does not typically resolve BSOD errors caused by anti-virus software compatibility. Option C, re-install the operating system, is an extreme measure and is not necessary for resolving compatibility issues with anti-virus software. Option D, replace the graphics card, is unlikely to resolve BSOD errors related to anti-virus software compatibility.

16. **Answer: A**

    Explanation: OS update failures can sometimes occur due to conflicts with temporary files or corrupted update data. Clearing temporary files helps eliminate potential issues and provides a clean environment for the update process. After clearing the temporary files, the user can retry the update to see whether the errors are resolved.

    Incorrect: Option B, install a different web browser, is not directly related to addressing OS update failures. Option C, upgrade the computer's power supply, is not generally connected to OS update failures. Option D, increase the screen resolution, does not address OS update failures and is unrelated to the update process.

17. **Answer: C**

    Explanation: When rolling back updates, it is important to create a system restore point. This allows you to revert your system to a previous state if any issues arise during the rollback process. System restore points capture the system's configuration and settings, enabling you to restore it to a known working state.

    Incorrect: Re-installing the latest updates is incorrect because the purpose of rolling back updates is to revert to a previous version, not to re-install the latest updates (option A). Disabling automatic updates is incorrect because disabling automatic updates does not address the process of rolling back updates. It simply prevents future updates from being installed automatically (option B). Increasing system resources is incorrect because it is unrelated to the process of rolling back updates. It pertains to improving system performance by allocating additional hardware resources, such as RAM or CPU, to address performance issues (option D).

18. **Answer: B**

    Explanation: When Windows fails to boot and displays a blue screen of death (BSOD), using System Restore to roll back to a previous working state is a recommended step. System Restore allows you to revert the system to a previously known good configuration, which can help resolve issues that caused the BSOD.

    Incorrect: Simply restarting the computer (option A) may not resolve the underlying issue. Re-installing all third-party applications (option C) is not necessary unless a specific application is causing the BSOD. Updating the computer's BIOS (option D) should be done cautiously and only if there is a specific indication that the BIOS update addresses the BSOD issue.

19. **Answer: C**

    Explanation: The correct answer is option C, when experiencing frequent application crashes. Running a Windows System File Checker can help identify and repair corrupted system files that may be causing frequent crashes. It is a troubleshooting step to address software-related issues.

    Incorrect: While hardware driver issues (option A) can also cause problems, they are better addressed by updating or re-installing the appropriate drivers. Running a file check is not directly related to installing new software updates (option B), although it can help ensure the stability of the system after updates. Performing a disk defragmentation (option D) is unrelated to running a Windows System File Checker, as defragmentation focuses on optimizing the storage layout on the disk.

20. **Answer: C**

    Explanation: Running the "sfc /scannow" command in Command Prompt initiates a Windows System File Checker. This command scans all protected system files and replaces incorrect versions with the correct Microsoft versions.

    Incorrect: The "sfc /scanfile" command (option A) is used to scan a specific file. "sfc /verifyonly" (option B) verifies the integrity of system files without making any repairs. "sfc /restorehealth" (option D) is used to repair system files using Windows Update as a source.

21. **Answer: C**

    Explanation: Windows reimaging can be used as a troubleshooting step when a computer is plagued by persistent crashes and blue screen errors. Reimaging can help eliminate software-related issues that might be causing system instability, providing a fresh and stable installation of Windows.

    Incorrect: Option A is incorrect because when a specific software application is not launching properly, it is usually an isolated issue related to that particular application. Troubleshooting steps specific to the application, such as re-installing or updating it, would be more appropriate. Option B is incorrect because an unstable internet connection is generally not resolved by using Windows reimaging. Troubleshooting network settings, checking hardware connections, or contacting the internet service provider would be more suitable for resolving internet connection issues. Option D is incorrect because adjusting the display resolution does not necessitate using Windows reimaging. Changing the display resolution is a configuration setting that can be adjusted within the OS without requiring a complete system re-installation.

3.2 Given a scenario, troubleshoot common personal computer (PC) security issues.

1. **Answer: A**

   Explanation: The first step in troubleshooting network connectivity issues is to verify the physical network connections and cables. This includes checking whether the network cable is securely plugged into the PC and the router or switch. By ensuring the physical connections are intact, any issues related to loose or faulty connections can be identified and resolved.

   Incorrect: Updating anti-virus software (option B) is not directly related to network connectivity issues. Re-installing the OS (option C) is an extreme step and should be considered only if all other troubleshooting steps fail. Increasing the PC's RAM (option D) does not directly address network connectivity issues.

2. **Answer: D**

   Explanation: False alerts regarding anti-virus protection can be caused by legitimate files being flagged as threats. By excluding the false positive files from anti-virus scans, the alerts will no longer appear, and the user can distinguish between genuine threats and false positives.

   Incorrect: Updating the anti-virus software (option A) may help improve its detection capabilities but may not directly address the false alert issue. Adjusting the settings of the firewall (option B) is unrelated to false alerts caused by the anti-virus software. Running a full system scan (option C) using an anti-virus program may detect threats but does not specifically address the false positive alerts.

3. **Answer: B**

   Explanation: A ransomware infection is a type of malware that encrypts or alters the user's files and demands a ransom to restore access. This aligns with the user's report of altered or missing/renamed files.

   Incorrect: Phishing attacks (option A) typically involve tricking users into revealing sensitive information and are less likely to directly affect file integrity. Rootkit installations (option C) and unauthorized access by network intruders (option D) can potentially lead to file tampering, but a ransomware infection is the most common cause of files being altered or held hostage.

4. **Answer: A**

   Explanation: Unwanted notifications within the OS can often be caused by unnecessary or malicious programs running at startup. By disabling startup programs, the technician can eliminate programs that may be responsible for generating unwanted notifications.

   Incorrect: Updating the BIOS (option B) is unrelated to OS notifications. Re-installing the OS (option C) is a drastic step and should be considered only if other troubleshooting methods fail. Cleaning the registry (option D) using a registry cleaner tool is unnecessary and may not directly address unwanted OS notifications.

5. **Answer: B**

   Explanation: Often, issues with OS update failures can be resolved by restarting the PC and attempting to install the updates again. This can help reset any temporary glitches or conflicts that may be preventing successful updates.

   Incorrect: Disabling the anti-virus software (option A) may temporarily help in some cases, but it is not the first step to take. Re-installing the OS (option C) should be considered only if all other troubleshooting methods fail. Clearing the browser cache (option D) is unrelated to OS updates and would not resolve this particular issue.

6. **Answer: A**

   Explanation: Adware or malware infections often result in the appearance of random or frequent pop-up advertisements on web browsers. These popups are usually unwanted and may lead to potentially harmful websites or downloads.

   Incorrect: Certificate warnings occur when a browser detects an issue with the security certificate of a website (option B). While certificate warnings may indicate potential security concerns, they are not directly associated with adware or malware infections. Option C, redirection, refers to instances where a web browser is automatically directed to a different website than the one intended by the user. While this can be caused by malware, it is not necessarily related to adware or malware infections alone. Slow internet speed can be caused by various factors, such as network congestion or issues with the internet service provider. While malware infections can impact internet performance, it is not a specific symptom associated with adware or malware infections (option D).

7. **Answer: C**

   Explanation: When a security certificate associated with a website expires, the browser generates certificate warnings to inform the user about the potential security risks. It is important to ensure that websites have up-to-date security certificates.

   Incorrect: An outdated browser can sometimes cause compatibility issues with new security certificates, but it is not the most likely cause for repeated certificate warnings (option A).

   While a firewall can block secure connections, it is unlikely to result in repeated certificate warnings (option B). Firewall-related issues typically prevent access to secure websites altogether rather than generating certificate warnings. DNS cache poisoning refers to an attack where incorrect or malicious information is inserted into the DNS cache. While this attack can lead to security issues, it is not the most likely cause for repeated certificate warnings (option D).

8. **Answer: C**

   Explanation: Browser hijacking is a form of malware attack where the settings of a web browser are modified without the user's consent, leading to frequent redirection to unwanted websites. This symptom is particularly associated with browser hijacking.

   Incorrect: Option A, random/frequent popups, can be associated with adware or malware infections but not specifically with browser hijacking. Certificate warnings can occur due to various reasons, including expired or invalid security certificates, but they are not directly linked to browser hijacking (option B). Option D, slow internet speed, can be caused by different factors, such as network congestion or performance issues, but it is not specifically associated with browser hijacking.

3.3 Given a scenario, use best practice procedures for malware removal

1. **Answer: A**

   Explanation: The best practice procedure for malware removal in this scenario is to disconnect the computer from the network to prevent further infection, perform a full system scan using updated anti-malware software to detect any malware, and then remove any detected malware. This approach ensures the thorough removal of the malicious software and helps restore the system's performance and stability.

   Incorrect: Option B is incorrect because manually deleting suspicious files and folders may not effectively remove all malware, and it does not address the potential for hidden or system-level malware. Option C is incorrect because re-installing the OS should be considered a last resort, as it involves significant time and effort. It should only be pursued if all other methods fail or if the system is severely compromised. Option D is incorrect because ignoring the issue can lead to further system instability, data loss, and potential security breaches. It is important to address malware infections promptly.

2. **Answer: C**

   Explanation: The recommended practice for updating anti-malware software is to configure it to update automatically and regularly. This ensures that the software receives the latest virus definitions, security patches, and feature updates, providing the most effective protection against new and emerging threats.

   Incorrect: Option A is incorrect because disabling automatic updates can leave the system vulnerable to new threats if the software is not regularly updated. It is important to maintain up-to-date protection. Option B is incorrect because relying solely on manual updates prompted by the OS can lead to delays in receiving critical updates and leave the system exposed to malware attacks. Option D is incorrect because uninstalling and re-installing the software is not necessary for routine updates. Most anti-malware software offers in-app update functionality that does not require a complete re-install.

3. **Answer: B**

   Explanation: It is important to investigate and verify malware symptoms before proceeding with the removal process because it allows for more accurate identification and selection of appropriate removal techniques. Different types of malware may exhibit different symptoms, and understanding these symptoms helps in determining the most effective course of action.

   Incorrect: The cost of malware removal can vary depending on factors such as the severity of the infection, the expertise required for removal, and the resources used, but it is not determined solely by investigating and verifying symptoms (option A). While investigating and verifying malware symptoms can provide some insights into the complexity of the infection, it does not directly help in estimating the time required to remove the malware (option C). The time required for removal depends on various factors, such as the nature of the malware, the extent of the infection, the efficiency of the removal tools, and the skill of the person performing the removal. Investigating and verifying malware symptoms may indirectly contribute to educating the end user about the potential risks of malware (option D). However, the primary purpose of investigating and verifying symptoms is to identify and select appropriate removal techniques. Educating the end user about malware risks is an important aspect but not directly related to the investigation and verification process.

4. **Answer: A**

   Explanation: Regularly updating anti-virus software is crucial for staying protected against new malware threats. Updates often include the latest virus definitions, improved detection algorithms, and security enhancements, ensuring the anti-virus software can effectively identify and remove the latest malware variants.

   Incorrect: Option B, disable the system's user account control (UAC) feature, removes an important layer of defense against unauthorized system changes and can make the system more susceptible to malware infections. It is recommended to keep UAC enabled. Option C, share user credentials with trusted colleagues, can lead to unauthorized access, compromising the security of the system and increasing the risk of malware infections. User credentials should be kept confidential and not shared. Option D, enable all browser extensions and plugins by default, increases the attack surface and potential vulnerabilities, making the system more prone to malware infections. It is advisable to review and disable unnecessary or untrusted extensions and plugins to reduce the risk.

5. **Answer: A**

    Explanation: Quarantining infected systems is necessary during the malware removal process to prevent the malware from spreading to other systems. By isolating the infected systems, the risk of further contamination is minimized, protecting other devices on the network.

    Incorrect: Option B, to disable System Restore in Windows, is not a primary reason for quarantining infected systems during the malware removal process. System Restore is a feature that allows users to revert their system's state to a previous point in time, which can be useful in case of system errors or issues. However, it is not directly related to quarantining infected systems. Option C, to create a restore point for future use, is also not a primary reason for quarantining infected systems. Restore points are typically created to provide a fallback option in case of system issues or changes. While it can be a good practice to create a restore point before performing malware removal, it is not the main purpose of quarantining infected systems. Option D, to schedule scans and run updates, is an important part of the malware removal process, but it is not directly related to quarantining infected systems. Quarantining infected systems is primarily done to isolate the malware and prevent its spread to other systems. Scans and updates can be performed after the quarantine to detect and remove the malware effectively.

6. **Answer: B**

    Explanation: Disabling System Restore in Windows during malware removal is done primarily to remove any infected restore points. Malware can hide in these restore points, allowing it to survive even after the malware removal process. By disabling System Restore, all existing restore points are deleted, reducing the chances of the malware reappearing.

    Incorrect: Option A is incorrect because disabling System Restore does not directly prevent the malware from spreading to other systems. It mainly focuses on removing infected restore points. Option C is incorrect because disabling System Restore alone does not guarantee that the malware cannot re-infect the system. Other security measures, such as using reliable anti-virus software and updating system patches, are also necessary. Option D is not correct as System Restore does not directly speed up the malware removal process. It is primarily done to remove infected restore points rather than affect the speed of the removal process.

7. **Answer: B**

    Explanation: When System Restore is disabled during malware removal, all existing restore points are deleted. This action helps remove any potential hiding places for the malware, making it harder for it to survive and re-infect the system.

    Incorrect: Disabling System Restore does not immediately delete the malware from the system. It primarily focuses on removing infected restore points rather than directly eliminating the malware (option A). Disabling System Restore does not directly isolate or prevent the malware from executing (option C). It primarily deals with removing infected restore points. Disabling System Restore does not make the system immune to further malware infections (option D). It is a precautionary step in the malware removal process, but additional security measures are required to ensure the system's ongoing protection.

8. **Answer: C**

    Explanation: Educating the end user is crucial in reducing the likelihood of future malware incidents. By teaching the end user about safe browsing habits, recognizing phishing attempts, and avoiding suspicious downloads, they become more aware of potential threats and are less likely to fall victim to malware. This helps minimize the risk of re-infection.

    Incorrect: Option A is incorrect because educating the end user should not be done to shift the responsibility of malware removal to them entirely. It is a collaborative effort between the end user and IT professionals. Option B is incorrect because while enhancing the end user's technical skills can be beneficial, it is not the primary reason for educating them as part of the malware removal process. Option D is incorrect because creating a sense of panic and urgency is counterproductive. Educating the end user should focus on providing them with the necessary knowledge and tools to prevent malware incidents, rather than inducing panic.

9. **Answer: C**

    Explanation: Educating the end user about malware removal can lead to faster incident response times. When end users are aware of potential malware threats and know how to report suspicious activities promptly, IT professionals can respond quickly and mitigate the impact of the incident.

    Incorrect: Option A is incorrect because educating the end user should not result in decreased user productivity. Instead, it should empower them to be proactive and take appropriate actions to prevent malware incidents. Option B is incorrect because the goal of educating the end user is to reduce reliance on IT support. By educating them about safe practices and self-help measures, end users can take more responsibility for their own security. Option D is incorrect because educating the end user about malware removal should lead to an increased likelihood of preventing data breaches, not the other way around.

10. **Answer: C**

    Explanation: Neglecting to educate the end user about malware removal can lead to a higher incidence of successful malware attacks. If end users are not aware of safe practices and do not know how to identify and report potential threats, they become more vulnerable to malware attacks.

    Incorrect: Option A is incorrect because neglecting to educate the end user does not necessarily result in increased IT budget allocation. While malware incidents can incur costs, allocating a higher budget may not address the root cause. Option B is incorrect because neglecting to educate the end user does not directly cause decreased system performance. Malware infections can impact system performance, but that is a consequence of the malware itself, not the lack of end user education. Option D is incorrect because neglecting to educate the end user does not directly cause decreased network bandwidth. Malware infections can consume network bandwidth if they engage in malicious activities, but that is a consequence of the malware itself, not the lack of end user education.

3.4 Given a scenario, troubleshoot common mobile OS and application issues.

1. **Answer: A**

   Explanation: Background app refresh is a feature that allows apps to refresh their content in the background, even when they are not actively being used. Enabling this feature for multiple apps can consume significant battery power, causing rapid battery drain.

   Incorrect: Option B is incorrect. Low screen brightness can conserve battery life, so it is unlikely to be the cause of the rapid battery drain. Option C is also incorrect. Mobile data usage affects data consumption but does not directly impact battery drain when the device is not actively using data. Option D is incorrect because overcharging the device can potentially damage the battery over time, but it does not cause immediate rapid battery drain.

2. **Answer: C**

   Explanation: AirDrop requires both Bluetooth and Wi-Fi to be enabled on both devices for the file transfer to take place. Bluetooth is used for device discovery, and Wi-Fi is used for the actual file transfer.

   Incorrect: Option A is incorrect as AirDrop can work even when both devices are not connected to the same Wi-Fi network. It uses a combination of Bluetooth and Wi-Fi to establish a direct connection between devices. Option B is not correct as AirDrop can be used to transfer files between various Apple devices, including iPhones, iPads, and Mac computers. Option D is incorrect as AirDrop is exclusive to Apple devices and cannot be used to transfer files to non-Apple devices.

3. **Answer: A**

   Explanation: Performing a soft reset on the device is the first troubleshooting step to attempt when a smartphone becomes unresponsive. This can be done by holding down the power button until the device restarts. It helps to clear temporary issues or software glitches that may be causing the unresponsiveness.

   Incorrect: Option B, clear the cache of all installed applications, may help with specific app-related issues, but it is not the most appropriate step for addressing a generally unresponsive device. Option C, re-install the mobile operating system, is a drastic measure that should be considered as a last resort when all other troubleshooting steps have failed. As many modern smartphones have non-removable batteries, option D may not be applicable. Even if the battery is removable, removing and reinserting it is not likely to resolve an unresponsiveness issue.

4. **Answer: A**

   Explanation: Frequent battery drain is a common symptom of a malware-infected mobile device. Malware running in the background can consume system resources and drain the battery more quickly than usual.

   Incorrect: Option B, improved device performance, is not a common symptom of a malware-infected mobile device. Malware tends to slow down the device and negatively impact its performance. Option C, enhanced battery life, is also not a common symptom of a malware-infected mobile device. Malware typically increases battery drain rather than improving battery life. Option D, app icons rearranging automatically, can be caused by various factors, such as a user's unintentional actions or a bug in the OS, but it is not directly indicative of a malware infection.

5. **Answer: A**

   Explanation: Near-field communication (NFC) enables contactless data exchange between two devices in close proximity. It allows devices to establish a connection by bringing them near each other, typically within a few centimeters.

   Incorrect: Option B, Bluetooth, is a wireless technology that enables data exchange between devices over short distances but not necessarily in close proximity or through contactless means. Option C, Wi-Fi, enables wireless communication between devices over longer distances and is not focused on contactless data exchange in close proximity. Option D, GPS (Global Positioning System), is a satellite-based navigation system used for determining the location and positioning of a device but does not facilitate contactless data exchange between devices.

6. **Answer: B**

   Explanation: The first troubleshooting step to resolve the issue of the screen not autorotating on a mobile device is to check the screen rotation settings. Sometimes, the autorotate feature may be disabled in the device's settings, preventing the screen from automatically rotating. By verifying and adjusting the screen rotation settings, the issue can often be resolved without further action.

   Incorrect: While restarting the device can fix various issues, it may not specifically address the screen autorotation problem (option A). Checking the screen rotation settings is a more targeted approach. Option C, update the mobile operating system, can be beneficial for overall system stability and bug fixes, but it is less likely to directly resolve the specific issue of the screen not autorotating. It is not the most immediate troubleshooting step. Option D, perform a factory reset, should be considered as a last resort. It erases all data and settings on the device, which can be inconvenient and time-consuming. It should only be attempted if other troubleshooting steps have failed to resolve the issue.

7. **Answer: B**

   Explanation: The most appropriate troubleshooting step to address a mobile device that randomly reboots while using an application is to update the OS to the latest version. This step is crucial as outdated OSs can cause compatibility issues, leading to system instability. Updating the OS ensures that any known bugs or vulnerabilities are addressed, providing a more stable environment for running applications.

   Incorrect: Option A, clear the cache and data of the application, might resolve issues related to the application's performance or data corruption, but it is unlikely to fix the problem of the device randomly rebooting. This step is more focused on resolving application-specific issues rather than system-wide problems. Option C, re-install the application, may help if the issue is isolated to that specific application, but if the device is randomly rebooting regardless of the application in use, re-installing the app is unlikely to solve the problem. Option D, factory reset the mobile device, should only be considered as a last resort. It erases all data and settings, returning the device to its original factory state. Performing a factory reset is a drastic step and should only be used when all other troubleshooting steps have failed to resolve the issue.

8. **Answer: B**

   Explanation: Uninstalling unnecessary applications will free up storage space on the mobile device and allow the user to install new applications.

   Incorrect: Option A, clear the device cache, may improve performance but will not directly address the storage space issue. Option C, perform a factory reset, will erase all data and settings on the device, which is not necessary in this scenario. Option D, upgrade the device's operating system, is unrelated to the storage space problem.

9. **Answer: A, B**

   Explanation: Closing background applications can help conserve battery power by preventing unnecessary processes from running. Enabling battery optimization settings can also extend battery life.

   Incorrect: Option C, replace the device battery, is not necessary unless the battery is old or damaged. On many mobile devices, it is not possible to replace the battery. Option D, disable push email notifications, may reduce battery usage but is unlikely to be the primary cause of rapid battery drain.

10. **Answer: A**

    Explanation: Restarting the device is the initial troubleshooting step to address various software-related issues, including unresponsive touchscreens.

    Incorrect: Options B, C, and D – calibrate the touchscreen, update the device's firmware, and clean the touchscreen – are secondary steps that can be performed if the issue persists after restarting the device.

11. **Answer: B**

    Explanation: Uninstalling and re-installing the app can resolve app crashes caused by corrupted installation files.

    Incorrect: Option A, clear the app cache, can improve performance but may not directly address the crashes. Options C and D, update the device's operating system and restart the device, are general troubleshooting steps and may not specifically resolve the app-crashing issue.

12. **Answer: A**

    Explanation: Clearing app cache and data can help improve performance by removing temporary files and resetting app settings.

    Incorrect: Option B, perform a factory reset, would erase all data and settings, which should be avoided unless necessary. Option C, install a performance optimization app, may help but is not the first troubleshooting step. Option D, upgrade the device's memory (RAM), is unrelated to the slow performance issue.

13. **Answer: A, B**

    Explanation: Resetting the device's network settings can resolve Wi-Fi connectivity issues caused by misconfigured network settings. Forgetting and reconnecting to the Wi-Fi network is a less drastic step and can also help establish a stable connection.

    Incorrect: Option C, replace the device's Wi-Fi antenna, is unnecessary unless it is physically damaged. Option D, update the device's firmware, is a general troubleshooting step and may not specifically address the Wi-Fi connectivity problem.

14. **Answer: C**

    Explanation: Deleting unnecessary files and applications will free up storage space on the device and resolve the "Insufficient storage available" issue.

    Incorrect: Option A, clear the app cache, can also help, but it may not be sufficient in this case. Options C and D, move apps and data to an external storage device and upgrade the device's storage capacity, are possible solutions but not the first steps to consider.

15. **Answer: A, B**

    Explanation: Option A, update the device's firmware, can fix known issues and bugs that may cause frequent reboots and freezes. Option B, perform a factory reset, is a more drastic step and should be a step to consider if option A is unsuccessful.

    Incorrect: Option C, replace the device's battery, is unlikely to solve the problem. Option D, disable unnecessary background processes, can improve performance but may not directly address reboots and freezes.

180　Solutions

3.5 Given a scenario, troubleshoot common mobile OS and application security issues.

1. **Answer: B**

   Explanation: APK (Android Package Kit) is a file format used to distribute and install applications on Android devices. It contains all the necessary files and resources needed to run an Android application.

   Incorrect: Option A is incorrect because an APK file is not specifically used for storing music files.

   Option C is incorrect because APK files are not used on iOS devices; they are specific to the Android OS. Option D is incorrect because a system file responsible for managing network connections is not related to APK files.

2. **Answer: A**

   Explanation: Enabling developer mode on a mobile device grants access to advanced system settings and debugging features, allowing developers to test and troubleshoot applications more effectively.

   Incorrect: Option B is incorrect because the ability to install applications from unofficial sources is typically controlled by a separate setting called "Unknown sources" or "Allow installation from unknown sources." Option C is incorrect because enabling developer mode does not directly optimize battery life. Option D is incorrect because the screen resolution is generally fixed and cannot be increased by enabling developer mode.

3. **Answer: C**

   Explanation: Rooting an Android device grants the user administrative access and control over the OS. It allows for customization, installing custom ROM, and using advanced system-level features.

   Incorrect: Option A is incorrect because removing malicious applications does not require rooting the device. Option B is incorrect because rooting, if not done properly, can potentially compromise device security. Option D is incorrect because while rooting can provide certain performance benefits, it is not its primary purpose.

4. **Answer: A**

   Explanation: Jailbreaking refers to the process of bypassing software restrictions imposed by Apple on iOS devices. It allows users to access the root filesystem and install unauthorized applications.

   Incorrect: Option B is incorrect because bootlegging refers to the unauthorized reproduction or distribution of copyrighted material. Option C is incorrect because application spoofing involves creating a fake or imitation application to deceive users. Option D is incorrect because a malicious application is a type of harmful software that can compromise the security of a device, but it is not directly related to bypassing software restrictions.

5. **Answer: C**

   Explanation: A bootleg application is a term used to describe a pirated or unauthorized copy of a mobile application, typically obtained from unofficial sources.

   Incorrect: Option A is incorrect because APK is a file format used to distribute and install Android applications, but it does not specifically refer to pirated or unauthorized copies. Option B is incorrect because developer mode is an unrelated term. Option D is incorrect because root access refers to gaining administrative privileges on an Android device, which is not directly related to pirated or unauthorized copies of applications.

6. **Answer: A**

   Explanation: High network traffic can cause a mobile device to have a sluggish response time, leading to delays in loading apps or web pages.

   Incorrect: Limited internet connectivity (option B) usually indicates a problem with the device's connection to the network but may not necessarily be related to high network traffic. A high number of ads (option C) is more likely to be caused by adware or malicious apps rather than high network traffic. Fake security warnings (option D) are typically associated with malware or phishing attempts, not specifically high network traffic.

7. **Answer: A**

   Explanation: When a mobile device reaches its data usage limit, it may experience no internet connectivity until the limit is reset or additional data is purchased.

   Incorrect: Unexpected application behavior (option B) could be caused by various factors, but reaching a data usage limit is not directly related to this symptom. Leaked personal files/data (option C) suggests a security breach or privacy issue rather than a specific symptom of reaching a data usage limit. Sluggish response time (option D) could be a symptom of other issues but is not specifically related to reaching a data usage limit.

8. **Answer: A**

   Explanation: A compromised mobile OS or application often exhibits slow device performance and frequent crashes because of malicious activities or vulnerabilities. This can indicate the presence of malware or unauthorized access.

   Incorrect: Option B suggests improved battery life and faster processing speed, which are not typical symptoms of a compromised mobile OS or application. Option C mentions enhanced security features and increased app compatibility, which are positive outcomes rather than symptoms of security issues. Option D suggests a smooth user interface and seamless multitasking, which are not directly related to security issues and compromises.

9. **Answer: A**

   Explanation: Excessive battery usage can indicate a security issue with a mobile application, such as background processes or malicious activities consuming resources without the user's knowledge. It can be a symptom of malware or poorly optimized app code.

   Incorrect: Option B suggests regular software updates, which is generally considered a good practice for security but does not represent a security issue. Option C mentions limited app permissions, which actually contribute to better security by restricting access to sensitive device functions. Option D refers to encrypted data storage, which is a security feature rather than an issue.

10. **Answer: A**

    Explanation: Unexpected app crashes can be a symptom of a mobile OS vulnerability, where a flaw in the OS or its components causes apps to malfunction or terminate abruptly. These crashes can potentially be exploited by attackers.

    Incorrect: Option B mentions enhanced device performance, which is not a symptom of an OS vulnerability and is more likely a positive outcome. Option C suggests improved battery life, which is not typically associated with OS vulnerabilities. Option D refers to seamless network connectivity, which is not directly related to OS vulnerabilities and can occur even in secure systems.

11. **Answer: D**

    Explanation: Unauthorized app installations represent a common security issue with mobile devices. When users unknowingly install apps from untrusted sources or with malicious intent, it can lead to privacy breaches, data theft, or compromise of the device's security.

    Incorrect: Option A mentions weak network signal strength, which may affect connectivity but is not directly linked to security issues. Option B suggests strong device encryption, which is actually a security measure rather than an issue. Option C refers to regular backups of data, which are essential for data protection but not a security issue themself.

12. **Answer: A**

    Explanation: Unwanted pop-up advertisements can be a symptom of a mobile application security breach, indicating the presence of adware or malware. These advertisements can disrupt the user experience, compromise privacy, and potentially lead to further security issues.

    Incorrect: Option B mentions enhanced app functionality, which is not typically associated with security breaches. Option C suggests increased device storage capacity, which is unrelated to application security breaches. Option D refers to improved user experience, which may occur in well-designed applications but does not directly signify a security breach.

13. **Answer: A**

    Explanation: Excessive RAM utilization is a common indication of a security issue associated with mobile OSs. It can indicate memory leaks or poorly optimized processes, potentially leading to system instability and unauthorized access to sensitive information.

    Incorrect: Option B suggests prompt security updates, which is generally considered a good practice for addressing security issues rather than being a security issue. Option C mentions a secure boot process, which is a security feature rather than an issue. Option D refers to encrypted user data, which is a desirable security measure.

14. **Answer: A**

    Explanation: Application crashes upon launch can be a symptom of a mobile application vulnerability, indicating potential coding or implementation flaws that result in instability. Such vulnerabilities can be exploited by attackers to gain unauthorized access or perform malicious actions.

    Incorrect: Option B mentions faster battery charging, which is unrelated to application vulnerabilities. Option C suggests enhanced network connectivity, which is not typically associated with application vulnerabilities. Option D refers to increased app compatibility, which is a positive outcome rather than a symptom of vulnerabilities.

15. **Answer: C**

    Explanation: Outdated software versions represent a common security issue with mobile OSs. Failure to install software updates promptly can leave devices vulnerable to known exploits and security vulnerabilities that have been patched in newer versions.

    Incorrect: Option A mentions frequent app updates, which are generally considered beneficial for functionality and security. Option B suggests encrypted device backups, which actually contribute to better security rather than being a security issue. Option D highlights optimized power-saving features, which are unrelated to security issues with mobile OSs.

16. **Answer: A**

    Explanation: Unexpected data usage can be a symptom of a compromised mobile application, indicating unauthorized background activities, data exfiltration, or communication with malicious servers. It may result in additional charges, privacy breaches, or other security risks.

    Incorrect: Option B mentions improved device performance, which is not typically associated with compromised applications. Option C suggests enhanced battery longevity, which is not directly related to compromised applications. Option D refers to seamless app integration, which is unrelated to security compromises and can occur even in secure applications.

Chapter 4: Operational Procedures

4.1 Given a Scenario, Implement Best Practices Associated with Documentation and Support Systems Information Management

1. **Answer: C**

   Explanation: Splash screens are an effective way to communicate important information to users before they access a system. They can display regulatory compliance requirements, organization policies, and other essential information. By implementing splash screens, the company can ensure that users are informed and aware of the necessary guidelines and procedures.

   Incorrect: While password complexity rules are important for security (Option A), they are not directly related to regulatory compliance requirements or splash screens. Network segmentation is a technique used to divide a network into smaller segments for security and performance purposes (Option B). It is not directly related to splash screens or regulatory compliance requirements.

   Incident reports are typically used to document and track security incidents or system failures (Option D). While important for incident management, they are not directly related to regulatory compliance requirements or splash screens.

2. **Answer: C**

   Explanation: Incident reports are the appropriate documents for recording detailed information about each incident that occurs during support activities. They provide a structured format to document the incident, including the nature of the issue, the steps taken to resolve it, and any relevant details. Incident reports are essential for tracking, analysis, and compliance purposes.

   Incorrect: Knowledge base articles contain information about common issues, solutions, and best practices (Option A). They are not specifically used for recording detailed information about individual incidents. Splash screens are typically used to display important information to users before accessing a system (Option B). They are not intended for recording incident details. Service-level agreements (SLAs) are contractual agreements between service providers and customers, defining the level of service expected (Option D). While SLAs may include incident management processes, they are not the primary documents for recording detailed incident information.

3. **Answer: D**

   Explanation: Training employees on data handling and privacy policies is a best practice for complying with regulatory requirements related to incident reporting. By providing proper training, employees are equipped with the necessary knowledge and skills to handle incidents appropriately, ensuring compliance with regulatory guidelines. This includes understanding incident reporting procedures, incident classification, and the importance of documenting incidents accurately.

   Incorrect: While splash screens can be used for various purposes, such as displaying company logos or legal disclaimers, they are not directly related to incident reporting or regulatory compliance requirements (Option A). Vulnerability assessments are important for identifying security weaknesses in systems and networks (Option B). While they are crucial for overall security, they are not specific to incident reporting or regulatory compliance requirements. Encryption of sensitive customer data during transit is an essential security measure (Option C). However, it specifically focuses on protecting data during transmission and does not directly address incident reporting or regulatory compliance requirements.

4. **Answer: A**

   Explanation: Network diagrams provide visual representations of the network infrastructure and help support technicians understand the layout and connectivity, making them an essential part of the documentation for support system information management.

   Incorrect: The other choices are important but not directly related to support system information management.

5. **Answer: C**

   Explanation: A knowledge base is a centralized repository of information that contains troubleshooting guides, FAQs, and solutions to known issues. It serves as a valuable resource for support technicians when resolving customer problems.

   Incorrect: The other choices are unrelated to the purpose of a knowledge base.

6. **Answer: B**

   Explanation: When documenting a support request, it is crucial to include the date and time of the request. This information helps establish the order of requests and allows for proper tracking and prioritization.

   Incorrect: The other choices are irrelevant details that do not contribute to support system information management.

7. **Answer: C**

    Explanation: Regularly updating and reviewing documentation is a best practice to ensure that the information remains accurate and relevant.

    Incorrect: Storing documents in multiple physical locations may lead to version control issues (Option A). Sharing sensitive information via email can compromise security (Option B). Printing documentation unnecessarily wastes resources (Option D).

8. **Answer: B**

    Explanation: ServiceNow is an example of a ticketing system commonly used in support systems. It allows support technicians to create, track, and manage support tickets, ensuring efficient resolution of customer issues.

    Incorrect: The other choices are software applications unrelated to ticketing systems.

9. **Answer: C**

    Explanation: A service level agreement (SLA) in support system documentation defines the agreed-upon response and resolution times for support requests. It sets expectations for both the support provider and the customer.

    Incorrect: The other choices are not directly related to the purpose of an SLA.

10. **Answer: C**

    Explanation: A support system knowledge base article should include tested solutions to known issues. It should provide accurate and reliable information to assist support technicians in resolving customer problems.

    Incorrect: The other choices are irrelevant or inappropriate for inclusion in a knowledge base.

11. **Answer: C**

    Explanation: Organizing and categorizing support system documentation using color-coded labels helps improve accessibility and ease of navigation. It allows support technicians to quickly locate the relevant information they need.

    Incorrect: The other choices do not provide an efficient method of organization.

12. **Answer: A**

    Explanation: Salesforce is an example of a customer relationship management (CRM) system used in support systems. It helps manage customer information, interactions, and support requests, ensuring a streamlined customer support experience.

    Incorrect: The other choices are unrelated to CRM systems.

13. **Answer: C**

    Explanation: Creating an inventory list in support system documentation helps track spare parts and equipment available for repair and replacement. It ensures that support technicians have the necessary resources to address customer issues effectively.

    Incorrect: The other choices are unrelated to the purpose of an inventory list.

14. **Answer: B.**

    Explanation: An acceptable use policy (AUP) is a set of rules and guidelines that define the acceptable and appropriate use of computer systems and networks within an organization. It outlines the expected behavior of users and helps protect against misuse or abuse of resources. AUPs typically cover topics such as authorized access, prohibited activities, confidentiality, and consequences for non-compliance.

    Incorrect: Option A is incorrect because backups of critical data are not directly related to an AUP. While data backup may be mentioned in other policies, an AUP specifically focuses on user behavior and system usage. Option C is incorrect because troubleshooting hardware issues is a separate topic from an AUP. Troubleshooting processes and procedures are covered under different policies or guidelines. Option D is incorrect because documenting software license agreements is not directly related to an AUP. Software license agreements are usually governed by legal and compliance policies rather than an AUP.

4.2 Explain Basic Change-Management Best Practices

1. **Answer: C**

    Explanation: Documenting changes thoroughly is a basic change-management best practice because it helps maintain a record of all modifications made, making it easier to track and troubleshoot issues if they arise.

    Incorrect: Option A is incorrect because implementing changes without proper planning can lead to unexpected consequences and disruptions in the system. Option B is incorrect because communicating changes only after they have been implemented can cause confusion and resistance among users. Option D is incorrect because ignoring user feedback can result in overlooking important insights and requirements for successful change implementation.

2. **Answer: C**

   Explanation: Assessing and managing risks is a key element of change management. By identifying potential risks and implementing appropriate mitigation strategies, organizations can ensure a smoother transition during change implementation.

   Incorrect: Option A is incorrect because user involvement is crucial during change management to gather feedback, address concerns, and ensure user acceptance. Option B is incorrect because effective communication with stakeholders is essential for managing expectations and ensuring their understanding and support. Option D is incorrect because rushing the implementation process can lead to errors and overlook critical steps, increasing the likelihood of failure.

3. **Answer: B**

   Explanation: Providing clear communication and training is a recommended practice for managing user resistance during change implementation. By keeping users informed about the changes and their benefits, and by providing adequate training, organizations can address concerns and increase user acceptance.

   Incorrect: Option A is incorrect because ignoring user concerns can lead to increased resistance and negatively impact the success of change implementation. Option C is incorrect because limiting user access to system documentation can hinder their understanding and ability to adapt to the changes effectively. Option D is incorrect because implementing changes abruptly without prior notice can cause confusion and resistance among users.

4. **Answer: C**

   Explanation: The purpose of a change advisory board (CAB) is to evaluate and prioritize proposed changes. The CAB ensures that changes align with organizational goals, assesses their impact, and decides their priority for implementation.

   Incorrect: Option A is incorrect because approving all changes without review can lead to uncontrolled modifications and potential disruptions. Option B is incorrect because while the CAB may monitor the progress of change implementation, its primary purpose is to evaluate and prioritize proposed changes. Option D is incorrect because user involvement is important in the change process to gather feedback and ensure successful adoption.

5. **Answer: C**

   Explanation: Temporary service disruptions are a common risk associated with change management. Implementing changes can sometimes result in system downtime or disruptions, affecting user productivity during the transition.

   Incorrect: Option A is incorrect because improved system performance is a potential benefit of change management rather than a risk. Option B is incorrect because increased user satisfaction is a desired outcome of successful change management. Option D is incorrect because enhanced security measures are typically a positive outcome of change management efforts.

6. **Answer: B**

   Explanation: Performing regular backups is an example of a change management best practice for software deployments. Backups ensure that data can be restored if there are any issues or failures during the deployment process.

   Incorrect: Option A is incorrect because skipping the testing phase can lead to the deployment of faulty software and potential system disruptions. Option C is incorrect because implementing changes during peak hours can increase the impact on users and affect system availability. Option D is incorrect because effective user communication is crucial for managing expectations and ensuring a smooth transition.

7. **Answer: B**

   Explanation: Conducting a thorough inventory assessment is an example of a change management best practice for hardware replacements. It ensures that organizations have accurate information about existing hardware, facilitating proper planning and decision-making during replacements.

   Incorrect: Option A is incorrect because ignoring user feedback can lead to overlooking important insights and requirements during hardware replacements. Option C is incorrect because implementing changes without testing can result in the deployment of faulty hardware and potential disruptions. Option D is incorrect because involving stakeholders in the process is essential for their understanding and support during hardware replacements.

8. **Answer: C**

   Explanation: The purpose of a rollback plan in change management is to identify potential issues that may occur during the change implementation and outline the steps to revert back to the previous state if necessary.

   Incorrect: Option A is incorrect because the purpose of a rollback plan is not to prevent changes from being implemented but rather to provide a contingency plan if issues arise. Option B is incorrect because documenting the reasons for change implementation is important, but it is not the primary purpose of a rollback plan. Option D is incorrect because user feedback is valuable during the change process and should be considered, rather than excluded.

9. **Answer: C**

   Explanation: Conducting regular risk assessments is a recommended practice for managing change-related risks. By periodically assessing potential risks associated with changes, organizations can proactively identify and mitigate them to minimize negative impacts.

   Incorrect: Option A is incorrect because avoiding risk assessment altogether can lead to overlooking potential risks and their consequences. Option B is incorrect because implementing changes without backup plans can result in unanticipated issues and difficulties during the change process. Option D is incorrect because ignoring risk mitigation strategies can leave organizations vulnerable to the negative impacts of potential risks.

10. **Answer: C**

   Explanation: Tailoring the message to the target audience is a key consideration when communicating changes to users during change management. Different users may have varying levels of technical knowledge and concerns, so customizing the communication helps ensure their understanding and acceptance.

   Incorrect: Option A is incorrect because providing vague and general information can lead to confusion and misunderstanding among users. Option B is incorrect because overemphasizing the negative aspects of the changes can create resistance and hinder user acceptance. Option D is incorrect because delaying communication until after the changes are implemented can cause uncertainty and negatively impact user readiness for the changes.

4.3 Given a Scenario, Implement Workstation Backup and Recovery Methods

1. **Answer: A**

   Explanation: A full backup creates a complete copy of all data and settings, providing a comprehensive snapshot of the workstation at that particular moment. This method allows for a complete restoration in case of data loss.

   Incorrect: Option B only includes the data that has changed since the last full backup, not all data at a specific point in time. Option C only includes data that has changed since the last backup, which could be either a full or incremental backup, but it does not capture all data at a specific point in time. Option D is not a standard backup method. It refers to manually choosing specific files or folders for backup, not creating a complete snapshot of the workstation.

2. **Answer: A**

   Explanation: Bare-metal recovery involves restoring an entire workstation's operating system, applications, and data from a complete backup, often in situations where the system needs to be rebuilt from scratch or migrated to new hardware.

   Incorrect: Option B refers to restoring data or applications from backups stored in the cloud, but it does not address restoring the entire workstation's hard drive. Option C focuses on recovering individual files or folders rather than the entire workstation's hard drive. Option D is not a standard term. Incremental backups are used to restore only the data that has changed since the last backup, not the entire system.

3. **Answer: A**

   Explanation: Tape drives offer fast transfer rates compared to other backup storage media, but they tend to be costly compared to other options.

   Incorrect: Option B (external hard drives) is a popular backup medium due to its relatively fast transfer rate and cost-effectiveness compared to tape drives. Option C (network-attached storage (NAS)) provides a convenient and network-accessible backup solution, but its transfer rate will not be as fast as tape drives. Option D (cloud storage) is cost-effective and easy to scale, but transfer rates will be slower compared to tape drives, especially when dealing with large amounts of data.

4. **Answer: B**

   Explanation: An incremental backup is designed to only back up data that has changed since the last backup. This type of backup is designed to reduce backup time and requires less storage space.

   Incorrect: Option A (differential backup) backs up all data that has changed since the last full backup, not considering previous incremental backups. Option C (synthetic backup) is a method that creates a new full backup by combining a previous full backup and subsequent incremental backups. It does not directly address only backing up changed data since the last backup. Option D (continuous backup) involves backing up data in real-time as changes occur, ensuring minimal data loss in the event of a failure. It does not differentiate between full and incremental backups.

5. **Answer: A**

   Explanation: The grandfather-father-son rotation scheme involves using a set of backup media and cycling through them on a daily basis. The oldest backup is overwritten when the set becomes full. This scheme provides a combination of daily, weekly, and monthly backups.

   Incorrect: Option B (Tower of Hanoi) is a backup rotation scheme that uses a set of backup media, but it involves a more complex rotation pattern that includes multiple levels of backups based on specific rules. Option C (back up to disk) refers to storing backups on disk-based storage media but does not specify a rotation scheme. Option D (back up to tape) is a backup method that utilizes tape drives as the storage medium, but it does not imply a specific rotation scheme.

6. **Answer: C**

   Explanation: Snapshot backup provides the fastest recovery time when compared to other backup methods. Snapshots capture the state of the workstation's system and data at a specific point in time, allowing for quick restoration to that exact state.

   Incorrect: Option A (incremental backup) requires restoring data from multiple backups, including the last full backup and subsequent incremental backups, which can take longer. Option B (differential backup) also requires restoring data from multiple backups, including the last full backup and subsequent differential backups, which can be slower than snapshot backup. Option D (full backup) provides a complete copy of all data, but recovery time can be longer as it involves restoring all data rather than just the changes since the last backup.

7. **Answer: A**

   Explanation: Mirroring ensures data redundancy by creating identical copies of backups on different backup media simultaneously. This method enhances data availability and fault tolerance.

   Incorrect: Option B (replication) involves creating copies of data on different systems or locations, but it does not specifically refer to creating multiple copies of backups on different media. Option C (archiving) refers to the long-term storage of data that is no longer actively used but still needs to be retained for compliance or historical purposes. Option D (versioning) involves creating and storing multiple versions of a file or document to track changes over time but does not necessarily create multiple copies of backups.

8. **Answer: D**

   Explanation: Offsite backup involves storing backups in a location outside the primary site, providing protection against disasters or physical damage that could affect the original location. By storing backups in different geographical locations, data is safeguarded against localized events.

   Incorrect: Option A (cloud-based backup) offers remote storage of backups, but it does not inherently guarantee multiple copies across different geographical locations. Option B (tape backup) and Option C (disk-to-disk backup) can be used for offsite backup, but they do not inherently provide the highest level of data protection as they depend on the specific implementation and location of the backup media.

9. **Answer: A**

   Explanation: Image backup captures an exact copy of the workstation's operating system, applications, and data, allowing for quick restoration to a functional state. It creates a snapshot of the entire workstation's configuration.

   Incorrect: Option B (file-level backup) focuses on backing up individual files or folders rather than capturing the entire workstation's configuration. Option C (incremental backup) captures only the changes since the last backup, which might not include the full workstation's operating system and applications. Option D (differential backup) captures the changes since the last full backup, but it does not provide an exact copy of the entire workstation's configuration.

10. **Answer: A**

    Explanation: Continuous backup involves automatically backing up data in real time as changes occur. This method ensures minimal data loss in the event of a failure, as the backups are kept up to date at all times.

    Incorrect: Option B (synchronization backup) refers to maintaining identical copies of data in different locations, but it does not necessarily involve real-time backup. Option C (manual backup) refers to the process of manually initiating backups, which might not be as efficient or provide real-time data protection. Option D (snapshot backup) captures the state of the workstation at a specific point in time but does not continuously back up data as changes occur.

4.4 Given a Scenario, Use Common Safety Procedures

1. **Answer: A**

   Explanation: Wearing an ESD (electrostatic discharge) wrist strap helps prevent static electricity from damaging computer components. It safely discharges any static electricity built up on your body.

   Incorrect: Option B (disconnecting the power supply without turning it off) can cause damage to the hardware and potentially harm the individual. Option C (handling circuit boards with bare hands) can introduce static electricity and damage sensitive components. Option D (standing on a wet surface) increases the risk of electric shock, which is hazardous when working with computer hardware.

2. **Answer: A**

   Explanation: Using compressed air to clean debris from fans and heatsinks helps maintain proper airflow and prevents overheating. It's important to clean the components safely and without causing damage.

   Incorrect: Option B (using a magnetized screwdriver) can potentially damage or interfere with sensitive electronic components. Option C (storing liquids near the computer) increases the risk of accidental spills, which can cause damage to the equipment. Option D (placing the computer on an unstable surface) increases the chances of it falling or toppling over, potentially causing damage.

3. **Answer: C**

   Explanation: Securing cables using cable ties or clips helps maintain an organized and tidy workspace, prevents tripping hazards, and protects the cables from damage due to pulling or tangling.

   Incorrect: Option A (pulling the cable from a distance) can cause stress on the connector and potentially damage it. Option B (bending the cable sharply) can lead to cable breakage or damage to the connector. Option D (leaving cables loose and tangled) increases the risk of tripping over them and can cause damage or disconnections.

4. **Answer: A**

   Explanation: Before opening a computer case, it is crucial to ensure the computer is turned off and unplugged. This eliminates the risk of electrical shock and protects both the technician and the hardware.

   Incorrect: Option B (wearing gloves) can increase the risk of static electricity discharge and potentially damage sensitive components. Option C (using a metal tool to open the case) can lead to accidental damage or short circuits if it comes into contact with live electrical components. Option D (keeping the case on a soft, cushioned surface) can interfere with proper ventilation and cooling, potentially causing overheating.

5. **Answer: A**

   Explanation: Following ergonomic practices, such as maintaining proper posture, using adjustable furniture, and taking regular breaks, helps prevent injuries such as musculoskeletal disorders and eye strain.

   Incorrect: Option B (wearing heavy jewelry and accessories) increases the risk of getting caught on components, causing damage or injury. Option C (using damaged tools) can lead to accidents, injuries, or damage to the hardware. It's important to use functional tools. Option D (skipping breaks and working for long periods without rest) can lead to fatigue, reduced focus, and increased chances of accidents or mistakes.

6. **Answer: A**

   Explanation: Using an antistatic vacuum cleaner is a safe way to remove dust and debris from the inside of a computer. It helps prevent the buildup of static electricity and reduces the risk of damaging sensitive components.

   Incorrect: Option B (spraying cleaning solution directly onto components) can cause damage or short circuits. It's best to use a cleaning solution on a cloth or sponge first. Option C (cleaning the computer while it is still powered on) poses the risk of electrical shock and potential damage to the hardware. Option D (using a dry cloth to wipe the motherboard) can generate static electricity and potentially damage the components. It's better to use an antistatic cloth or cleaning solution.

7. **Answer: A**

   Explanation: Disposing of old computer equipment should be done responsibly by recycling it according to local regulations. This helps prevent environmental contamination and ensures the proper handling of potentially hazardous materials.

   Incorrect: Option B (disassembling the equipment without protective gear) can expose individuals to potentially harmful substances or components, such as chemicals or sharp edges. Option C (throwing the equipment in regular household waste) can lead to improper disposal and can have negative environmental impacts. Option D (storing the equipment in a humid environment) can cause corrosion and damage to the components.

8. **Answer: A**

   Explanation: When working with high-voltage equipment, it is essential to wear insulated gloves and safety glasses. These safety measures protect against electric shocks and potential eye injuries.

   Incorrect: Option B (working alone with high-voltage equipment) is not recommended. It's safer to have a colleague nearby or follow proper procedures for working with others in hazardous situations. Option C (using a metal ladder when working at heights) can create a risk of electric shock if it comes into contact with live electrical equipment. It's safer to use non-conductive ladders. Option D (using equipment with damaged cords) can be hazardous and may result in electrical shock or short circuits. Damaged cords should be repaired or replaced.

9. **Answer: C**

    Explanation: In the event of a chemical spill near computer equipment, it is important to follow proper procedures for chemical cleanup. This may involve using appropriate safety equipment, containment measures, and contacting the appropriate authorities if necessary.

    Incorrect: Option A (shutting down the equipment immediately) may be necessary if there is an immediate risk of electrical damage, but the focus should be on addressing the chemical spill and ensuring safety. Option B (using a vacuum cleaner to remove the spill) can potentially spread the chemical or cause damage to the equipment. It's best to follow proper cleanup procedures. Option D (ignoring the spill and continuing to work) is not safe and can lead to potential damage to the equipment or harm to individuals in the area.

10. **Answer: A**

    Explanation: When installing or replacing computer hardware components, it is important to use proper lifting techniques for heavy components. This helps prevent strains, back injuries, and damage to the hardware.

    Incorrect: Option B (using excessive force when inserting connectors) can damage the connectors or the components themselves. It's important to use gentle pressure and ensure proper alignment. Option C (installing components in an unventilated area) can lead to overheating, which can damage the components and affect the overall performance of the system. Proper ventilation is essential. Option D (installing components without grounding yourself) increases the risk of static electricity discharge, which can damage sensitive components. It's important to ground yourself to prevent static electricity buildup.

4.5 Summarize Environmental Impacts and Local Environmental Controls

1. **Answer: B**

    Explanation: Material Safety Data Sheets (MSDSs) are important documents that provide detailed information about potential hazards associated with specific materials. They outline the necessary precautions and safety measures to be followed when handling, using, or disposing of hazardous substances. The purpose of MSDSs is to ensure that individuals have access to accurate and relevant information to minimize the risks associated with hazardous materials.

    Incorrect: Option A is incorrect because transportation guidelines for hazardous materials are usually covered by separate regulations and documentation, such as the hazardous materials regulations (HMR). Option C is incorrect because the proper procedures for recycling electronic waste are typically outlined in different documents or guidelines, such as e-waste recycling regulations. Option D is incorrect because MSDSs do not certify the quality or durability of protective equipment. Such certifications are usually provided by relevant standards organizations or testing agencies.

2. **Answer: C**

   Explanation: The primary purpose of reviewing material safety data sheets (MSDSs) before handling or disposing of hazardous materials is to understand the potential health and safety risks associated with the materials. MSDSs provide crucial information about the hazards, precautions, and safe handling procedures for the substances involved. By reviewing the MSDSs, individuals can make informed decisions and take necessary precautions to minimize the risks to their health and safety.

   Incorrect: Option A focuses on the financial cost associated with the materials, which is not the primary purpose of reviewing MSDSs. Option B relates to the expiration date of the materials, which may be mentioned in the MSDSs but is not the primary purpose of reviewing it. Option D refers to identifying potential sources of the materials, which is unrelated to the primary purpose of reviewing MSDSs.

3. **Answer: C**

   Explanation: Recycling used batteries at designated centers or facilities ensures proper handling and environmentally friendly disposal.

   Incorrect: Option A is incorrect because throwing used batteries in the regular trash can lead to environmental pollution and the release of harmful chemicals. Option B is incorrect because while some electronics stores may offer battery disposal, it is not a standard practice, and not all stores have this service. Option D is incorrect because burying batteries in the backyard can contaminate the soil and pose risks to the environment and human health. Batteries should not decompose naturally in this manner.

4. **Answer: C**

   Explanation: Returning used toner cartridges to the manufacturer or participating in a designated recycling program ensures they are properly recycled and disposed of in an environmentally responsible manner.

   Incorrect: Option A is incorrect because not all recycling bins are suitable for toner cartridge disposal, and improper recycling may harm the environment. Option B is incorrect because toner cartridges can contain harmful substances and should not be treated as regular trash. Option D is incorrect because burning toner cartridges releases toxic fumes and is highly hazardous.

5. **Answers: A, B, and D**

   Explanation: Option A (selling devices to unknown parties) may lead to data breaches or unauthorized access to sensitive information. Option B (donating devices without properly wiping their data) may expose personal or confidential data to others. Option D (disassembling devices and disposing of their parts separately without proper knowledge) can lead to environmental damage, and some components may require specialized recycling facilities for safe disposal. Proper disposal of electronic devices and assets often involves data wiping, recycling, or returning them to the manufacturer or designated recycling programs. This ensures both data security and environmental protection.

   Incorrect: Option C (erasing all data before recycling or disposal) is essential to protect privacy; it is not a method to avoid.

6. **Answer: A**

   Explanation: Temperature, humidity, and proper ventilation are important factors to consider for maintaining optimal equipment performance and longevity. Extreme temperatures can cause damage to sensitive components, while high humidity levels can lead to condensation and moisture-related issues. Proper ventilation ensures adequate airflow and helps prevent overheating.

   Incorrect: Option B – noise level, cable management, and power supply – are important considerations for a well-organized and efficient setup, but they are not directly related to temperature, humidity, and ventilation. Option C – lighting conditions, firewall settings, and antivirus software – are more focused on security and user experience rather than environmental factors. Option D – backup systems, network security, and data encryption – are essential for data protection but do not directly relate to temperature, humidity, and ventilation considerations.

7. **Answer: A**

   Explanation: A UPS is specifically designed to provide backup power during power surges, under-voltage events, and power failures. It offers a continuous supply of power to connected devices, protecting them from potential damage or data loss.

   Incorrect: Option B, Power over Ethernet (PoE), refers to a technology that enables the delivery of power and data through an Ethernet cable to compatible devices, such as IP cameras or VoIP phones. This option is not directly related to protecting against power surges or failures. Option C, Network Attached Storage (NAS), is a storage device connected to a network that provides centralized file storage and sharing capabilities. While NAS devices may have some built-in surge protection, they are not primarily designed to protect against power surges or failures. Option D, Wireless Access Point (WAP), is a networking device that allows wireless devices to connect to a wired network. It is not designed to protect against power surges, under-voltage events, or power failures.

8. **Answer: A**

   Explanation: A surge protector, commonly referred to as a surge suppressor, is a specialized device created with the purpose of safeguarding electronic devices against sudden increases in voltage and power surges. Its primary function is to absorb and redirect excess electrical energy, shielding the connected devices from potential damage caused by these voltage spikes. By offering this protective barrier, surge protectors play a vital role in maintaining the longevity and reliability of electronic equipment.

   Incorrect: Option B, Uninterruptible Power Supply (UPS), is primarily used to provide backup power during power outages and protect against power failures. While some UPS models may have surge protection features, their primary function is not surge suppression. Option C, a power inverter, is used to convert DC power from a battery or other sources into AC power. It is not designed to suppress power surges or protect against voltage spikes. Option D, a power strip, is a device that provides multiple electrical outlets from a single power source. While some power strips may include surge protection features, not all power strips offer this functionality, and it is not their primary purpose.

9. **Answer: A**

   Explanation: A battery backup system, also known as an Uninterruptible Power Supply (UPS), is used to provide backup power to connected devices during power outages. It ensures that critical equipment remains operational and prevents data loss or damage caused by sudden power loss.

   Incorrect: Option B, increasing network bandwidth, is unrelated to the purpose of a battery backup system. Network bandwidth refers to the capacity of a network to transmit data. Option C, protecting against electromagnetic interference, is typically accomplished using devices such as shielding or filters. While a battery backup system may provide some level of protection against electrical noise, its primary purpose is to provide backup power. Option D, preventing power surges, is the function of a surge protector or surge suppressor, not a battery backup system.

10. **Answer: C**

    Explanation: Positioning the computer away from electrical interference helps reduce potential disruptions and ensures optimal performance.

    Incorrect: Placing the computer on an uneven surface (Option A) can cause stability issues and affect airflow. Locating the computer near direct sunlight (Option B) can lead to overheating and damage to the components. Stacking multiple computers on top of each other (Option D) can result in heat buildup and compromise ventilation.

11. **Answer: D**

    Explanation: Utilizing a vacuum designed for electronics is a suitable method for dust cleanup, as it minimizes the risk of static discharge and safely removes debris.

    Incorrect: Blowing compressed air directly into the components (Option A) can push the dust deeper into the system and potentially damage sensitive parts. Using a dry cloth to wipe the components (Option B) may cause static discharge and harm the computer. Applying water or liquid cleaning agents on the components (Option C) can lead to damage and short circuits.

4.6 Explain the Importance of Prohibited Content/Activity and Privacy, Licensing, and Policy Concepts

1. **Answer: A**

    Explanation: The chain of custody is the process of documenting the handling and transfer of evidence during an incident response. It ensures the integrity and preservation of data by maintaining a clear record of who had control over the evidence at any given time.

    Incorrect: Option B, incident escalation, refers to the process of escalating an incident to a higher authority or management. Option C, password recovery, is unrelated to data integrity and preservation. Option D, data compression, is a technique used to reduce the size of data, but it does not directly address the importance of preserving data integrity during an incident response.

2. **Answer: A**

    Explanation: When encountering prohibited content/activity during an incident response, it is important to inform management or law enforcement, if necessary. This ensures that appropriate actions are taken to address the issue and comply with legal requirements.

    Incorrect: Option B, continuing the investigation without involving anyone else, is not advisable as it may hinder the resolution of the incident. Option C, deleting the prohibited content/activity immediately, may compromise the chain of custody and hinder further investigation. Option D, performing a system reboot, is not a sufficient response to handling prohibited content/activity.

3. **Answer: A**

    Explanation: Making a copy of a drive during an incident response is done to preserve data integrity and evidence. It ensures that the original data remains intact and can be analyzed without any modifications.

    Incorrect: Option B, speeding up the incident resolution process, may not be the primary purpose of making a drive copy. Option C, minimizing the impact on system performance, is unrelated to the need for preserving data integrity. Option D, reducing the risk of future incidents, is not directly addressed by making a drive copy.

4. **Answer: A**

   Explanation: The concept that involves documenting the handling and transfer of evidence during an incident response is the chain of custody. It ensures a clear record of who had control over the evidence at any given time.

   Incorrect: Option B, incident containment, refers to the process of preventing an incident from spreading or causing further damage. Option C, data classification, is the process of categorizing data based on its sensitivity and importance. Option D, system hardening, involves implementing security measures to reduce vulnerabilities but does not directly relate to evidence handling.

5. **Answer: D**

   Explanation: Documenting an incident during an incident response serves the purpose of creating a detailed record for analysis and accountability. It provides a comprehensive account of the incident, aiding in understanding the root cause and taking appropriate actions.

   Incorrect: Option A, providing a reference for future incidents, may be a secondary benefit but is not the primary purpose of documenting an incident. Option B, informing management of ongoing activities, may be necessary but is not the main purpose of documentation. Option C, facilitating collaboration with other teams, can be a benefit but is not the primary reason for documenting an incident.

6. **Answer: C**

   Explanation: The end-user license agreement (EULA) outlines the permissions, restrictions, and liabilities associated with the use of software by an individual or organization.

   Incorrect: Option A, privacy policy, focuses on data protection. Option B, open source license, pertains to the distribution and modification of open source software. Option D, digital rights management (DRM), deals with copyright protection and access control to digital content.

7. **Answer: A**

   Explanation: Personal use licenses typically require individual registration, allowing the software to be used by a single user for personal purposes. On the other hand, corporate use licenses are designed for organizations and allow the software to be used by multiple users within the organization.

   Incorrect: Option B, personal use licenses, are not defined by the length of the license. Option C, the restrictions within the terms of the license, may be different between personal and corporate licenses, often personal licenses are more restrictive. As for Option D, in some cases, a personal license may be free (with restricted use), but this is not always the case.

8. **Answer: D**

    Explanation: Digital rights management (DRM) is a licensing concept that focuses on copyright protection and access control to digital content. It ensures that users comply with the terms of the software license and prevents unauthorized copying or distribution.

    Incorrect: Option A, open source license, refers to the distribution and modification of open-source software. Options B and C, valid license and non-expired license, pertain to the legal status of a license.

9. **Answer: B**

    Explanation: Licensing, digital rights management (DRM), and the end-user license agreement (EULA) are designed to prevent the use of prohibited content/activity. They outline the permissible uses of software and help restrict or block access to content or activities that are deemed prohibited or illegal.

    Incorrect: Option A is incorrect. Licensing, DRM, and EULAs are implemented to prevent or control the sharing of prohibited content or activities, not to facilitate them. As for Option C, while those mechanisms can include monitoring features to track usage and ensure compliance with terms, their primary purpose is not to monitor and report prohibited content or activities. They aim to prevent such usage in the first place. For Option D, while EULAs and licensing agreements can specify consequences for violating terms, their main purpose is not to establish penalties. Their primary focus is on setting forth the rights, obligations, and restrictions related to the use of the software or content.

10. **Answer: B**

    Explanation: An open source license allows users to view, modify, and distribute the source code of software. It promotes collaboration, transparency, and community-driven development.

    Incorrect: As for Option A, a privacy policy outlines how an organization collects, uses, and manages user data. It is not related to software source code or licensing that allows code modification and distribution. For Option C, an EULA defines the terms and conditions under which software can be used; it typically does not grant users the right to view, modify, and distribute the source code. EULAs often restrict users from accessing the source code. For Option D, DRM is focused on protecting intellectual property rights, such as preventing unauthorized copying or distribution of digital content. It is not related to open access to source code for software development.

11. **Answer: A**

    Explanation: Regulated data refers to information that is subject to government regulations and restrictions. This type of data may include personal government-issued information, credit card transactions, healthcare data, and other sensitive information that requires special protection and compliance with specific policies.

    Incorrect: Option B is incorrect because regulated data is not freely accessible to the public. Option C is incorrect because regulated data is typically stored with encryption and security measures to ensure its protection. Option D is incorrect because regulated data is not necessarily shared among employees within an organization without proper authorization.

12. **Answer: B**

    Explanation: Personally identifiable information (PII) refers to data that can be used to identify an individual. Examples of PII include names, addresses, social security numbers, email addresses, and other similar personal details. Protecting PII is crucial for maintaining privacy and complying with privacy regulations.

    Incorrect: Option A is incorrect because social media posts and comments may contain personal opinions and information but do not necessarily qualify as PII. Option C is incorrect because publicly available company information does not necessarily involve personal details about individuals. Option D is incorrect because even non-sensitive email communication can potentially contain PII, such as email addresses and names.

13. **Answer: B**

    Explanation: When handling credit card transactions, one of the key concerns is securing cardholder data. It is crucial to protect credit card information to prevent unauthorized access, fraud, and identity theft. Compliance with industry standards such as the Payment Card Industry Data Security Standard (PCI DSS) is essential for safeguarding cardholder data.

    Incorrect: Option A is incorrect because while data availability is important, the primary concern with credit card transactions is data security. Option C is incorrect because maintaining accurate financial records is important but not the primary concern when handling credit card transactions. Option D is incorrect because while transaction speed is desirable, it is not the key concern when it comes to securing credit card transactions.

14. **Answer: B**

    Explanation: A driver's license number is an example of personal government-issued information. It is a unique identifier issued by the government to individuals for the purpose of driving legally. Protecting personal government-issued information is important to prevent identity theft and misuse.

    Incorrect: Option A is incorrect because social media account usernames are not government-issued personal information. Option C is incorrect because Wi-Fi network passwords are not personal government-issued information. Option D is incorrect because a home address is not directly government-issued personal information.

15. **Answer: B**

    Explanation: Data retention requirements refer to the policies and procedures for storing and managing data. It includes determining how long data should be retained, what types of data should be stored, and how data should be protected and disposed of when no longer needed. Compliance with data retention requirements is essential for regulatory compliance and effective data management.

    Incorrect: Option A is incorrect because data retention requirements are not related to the time it takes to process data. Option C is incorrect because data backup frequency is a separate concern from data retention requirements. Option D is incorrect because data transmission speed is not directly related to data retention requirements.

4.7 Given a Scenario, Use Proper Communication Techniques and Professionalism

1. **Answer: C**

    Explanation: Active listening and paraphrasing the customer's concerns demonstrate professionalism by showing that you understand their needs and are actively engaged in finding a solution.

    Incorrect: Option A, interrupting the customer, may seem rude and dismissive. Option B, using technical jargon, can confuse the customer, and offering discounts or freebies (Option D) should only be considered if it aligns with company policies and the customer's issue.

2. **Answer: A**

    Explanation: Maintaining eye contact and nodding in agreement are non-verbal cues that demonstrate active listening and engagement, which are professional communication behaviors.

    Incorrect: Option B, checking personal emails on a mobile device, is unprofessional and distracts from the conversation. Option C, speaking softly, shows consideration for others but does not address the question requirements (non-verbal). Option D, using slang terms and informal language, is inappropriate in a professional setting.

3. **Answer: B**

    Explanation: Using "Dear [Recipient's First Name]," is the most appropriate and professional way to address the recipient in a business email.

    Incorrect: Options A and D are less formal and may not convey the necessary level of professionalism. Option C is an unusual way to address a business associate. It is more likely to be used in a legal undertaking (such as a court injunction).

4. **Answer: C**

   Explanation: Utilizing visual aids, diagrams, and illustrations is the most effective way to convey complex technical information to a non-technical audience.

   Incorrect: Options A, B, and D are incorrect because using technical terms extensively can confuse the audience, relying solely on written documentation may not be easily understood, and speaking rapidly can overwhelm the audience and hinder comprehension.

5. **Answer: B**

   Explanation: Option B demonstrates the use of professional language by describing the situation without being overly casual or judgmental.

   Incorrect: Options A, C, and D use unprofessional language and may not effectively address the customer's concerns.

6. **Answer: C**

   Explanation: Offering alternative solutions and compromises demonstrates professionalism when handling a disagreement or conflict with a customer.

   Incorrect: Raising your voice, blaming the customer, or ignoring their concerns are unprofessional and can escalate the situation.

7. **Answer: C**

   Explanation: Actively listening and respecting others' opinions is an example of appropriate professional behavior when interacting with colleagues.

   Incorrect: Options A, B, and D promote negative workplace dynamics and are considered unprofessional.

8. **Answer: C**

   Explanation: Holding individual face-to-face meetings is the best communication method for delivering sensitive or confidential information.

   Incorrect: Options A, B, and D can compromise confidentiality and may not allow for personal attention or support.

9. **Answer: B**

   Explanation: Keeping the microphone on mute when not speaking is an example of maintaining professionalism in a virtual meeting.

   Incorrect: Eating a meal on camera, using informal language in chat messages, and sharing irrelevant personal anecdotes are unprofessional and can disrupt the meeting.

10. **Answer: B**

    Explanation: Setting realistic expectations and providing updates is a professional approach to managing customer expectations.

    Incorrect: Overpromising can lead to disappointment, ignoring customer requests is unprofessional, and redirecting customers without addressing their concerns may be seen as dismissive.

11. **Answer: B**

    Explanation: Encrypting the customer's sensitive files and folders using strong encryption algorithms ensures their data remains confidential and protected.

    Incorrect: Option A is incorrect because regularly sharing the customer's data with colleagues compromises its confidentiality. Option C, uploading the customer's confidential data to a cloud storage service, increases the risk of unauthorized access. Option D, disposing of the customer's computer without securely wiping the hard drive, may expose their private materials to potential data breaches.

12. **Answer: C**

    Explanation: Implementing access controls on the printer ensures that only authorized individuals can use and access the customer's confidential materials, maintaining their security.

    Incorrect: Option A, sharing the printer's access credentials with other technicians, increases the risk of unauthorized access to the customer's confidential materials. Option B, disabling logging features, hampers the ability to track and investigate any potential privacy breaches. Option D, printing the customer's confidential documents in a public area, compromises their privacy and confidentiality.

13. **Answer: C**

    Explanation: Option C is the correct choice because implementing strong password policies and enabling full disk encryption on the customer's desktop computer provides an additional layer of security, ensuring the confidentiality of their materials.

    Incorrect: Option A, creating a shared user account with unrestricted access, compromises the confidentiality of the customer's materials. Option B, performing data backups without verifying the integrity and confidentiality of the backup media, may lead to potential data breaches. Option D, storing the customer's confidential files in publicly accessible folders, exposes them to unauthorized access.

4.8 Identify the Basics of Scripting

1. **Answer: C**

   Explanation: JavaScript is specifically designed for web development, allowing for dynamic and interactive elements on websites.

   Incorrect: Python, Bash, and PowerShell are commonly used scripting languages, allowing for automated tasks to be scheduled.

2. **Answer: D**

   Explanation: PowerShell is a scripting language developed by Microsoft for task automation and configuration management in Windows environments.

   Incorrect: Python, Bash, and JavaScript are not specifically designed for Windows automation.

3. **Answer: B**

   Explanation: Bash (Bourne Again SHell) is the default scripting language for Unix-like operating systems and is widely used for system administration tasks.

   Incorrect: Python, JavaScript, and PowerShell are not commonly used for this purpose.

4. **Answer: A**

   Explanation: Python is a versatile scripting language that can be used for various purposes, including web development, task automation, scientific computing, and data analysis.

   Incorrect: While Bash, JavaScript, and PowerShell have their own specific use cases, Python offers a broader range of applications.

5. **Answer: C**

   Explanation: JavaScript is primarily used for client-side scripting, allowing for dynamic and interactive elements on web pages.

   Incorrect: Python, Bash, and PowerShell are not typically used for this purpose.

6. **Answer: A**

   Explanation: Inadequate error handling can lead to unintended consequences such as introducing malware, changing system settings, or causing crashes. By implementing proper error handling mechanisms, script developers can minimize the risks and ensure safer execution of their scripts.

   Incorrect: Options B, C, and D are not directly related to the mentioned risks.

7. **Answer: B**

   Explanation: Implementing input validation and sanitization helps prevent malicious code injection through user input. It ensures that only expected and safe inputs are processed by the script, reducing the risk of unintentionally introducing malware.

   Incorrect: Regularly updating antivirus software (Option A) helps protect against known malware, but it does not directly address the risk associated with scripting. Options C and D are not recommended actions and can potentially introduce additional vulnerabilities.

8. **Answer: A**

   Explanation: Scripts that consume excessive memory resources can overload the browser or system, leading to crashes. This can occur when the script does not properly manage memory allocation or fails to release allocated resources.

   Incorrect: Options B, C, and D can cause performance issues but are not specifically related to mishandling of resources leading to crashes.

9. **Answer: C**

   Explanation: Downloading scripts from untrusted or unknown sources can lead to the inadvertent introduction of malware into the system.

   Incorrect: Option A is a good practice as reputable script repositories typically vet their content, reducing the risk of malware. Option B is also a good practice, but it doesn't directly address the concern of unintentionally introducing malware. Option D is a valid method to mitigate potential risks, but it doesn't specifically address the risk of malware.

10. **Answer: D**

    Explanation: When executing scripts, inadvertent changes to critical system settings may lead to system instability or malfunction.

    Incorrect: Options A, B, and C are positive outcomes that can result from intentional changes to system settings.

11. **Answer: C**

    Explanation: Optimizing resource usage in scripts helps avoid overloading system resources and reduces the likelihood of browser or system crashes.

    Incorrect: Options A and B are not directly related to preventing crashes due to resource mishandling. In fact, increasing script execution speed (Option A) could potentially exacerbate the issue. Option D is too extreme and may not be necessary if resource usage is properly optimized.

4.9 Given a Scenario, Use Remote Access Technologies.

1. **Answer: A**

   Explanation: Microsoft Remote Assistance (MSRA) is the appropriate remote access technology to use in this scenario. MSRA allows a technician to remotely connect to a user's computer running a Windows operating system. Since the user and the technician are connected to the same network, MSRA can be used to troubleshoot and provide assistance without requiring additional configuration or access permissions.

   Incorrect: For Option B, VNC is a remote access technology commonly used for cross-platform remote access. However, in this scenario, since both the technician and the user are using a Windows operating system and are on the same network, using MSRA would be a more suitable choice. For Option C, RDP is a remote access technology that allows users to connect to a remote computer and control it as if they were sitting in front of it. While RDP is commonly used in various scenarios, in this particular situation where the technician and the user are on the same network, MSRA would be a more appropriate choice for troubleshooting and assistance. For Option D, SSH is a network protocol used for secure remote access to Unix-like systems. However, in this scenario where the technician needs to troubleshoot a Windows computer on the same network, MSRA would be the preferred remote access technology, as it is specifically designed for Windows systems and provides the necessary features for remote assistance.

2. **Answer: D**

   Explanation: Remote monitoring and management (RMM) is the most appropriate remote access technology for remotely monitoring and managing multiple devices in a network. RMM tools allow IT technicians to proactively monitor the health, performance, and security of devices from a centralized location. They provide features such as remote control, software deployment, patch management, and reporting, enabling efficient and effective management of remote devices.

   Incorrect: For Option A, VPNs are primarily used to establish secure connections between remote users and a private network. For Option B, RDP is a protocol that allows users to access and control a remote computer. For Option C, Telnet is a network protocol that allows remote access to devices using a command-line interface.

3. **Answer: B**

   Explanation: Remote Desktop Protocol (RDP) enables users to connect to and control their office computer remotely, providing access to files, applications, and resources.

   Incorrect: Option A, a virtual private network (VPN), is used to establish secure connections between networks, not necessarily for accessing individual computers remotely. Option C, Telnet, is a network protocol used for remote administration of devices, but it does not provide graphical remote desktop access. Option D, Secure Shell (SSH), is a cryptographic network protocol used for secure remote access, but it is primarily used for command-line access to devices rather than full desktop access.

4. **Answer: A**

   Explanation: Remote Desktop Protocol (RDP) is the most suitable remote access technology for accessing a Windows server, as it provides graphical desktop access and control.

   Incorrect: Option B, File Transfer Protocol (FTP), is primarily used for transferring files between a client and a server, not for remote desktop access. Option C, Telnet, is a network protocol used for remote administration, but it does not provide graphical remote desktop access. Option D, Secure Shell (SSH), is commonly used for secure command-line access to Linux/Unix servers, but it may not provide graphical remote desktop access to Windows servers.

5. **Answer: C**

   Explanation: Secure Shell (SSH) is the most appropriate remote access technology for connecting to a Linux server using a command-line interface, as it provides secure encrypted connections.

   Incorrect: Option A, Telnet, sends data in plain text, which can pose a security risk, and it does not provide encryption for remote access. Option B, Remote Desktop Protocol (RDP), is primarily used for graphical remote desktop access, not command-line access to Linux servers. Option D, the virtual private network (VPN), is used to establish secure connections between networks, but it does not directly provide command-line access to Linux servers.

6. **Answer: A**

   Explanation: A virtual private network (VPN) is the most appropriate remote access technology for securely accessing a home network from a remote network, as it creates a secure tunnel between the user's device and the home network.

   Incorrect: Option B, Remote Desktop Protocol (RDP), is primarily used for remote desktop access within a network, and it may not be the most suitable option for remote access from a different network due to network configuration requirements. Option C, Telnet, is not a secure remote access technology and is generally not recommended for remote access purposes due to its lack of encryption and vulnerability to attacks. Option D, Secure Shell (SSH), is typically used for secure command-line access to servers, and while it can be used for remote access, a VPN is a more appropriate choice for accessing a home computer from a different network.

7. **Answer: A**

   Explanation: Remote Desktop Protocol (RDP) commonly uses port 3389 by default for establishing remote desktop connections.

   Incorrect: Option B, File Transfer Protocol (FTP), commonly uses port 21 for control connections and port 20 for data connections, not port 3389. Option C, Telnet, typically uses port 23 for establishing remote terminal connections, not port 3389. Option D, Secure Shell (SSH), commonly uses port 22 for secure remote access, not port 3389.

8. **Answer: A**

   Explanation: Apple Remote Desktop is the built-in remote access technology provided by Apple for remotely accessing Mac computers.

   Incorrect: Option B, Virtual Network Computing (VNC), is a cross-platform remote access technology and can be used to remotely access Mac computers, but Apple Remote Desktop is the built-in solution specifically designed for Mac-to-Mac remote access. Option C, Remote Desktop Protocol (RDP), is primarily used for Windows-based remote access, and while there are third-party clients available for Mac, it is not the built-in solution. Option D, Secure Shell (SSH), is used for secure command-line access to systems and does not provide graphical remote desktop access like Apple Remote Desktop.

9. **Answer: A**

   Explanation: A virtual private network (VPN) allows users to securely access their office network resources over the internet by establishing an encrypted connection.

   Incorrect: Remote Desktop Protocol (RDP) is primarily used for remote desktop access to individual computers rather than accessing network resources. Telnet is not a secure remote access technology and is generally not recommended for accessing network resources over the internet due to its lack of encryption and vulnerability to attacks. Secure Shell (SSH) is primarily used for secure command-line access to systems and may not provide the same level of network resource access as a VPN.

Mock Exam

1. **Answer: B**

   Explanation: This is a reasonable first step for addressing a suspected malware infection. Antivirus apps can scan the device for malware and potentially remove it. However, it's important to use a reputable antivirus app and keep the device disconnected from the internet until the scan is complete to prevent further infection.

   Incorrect: Option A: This option is a drastic measure and should only be considered as a last resort. It will erase all data on the phone, including apps, settings, and personal data. It's not the most appropriate first step for malware removal.

   Option C: While disconnecting the smartphone from the internet can prevent further malware downloads or communication with command-and-control servers, it doesn't address the existing malware infection. This step should be combined with other actions, such as running a malware scan.

   Option D: Keeping the operating system and apps up to date is essential for security. However, this step alone may not remove existing malware. It's a good practice but should be combined with malware scanning and removal efforts.

2. **Answer: D**

   Explanation: Once a change request has been approved by the change advisory board, the next logical step in the change process is sandbox testing. This is performed during the testing phase to isolate the change in a controlled environment and assess its impact on system functionality and performance. The purpose is to communicate the details of the approved change to the relevant stakeholders. Sandbox testing allows an organization to replicate a production environment.

   Incorrect: Option A: End user acceptance typically comes after the implementation of the change when end users are required to accept and adapt to the new or modified system.

   Option B: Risk analysis is generally conducted during the planning stage of the change process to identify potential risks and develop mitigation strategies.

   Option C: Stakeholder communication ensures that all parties involved are informed about the upcoming change, its potential impact, and any necessary actions or adjustments they may need to make. Effective stakeholder communication is crucial for maintaining transparency, minimizing disruptions, and ensuring a smooth implementation of the approved change.

3. **Answer: A**

   Explanation: The most effective solution for the technician to implement in this scenario is to disable the browser's capability to send notifications to the Windows 10 Action Center. By doing so, the unwanted advertisement notifications originating from the browser will no longer appear within the Action Center, providing relief to the user. This solution directly targets the source of the notifications, ensuring a focused resolution.

   Incorrect: Option B: Performing a comprehensive antivirus scan on the computer is not the best solution in this case, as the reported notifications do not indicate malicious content. The issue seems to be related to browser notifications rather than a potential virus or malware infection.

   Option C, turning off all notifications within the Action Center, is a broad approach that might negatively impact the user's experience. It is preferable to address the specific issue of advertisement notifications from the web browser rather than disabling all notifications.

   Option D, transferring specific site notifications from the Allowed category to Block, might help manage notifications from specific websites, but it does not address the broader issue of advertisement notifications originating from the browser. Disabling the browser's ability to send notifications is a more comprehensive solution in this case.

4. **Answer: D**

   Explanation: To address the issue of staff members frequently forgetting their passwords, implementing a single sign-on system with biometrics can be an effective solution. This approach allows users to authenticate themselves using unique physical characteristics, such as fingerprints or facial recognition, reducing the reliance on memorizing passwords and minimizing the chances of forgetting them.

   Incorrect: Option A is incorrect because enabling multifactor authentication adds an extra layer of security but does not directly address the problem of staff members forgetting their passwords.

   Option B is incorrect because increasing the failed login threshold may result in more unsuccessful login attempts before assistance is sought, but it does not address the underlying issue of forgotten passwords.

   Option C is incorrect because removing complex password requirements may make it easier for staff members to remember their passwords, but it also compromises the security of the system by weakening password strength and increasing vulnerability to unauthorized access.

5. **Answer: B**

   Explanation: The most effective solution for dealing with a suspected rootkit is to utilize anti-malware software. Rootkits are sophisticated types of malware that can deeply embed themselves within the operating system, making them difficult to detect and remove. Anti-malware software is specifically designed to identify and eliminate such threats, providing the best chance of successfully removing the rootkit from the system.

   Incorrect: Option A, updating applications, may enhance security by patching vulnerabilities but may not directly address the rootkit issue.

   Option C, reinstalling the operating system, can be a drastic measure that should be considered only if other methods fail or the rootkit is exceptionally persistent.

   Option D, file restoration, may help recover compromised files but does not directly target the rootkit itself.

6. **Answer: B**

   Explanation: Given the technology available in 2013 (at the time of writing), the most secure option for the wireless network would be WPA2 with AES encryption. WPA2 provides robust security measures, and Advanced Encryption Standard (AES) is a widely accepted and secure encryption algorithm for wireless communication. Although WPA3 and AES-256 or AES-128 are more recent advancements, they might not be supported by a 10-year-old wireless router. Therefore, selecting WPA2 with AES would offer the best available security configuration in this scenario. WPA2 was released in 2004.

   Incorrect: Option A, WPA3 with AES-128, offers a higher level of security than WPA2 with AES. However, choosing WPA3 with AES-256 provides even stronger encryption, making it the preferred choice for maximum security. It was released in 2018.

   Option C: WPA3 is the latest and most advanced Wi-Fi security protocol, providing strong protection against unauthorized access and attacks. AES-256 encryption ensures that the data transmitted over the network is securely encrypted with a robust encryption algorithm. It was released in 2018.

   Option D, WPA2 with TKIP, is not as secure as the other options. While WPA2 is still considered secure, TKIP is an old encryption method and has known vulnerabilities.

7. **Answer: C**

   Explanation: When assisting a user with updating Windows, the recommended approach for the call center technician is to guide the user through the process. In this case, the technician should instruct the user to click on the Search field, enter "Check for Updates," and then press the Enter key. This action initiates the Windows update process and allows the user to check for available updates and install them manually.

   Incorrect: Option A is incorrect because suggesting the use of a different system does not address the issue of updating Windows on the user's current device.

   Option B is incorrect and highly inappropriate as it involves sharing sensitive information (password) with the technician, which violates security protocols.

   Option D is incorrect because advising the user to wait for an upcoming automatic patch does not address the immediate need for updating Windows.

8. **Answer: A**

   Explanation: To ensure accurate association between the reported issue and the user, the technician should assign a unique ticket identifying number. This identifier makes it easier to track and manage the reported issue throughout the support process.

   Incorrect: Option B: This is not the best practice for associating a service ticket with a user. While protecting customer privacy is important, assigning a random ticket number without verifying the user's identity can lead to confusion and difficulty in resolving the issue. It's essential to link the ticket to the correct customer.

   Option C: Using the technician's personal identification is not a standard practice for associating service tickets with users. It could lead to confusion and is not a reliable way to track and resolve customer issues.

   Option D: Creating a generic ticket without associating it with any user is not an effective practice. It makes it challenging to provide personalized support and track issues for specific customers. Service tickets should always be associated with the appropriate user or customer to ensure a smooth resolution process.

9. **Answer: D**

   Explanation: The user's inability to log in to the network after an extended period of absence, with the network utilizing 802.1X and EAP-TLS for authentication on the wired network, can be attributed to various factors. However, the most probable cause in this scenario is an expired certificate. Since the user has been away for several months, it is possible that the certificate used for authentication has expired during that period, leading to the login issue.

   Incorrect: Option A is not directly related to the given situation involving network authentication and extended leave.

   Option B: Generally refers to services related to the operating system or applications, but it is not the primary cause of a login issue in this particular context.

   Option C is unrelated to network login issues caused by expired certificates.

10. **Answer: B**

    Explanation: To exclude specific folders from Windows search, the user should add those folders to the "Excluded Folders" list in the Windows search settings. This allows them to customize search preferences while keeping the search feature running.

    Incorrect: Option A: Disabling Windows Search Service will turn off the entire Windows search feature, which is not what the user wants. They want to exclude specific folders while keeping the search feature active.

    Option C: Deleting the folders will remove them from the hard drive entirely, which may not be what the user wants. They likely want to keep the folders but exclude them from search results.

    Option D: Reinstalling the entire operating system is a drastic and unnecessary step to exclude folders from Windows search. It would erase all data and settings, which is not the user's intention.

11. **Answer: B**

    Explanation: When the "cat" command is used in a Linux terminal with the filename "comptia.txt," it displays the content of that file on the terminal. It does not modify the file or create a new file. Therefore, option B is the correct answer.

    Incorrect: Option A is incorrect because executing the "cat" command does not replace the contents of the file with a new blank document.

    Option C is incorrect because the "cat" command does not perform any sorting operations on the contents of the file.

    Option D is incorrect because the "cat" command does not copy the contents of the file to another file.

12. **Answer: B**

    Explanation: This process, known as hard drive cloning, involves making an exact copy of the affected drives. By doing so, the original evidence remains intact and can be securely stored, ensuring its admissibility and maintaining the chain of custody.

    Incorrect: Option A: Encryption may be utilized for data protection but does not directly address evidence preservation.

    Option C: Contacting the cyber insurance company may be necessary for reporting incidents, but it does not specifically focus on evidence preservation.

    Option D: Informing law enforcement may be appropriate in certain cases, but creating hard drive duplicates is the primary action to preserve evidence in preparation for potential litigation.

13. **Answer: B**

    Explanation: To address the concerns of regularly modifying only a few files and limited storage space while mitigating regulatory requirements, the most effective backup method is incremental backup. Incremental backups only store the changes made since the last full or incremental backup, resulting in smaller backup sizes and quicker backup operations. This approach optimizes storage space utilization and reduces the time required for backup and restoration processes. Incremental backups allow the easy identification and restoration of specific modified files, minimizing potential data loss and downtime.

    Incorrect: Option A: A full backup would not be the best choice as it involves backing up all files and folders, regardless of whether they have been modified or not. This approach would consume significant storage space and require more time for backup operations.

    Option C: Off-site backup focuses on storing backup copies at a remote location for disaster recovery purposes. While it is a valuable strategy, it does not directly address the concerns of regularly modifying only a few files and limited storage space.

    Option D: Tape rotation has no bearing on the required storage space used for backups.

14. **Answer: A**

    Explanations: Setting a mobile device to silent or vibrate mode is a courteous practice when visiting a customer because it prevents incoming calls or notifications from causing disruptions or distractions during the visit. It shows respect for the customer's environment and ensures professional interaction.

    Incorrect: Option B: Setting the phone to silent or vibrate mode is not primarily done to conserve battery life. While it may have a minor impact on battery consumption, the main reason is to maintain a quiet and professional atmosphere during the customer visit.

    Option C: Setting the phone to silent mode does not prevent incoming calls from being recorded. Call recording settings are usually independent of the phone's audio settings and are controlled separately through specific apps or phone settings.

    Option D: Setting the phone to silent mode is unrelated to enabling location tracking for service records. Location tracking is typically a separate feature and is not affected by the phone's audio settings.

15. **Answer: D**

    Explanation: To handle the task of transferring a large number of files over an unreliable connection while allowing the ability to resume the process if the connection is interrupted, the recommended tool is Robocopy. Robocopy, short for "Robust File Copy," is a command-line utility designed for efficient file copying and mirroring. It includes features such as the ability to restart file transfers from where they left off in case of connection disruptions, making it an ideal choice for scenarios involving unreliable connections.

    Incorrect: Option A: System File Checker (sfc) is primarily used to scan and repair system files for errors, not for file transfers over an unreliable connection.

    Option B: Check Disk (chkdsk) is used for checking and repairing filesystem errors on a disk, not for file transfers.

    Option C: Git Clone (git clone) is a command used for cloning repositories from Git, a version control system. It is not intended for large file transfers over unreliable connections with the ability to resume the process if interrupted.

16. **Answer: D**

    Explanation: When implementing a new backup system, the initial backup that should be performed is a complete or full backup. A complete backup copies all data and files from the source system to the backup storage medium. This comprehensive backup captures the entire system and establishes a baseline for future backups. By starting with a complete backup, you ensure that all essential data and system configurations are securely stored, allowing efficient and effective restoration in the event of data loss or system failure. The full backup will clear the archive bit on all files, indicating that they have backed up.

    Incorrect: Option A: A copy backup can be made at any time; it is designed to backup all the files but does not set the archive bit.

    Option B: Mirror backups do not exist as a recognized backup type. This option is incorrect and not applicable in the context of backup and recovery.

    Option C: Differential backups capture the changes made since the last complete backup. Although differential backups are useful in subsequent backup cycles, they are not the initial backup type to be completed when installing a new backup and recovery system.

17. **Answers: A, B**

    Explanation: Option A is a valid recommendation. Installing a reputable ad blocker extension can effectively block unwanted pop-up ads and enhance the user's browsing experience by preventing intrusive ads from appearing.

    Option B is also a valid recommendation. Outdated browsers may have vulnerabilities that allow popups and other unwanted content to appear. Updating the browser to the latest version often includes security fixes that can help prevent such issues.

    Incorrect: Option C: Disabling the firewall is not a recommended solution for dealing with popups. Firewalls play a critical role in protecting the computer from various online threats, including malware. Disabling the firewall would leave the computer vulnerable.

    Option D: Ignoring popups is not a recommended solution. While some popups may be harmless, others could be related to malicious activities or potentially unwanted programs (PUPs). It's essential to investigate and address the issue rather than ignore it.

    Option E: Downloading and running registry cleaner tools is not a recommended solution for dealing with popups. Registry cleaners can sometimes do more harm than good and are unlikely to address the root cause of pop-up issues.

    Option F: Resetting the computer to factory settings should be a last resort and is generally unnecessary for dealing with pop-ups. It would result in the loss of all user data and settings, which is a drastic measure that should only be considered if all other solutions fail.

18. **Answer: D**

    Explanation: When working with macOS, the ".dmg" file extension is commonly used for software installation. A DMG (disk image) file contains the necessary files and folders required for installing applications on macOS systems. Technicians often encounter DMG files when installing software or applications on Apple devices. The DMG file acts as a virtual disk that can be mounted, allowing access to the installer package contained within. Once mounted, the technician can initiate the installation process to install the software onto the macOS computer. There may be an option to have an application (possibly an installer) run automatically upon mounting a disk image, but that's not the norm. An .app file is similar to an .exe file in Windows and is mainly used for small programs and tools.

    Incorrect: Option A: ".pkg" is incorrect because it is typically used for package installers on macOS, not the actual software installation files.

    Option B: ".bat" is incorrect because it is a file extension used for batch files primarily in Windows environments, not macOS.

    Option C: ".msi" is incorrect because it is a file extension used for Windows Installer packages and is not commonly used for software installation on macOS.

19. **Answer: A, F**

    Explanation: The technician can take the following actions to address the issues. Option A: Clearing app cache and data can help resolve issues with crashing applications. Updating apps ensures you have the latest bug fixes and optimizations. Ensuring proper ventilation can prevent overheating.

    Option F: By closing down unneeded applications, memory will be freed up and background processing may be using extra system resources, contributing to the overheating.

    Incorrect: Option B: This is not the best solution. Performing a factory reset should be a last resort as it erases all data on the device. Installing third-party cooling apps may not always be effective and can sometimes cause more problems.

    Option C: Disabling automatic updates is not recommended as it can leave the device vulnerable to security issues. Limiting background processes may help with performance but might not resolve overheating or media playback issues.

    Option D: This is an extreme solution and not necessary in most cases. It should only be considered if the device is severely outdated or damaged.

    Option E: Ignoring the issues is not a recommended solution. Overheating and app crashes can be indicative of underlying problems that may worsen if left unaddressed.

20. **Answer: A**

    Explanation: This is the recommended action. Performing a System Restore allows the user to revert their computer's state to a previous point in time when it was working correctly. This can often resolve issues caused by system changes or updates.

    Incorrect: Option B: Reinstalling the entire Windows operating system is a drastic step and should be considered a last resort. It involves a lot of time and effort and may lead to data loss. System Restore is a less intrusive solution that should be tried first.

    Option C: While reinstalling the affected applications might resolve the issue if it's isolated to those specific applications, it won't address potential underlying system problems. System Restore is a more comprehensive solution that can address system-wide issues.

21. **Answer: C**

    Explanation: In order to ensure secure physical access to a data center, a proximity card reader can be employed. Proximity card readers utilize radio frequency identification (RFID) technology to grant authorized individuals access to restricted areas. These readers detect and validate proximity cards, also known as access cards or keycards, allowing entry to authorized personnel while restricting unauthorized individuals from entering the data center.

    Incorrect: Option A, perimeter barrier, refers to physical barriers such as fences or walls that enclose the data center premises but does not specifically address secure access control. Option B, an intrusion detection system, is designed to detect and alert against unauthorized entry or activities within a facility, but it does not directly address access control. Option D, a surveillance camera, plays a crucial role in monitoring and recording activities within the data center but does not directly control physical access to the facility.

22. **Answer: B**

    Explanation: When troubleshooting a slow computer, the Performance Monitor tool is a valuable asset for a technician. Performance Monitor allows the technician to monitor various system resources, such as CPU usage, memory utilization, disk activity, and network performance. By analyzing the data collected by Performance Monitor, the technician can identify resource bottlenecks or abnormal behavior that may be causing the slow performance. This enables them to pinpoint the specific area requiring attention and take appropriate measures to resolve the issue.

    Incorrect: Option A, System Optimizer, focuses on optimizing system performance but may not provide detailed insights into the specific causes of a slow computer.

    Option C, Registry Editor, is a tool that's used to modify the Windows registry and is not directly related to identifying performance issues.

    Option D, Task Scheduler, is primarily used for automating tasks and scheduling processes and does not provide real-time monitoring of system performance.

23. **Answer: A**

   Explanation: This string is most likely a checksum or hash value. It is used to verify the integrity of the downloaded software image. By comparing the calculated checksum of the downloaded file to this value, the technician can ensure that the file has not been tampered with during the download process.

   Incorrect: Option B: This string is not likely to be an encryption key. Encryption keys are generally longer and more complex, and they are used for encrypting and decrypting data, not for verifying the integrity of downloaded files.

   Option C: This string is not a product license key. Product license keys are typically alphanumeric and are used to activate or license software legally. They are not used for verifying the integrity of software downloads.

   Option D: This string is not a network port number. Network port numbers are used to specify a specific communication endpoint in networking protocols, such as TCP or UDP. They are not related to verifying the integrity of software downloads.

24. **Answer: A, B**

   Explanation: Option A: App whitelisting is a mobile device management (MDM) policy that allows administrators to specify which applications are allowed to be installed on mobile devices. By creating a whitelist of approved applications, you can prevent users from sideloading unapproved applications because only the apps on the whitelist can be installed.

   Option B: You can restrict users from sideloading apps by enforcing policies that only allow app installations from official app stores (such as Google Play or the Apple App Store). This prevents users from downloading and installing apps from unofficial or third-party sources.

   Incorrect: Option C: Enabling or disabling USB debugging control is more related to developer options and doesn't directly prevent the sideloading of unapproved applications. It's not a typical MDM policy for this purpose.

   Option D: Full device encryption is essential for data security but doesn't directly prevent users from sideloading applications. It's a security feature to protect data in case the device is lost or stolen.

   Option E: Enabling remote wipe is a security measure that protects data in case a device is lost or stolen. It doesn't directly prevent sideloading of applications.

   Option F: Geofencing is used to define geographical boundaries and trigger actions when a device enters or exits those boundaries. It's not directly related to preventing sideloading of applications.

25. **Answer: B**

Explanation: The most likely reason why the technician is unable to join a Windows 10 laptop to a domain is because the laptop is running the Windows 10 Home edition. Windows 10 Home does not have the capability to join a domain; this functionality is only available in Windows 10 Professional or Enterprise editions.

Incorrect: Option A: This option is incorrect because processor compatibility is typically not a determining factor for joining a domain.

Option C: This option is incorrect because the absence of a touchscreen adapter would not be a reason that the laptop cannot be domain joined.

Option D: The laptop being connected to a docking station is not directly related to the laptop's ability to join a domain.

26. **Answer: C**

Explanation: The IT manager is likely to have concerns about the significant increase in network utilization caused by the larger size of CAD files being backed up to the software's cloud server. This increase in data transfer can put a strain on the network bandwidth and potentially affect the overall network performance.

Incorrect: Option A is not the most likely concern for the IT manager in this scenario. While compatibility testing is important, it is not directly related to the storage of CAD file backups on the cloud server.

Option B is not the primary concern here. While budget allocation for additional technician hours during installation is important, it is not the primary concern in this specific scenario.

Option D is not the most likely concern for the IT manager. Although large update and installation files may pose challenges for local hard drives, it is not the primary concern mentioned in the question.

27. **Answer: C**

Explanation: The incident described in the question is an example of impersonation. Impersonation occurs when someone fraudulently pretends to be another person or entity in order to deceive others. In this case, the caller is posing as a representative of a reputable bank, attempting to gain the trust of the company employee and potentially deceive them into revealing sensitive information or performing unauthorized actions. As the exploit involves the placing of a phone call, this could also be termed a Vishing exploit.

Incorrect: Option A: Social engineering refers to the manipulation of individuals to gain unauthorized access or information. While impersonation can be a form of social engineering, it specifically involves pretending to be someone else.

Option B: Phishing typically involves fraudulent emails or websites designed to deceive individuals into revealing sensitive information. Although the incident involves deception, it specifically describes a phone call, not an email or website.

Option D: Identity theft involves stealing someone's personal information with the intention of using it for fraudulent purposes. While impersonation can be a component of identity theft, the incident described in the question does not specifically involve stealing the employee's identity.

28. **Answer: E**

    Explanation: An account lockout is a security measure typically implemented by computer systems to prevent unauthorized or malicious access to user accounts. If a user enters incorrect login credentials multiple times, their account may be locked out for a certain period of time or until it is manually unlocked by an administrator. This helps protect against dictionary or brute-force attacks, where an attacker repeatedly tries to guess login credentials in order to gain access to an account.

    Incorrect: Option A (two-factor authentication) is not the best choice for mitigating a dictionary attack specifically. While two-factor authentication enhances security overall, it does not directly address the dictionary attack issue.

    Option B: An IDS monitors network traffic and detects any suspicious activity or unauthorized access attempts. By analyzing patterns and signatures associated with dictionary attacks, the IDS can promptly alert network administrators, enabling them to take immediate action and prevent further unauthorized access. As this was during the night, it is likely there would be no staff to respond to the threat.

    Option C can improve password strength, but it alone cannot prevent a dictionary attack. Attackers can still guess complex passwords if they are present in the dictionary.

    Option D (network segmentation) is a security measure that isolates different parts of the network, but it may not directly mitigate a dictionary attack on a specific user's account.

    An IDS monitors network traffic and detects any suspicious activity or unauthorized access attempts. By analyzing patterns and signatures associated with dictionary attacks, the IDS can promptly alert network administrators, enabling them to take immediate action and prevent further unauthorized access.

29. **Answer: C**

Explanation: To assist the manager in hiding the file and preventing accidental deletion by others, the technician should recommend using File Explorer. By modifying the file's properties, the user can mark it as hidden, making it less visible to other users accessing the shared drive. This provides an additional layer of protection and helps maintain the file's privacy and integrity.

Incorrect: Option A: Disk Cleanup is used to free up disk space by removing unnecessary files, but it does not offer a feature to hide specific files.

Option B: Task Scheduler is a tool used to automate tasks at specific times or events and does not provide functionality to hide files.

Option D: Control Panel provides various system settings and configuration options, but it does not offer a direct solution for hiding files on shared drives.

30. **Answer: D**

Explanation: Given the time constraint and the importance of resolving the issue promptly for the CEO, the technician should escalate the support ticket to higher-level technicians. By escalating the ticket, the technician ensures that the problem receives immediate attention from individuals with more expertise or resources to expedite the resolution process.

Incorrect: Option A is incorrect because continuing research might consume additional time, which conflicts with the CEO's urgent need to have the device returned promptly.

Option B is incorrect because restarting the diagnostic process would lead to redundant efforts, further delaying the resolution and not addressing the time-sensitive nature of the situation.

Option C is incorrect because informing the CEO that the repair will take a few weeks is not a suitable course of action when there is an immediate need to return the device.

31. **Answer: A**

Explanation: To maintain a consistent IP address for the server while adhering to the company's policy against static IP addresses, the technician should utilize IP address reservation through DHCP. By assigning a specific IP address to the server's MAC address within the DHCP server's configuration, the server will always receive the same IP address when it requests an IP address lease. This approach ensures that the server is easily identifiable and accessible on the network without relying on a static IP configuration.

Incorrect: Option B: Network address translation (NAT) involves translating IP addresses between private and public networks and does not provide a solution for maintaining a consistent IP address for the server.

Option C: Dynamic Name System (DNS) records associate domain names with IP addresses and are not directly related to ensuring a server maintains the same IP address.

Option D: Virtual private network (VPN) configuration establishes secure connections over public networks and is not specifically relevant to maintaining a consistent IP address for a server.

32. **Answer: D**

   Explanation: The most efficient solution in this scenario would be setting up a virtual machine within the Windows OS to run Linux and the required application. This allows Windows and Linux applications to be run at the same time.

   Incorrect: Option A suggests utilizing a cloud environment. This will require network connections to the cloud provider.

   Option B: The Windows Linux Subsystem is a feature that can be installed on a Windows desktop computer. It allows basic command-line applications to be supported. However, it will not support all applications as it is an emulator, in contrast to a full installation of Linux with access to graphical applications.

   Option C: This approach will allow the user to swap between Linux and Windows as needed but will incur additional costs.

33. **Answer: A**

   Explanation: When working on internal computer components like processors and memory modules, it's crucial to prevent electrostatic discharge (ESD), which can damage sensitive electronic parts. Using an anti-static wrist strap helps to discharge any static electricity from your body, protecting the components.

   Incorrect: Option B: The order of upgrades is not necessarily critical as long as you follow proper procedures. However, this statement doesn't address the ESD concerns, which are essential for preventing damage during the upgrade process.

   Option C: Keeping the computers powered on during upgrades is not recommended. You should shut down and unplug the computers before making any hardware changes to avoid electrical hazards and ensure a safe upgrade process.

   Option D: This is incorrect. ESD precautions are essential during desktop upgrades, just as they are for laptops or any other electronic devices. Failing to take anti-static precautions can result in damaging the components, leading to costly repairs or replacements.

34. **Answer: B**

   Explanation: To enable speech recognition on a PC, the user should navigate to the Accessibility settings. Within the Accessibility settings, there is an option to enable speech recognition, allowing the user to interact with their computer using voice commands.

   Incorrect: Option A is incorrect as it primarily deals with language, date, time, and location settings.

   Option C is incorrect as it focuses on personalizing the display, themes, and visual aspects of the operating system.

   Option D is incorrect as it pertains to privacy settings and permissions for various applications and system features.

35. **Answer: D**

    Explanation: The acceptable use policy (AUP) should be updated to incorporate the new requirement of prohibiting cryptocurrency mining on work desktops. The AUP outlines the rules and guidelines for acceptable behavior and usage of company resources. By explicitly including this restriction in the AUP, the company can address the violation and prevent future instances.

    Incorrect: Option A: Enterprise mobility management (EMM) is not directly related to updating guidelines and policies regarding cryptocurrency mining on work desktops. EMM primarily focuses on managing mobile devices and their associated security and policies.

    Option B: A service level agreement (SLA) is a contractual agreement between a service provider and a customer, typically specifying the level of service and support to be provided. It does not specifically address updating guidelines and policies.

    Option C: Data loss prevention (DLP) is a set of technologies and practices aimed at preventing unauthorized disclosure or loss of sensitive data. While it is important for data protection, it does not directly relate to updating guidelines for cryptocurrency mining on work desktops.

36. **Answer: A**

    Explanation: This is the correct answer because one of the major benefits of moving to a 64-bit OS is the ability to access and utilize larger amounts of random access memory (RAM) than a 32-bit OS. This is particularly important for tasks such as video editing, 3D rendering, and other memory-intensive applications.

    Incorrect: Option B: This is not the primary benefit of moving to a 64-bit OS. While a 64-bit OS can offer performance improvements for certain tasks, the major advantage lies in its ability to address more RAM.

    Option C: The transition to a 64-bit OS primarily impacts memory access, and while it can indirectly benefit graphics performance by allowing for larger textures and smoother multitasking, it's not the primary benefit.

    Option D: The move to a 64-bit OS doesn't directly affect network connectivity or data transfer rates. These aspects are more dependent on network hardware and infrastructure.

37. **Answer: A**

    Explanation: The most likely cause of the issue is network connectivity problems. Since the laptop PC is functioning properly on the same network, it suggests that the network connection is not the root cause. However, the desktop PC's inability to log in to the domain and the technician's inability to access the secure intranet site indicate that there may be issues with network connectivity specific to the desktop PC. This can be due to factors such as network cable disconnection, faulty network adapter, or misconfiguration.

Incorrect: Option B: Incorrect domain credentials would prevent both the laptop PC and the technician from accessing the domain, not just the desktop PC.

Option C: Browser compatibility problems would typically affect the user's ability to access websites in general, rather than being specific to the secure intranet site.

Option D: Firewall restrictions, while a possibility, would likely affect both the laptop PC and the technician's ability to access the secure intranet site, rather than being limited to the desktop PC.

38. **Answer: A**

    Explanation: Setting the network configuration to private allows access to shared files on the Windows firewall. Public profiles do not allow file and print sharing.

    Incorrect: Option B: Establishing a proxy server connection is not necessary for accessing shared drives on the network. Proxy servers are typically used for accessing the internet through an intermediary server, not for internal network file access.

    Option C: Granting the user with network administrator privileges is not required for accessing shared drives. Network administrator privileges are typically reserved for managing network resources and performing administrative tasks.

    Option D: Creating a shortcut to the shared drive's public documents is not the appropriate configuration for accessing files on a shared drive. The shortcut would only provide access to the public documents folder, limiting the user's ability to access other files on the shared drive.

39. **Answer: B**

    Explanation: To resize a partition on the internal storage drive of a computer running macOS, the technician should employ the Disk Utility tool. Disk Utility is a built-in utility in macOS that allows users to manage, format, and resize storage drives and partitions. With Disk Utility, the technician can easily modify the size of existing partitions to allocate space according to specific requirements.

    Incorrect: Option A: Activity Monitor is a utility used for monitoring system processes and resource usage, not for resizing partitions.

    Option C: Time Machine is a backup utility that enables users to create regular backups of their system, but it is not designed for partition resizing.

    Option D: Terminal is a command-line interface tool in macOS, primarily used for executing commands and scripts, but it is not specifically intended for resizing partitions.

40. **Answer: B**

   Explanation: The "Reset This PC" feature in Windows 10 allows you to reinstall Windows while keeping all previous user files and settings. It's a quick and efficient way to prepare a laptop for a new user while maintaining the base operating system.

   Incorrect: Option A: This is a valid method but not the most efficient for high staff turnover. Manually reinstalling Windows from installation media involves more time and effort compared to using built-in features such as "Reset This PC."

   Option C: Cloning the hard drive is not the best solution for re-purposing laptops for new staff members. It creates a copy of the existing system, including software and settings, which may not be suitable for a new user. It's also time-consuming.

   Option D: Windows 10 System Restore is designed to restore the system to its previous state, not to reinstall the operating system. It's not an efficient method for re-purposing laptops.

41. **Answer: A**

   Explanation: To resolve the issue of receiving unexpected pictures, the executive should set AirDrop to accept transfers solely from known contacts. This action restricts the reception of unsolicited files and ensures that only trusted sources can send content to the executive's iPhone during the flight.

   Incorrect: Option B is incorrect because disabling all wireless systems would hinder the executive's ability to use in-flight Wi-Fi for legitimate purposes.

   Option C is incorrect because discontinuing iMessage usage does not directly address the issue of receiving unexpected pictures through in-flight Wi-Fi.

   Option D is incorrect because limiting messages and calls to saved contacts only does not specifically address the problem of receiving unsolicited images during the flight.

42. **Answer: B**

   Explanation: The best solution for enhancing building security while allowing easy customer access is to install protective barriers such as bollards. Bollards are sturdy posts or barriers strategically placed around the building perimeter to physically prevent vehicles from breaching the area. They provide an effective physical deterrent and minimize the risk of unauthorized vehicle access, ensuring the safety of the premises.

   Incorrect: Option A, security personnel, may help with surveillance and monitoring but may not provide a sufficient physical barrier against vehicles.

   Option C, motion detection systems, are useful for detecting movement but do not directly address the issue of preventing vehicles from driving into the building.

   Option D, a controlled entryway or access control vestibule, primarily focuses on regulating access for individuals and may not offer the same level of protection against vehicle intrusions.

43. **Answer: A**

    Explanation: The best solution for addressing interference caused by nearby SSIDs is to adjust the channel settings of your wireless network. By changing the channel, you can avoid overlapping frequencies with neighboring networks and reduce interference. This allows your wireless network to operate on a clear and less congested channel, resulting in improved performance and reduced interference issues.

    Incorrect: Option B will definitely disrupt operations and is not a realistic option when considering the store may need to support wireless devices.

    Option C, switching the equipment off and then back on is not a solution to fix the problem.

    Option D, renaming the access point, does not directly resolve the interference issue caused by nearby SSIDs. Changing the access point name might be useful for identification purposes but does not mitigate the impact of interference on the wireless network.

44. **Answer: C**

    Explanation: Given the concerns regarding sensitive, legacy, unmaintained PII and the regulatory requirement for long-term data retention, the best approach would be to perform a complete backup of the data. Storing this backup on an offline, encrypted tape storage ensures that the data remains secure and protected from ransomware attacks. The transfer of data to offline storage provides an added layer of protection against potential data loss.

    Incorrect: Option A suggests a daily incremental backup to the corporate file server, which may not provide sufficient protection in case of a ransomware outbreak. Incremental backups only store changes since the last full backup, and in the event of an outbreak, the data could be compromised.

    Option B proposes using snapshots stored on a network-attached storage (NAS) device. While snapshots offer some level of data protection, they are still vulnerable to ransomware attacks if the NAS device itself becomes compromised.

    Option D suggests weekly, differential backups stored in a cloud-hosting provider. While offsite backups are good practice, differential backups only store changes since the last full backup, which may not provide adequate protection for sensitive data if a ransomware outbreak occurs.

45. **Answer: A**

Explanation: Using a key combination to lock the computer when leaving the workstation is the best way for the police officer to quickly secure the workstation. This action immediately restricts access to the computer, ensuring that any sensitive or confidential information remains protected from unauthorized access during the officer's absence. Windows Key + L will lock the workstation.

Incorrect: Option B: While ensuring the absence of unauthorized individuals is important for security, it does not provide an immediate and direct method of securing the workstation.

Option C: Configuring a screensaver with an automatic lock after a set period of inactivity is a good security practice but may not be the most efficient solution when the officer needs to secure the workstation quickly.

Option D: Turning off the monitor only addresses the issue of unauthorized visibility of information but does not provide a comprehensive solution to secure the entire workstation and its data.

46. **Answer: B, E**

Explanation: To achieve automatic application boot-up upon logging in to a conference room computer, a technician would employ two specific options. First, utilizing the Task Scheduler feature allows them to schedule the application to launch automatically upon user login. Second, the Startup Folder option enables the technician to add a shortcut of the application to the system's designated startup folder, ensuring it initiates during the login process.

Incorrect: Option A: Windows Explorer is a file management tool and does not pertain to the automatic launch of applications upon login.

Option C: System Overview, or System Information, does not provide the functionality to enable automatic application boot-up on login.

Option D: Programs and Features is unrelated to the task of initiating application launch during login.

Option F: Device Manager deals with managing and configuring hardware devices and does not apply to the automatic launching of applications on login.

47. **Answer: A**

    Explanation: After resetting the user's password, enabling the requirement for the user to change the password at the next login adds an extra layer of security. This ensures that the user creates a new password unique to them and helps prevent unauthorized access to the account.

    Incorrect: Option B is incorrect because prohibiting the user from changing the password restricts their ability to enhance their account's security by regularly updating their password.

    Option C is incorrect because disabling the user's account would prevent them from accessing any resources or performing their tasks. It is an extreme measure that should be reserved for cases where there is a specific reason for disabling the account.

    Option D is incorrect because setting a password with no expiration date poses a security risk. Regularly changing passwords reduces the likelihood of compromised accounts and enhances overall security.

48. **Answer: C**

    Explanation: In this scenario, the most likely agreement being utilized is an end user license agreement (EULA). EULAs are commonly encountered when installing software and typically require users to scroll through the agreement text and click an "Accept" button to indicate their consent to the terms and conditions set forth by the software vendor.

    Incorrect: Option A, service level agreement, is incorrect because SLAs are usually related to service delivery and performance metrics between parties, rather than software installation agreements.

    Option B, non-disclosure agreement, is incorrect because NDAs are used to protect confidential information, not typically encountered during software installation.

    Option D, memorandum of understanding, is incorrect because MOUs are typically used to outline agreements or collaborations between organizations, not for software installation purposes.

49. **Answer: C**

    Explanation: Multi-factor authentication (MFA) involves the use of multiple authentication factors to verify the identity of a user. In this case, the combination of a one-time password (OTP) and a fingerprint scan serves as an example of MFA. The OTP provides a temporary code that is unique for each authentication attempt, adding an additional layer of security. Meanwhile, the fingerprint scan verifies the user's biometric data, such as their unique fingerprint pattern, adding another layer of authentication.

    Incorrect: Option A, voice recognition and facial recognition, are both components of biometric authentication but do not specifically represent MFA.

    Option B, username and password, are both something you know.

    Option D, password and PIN, represents a single-factor authentication method, not MFA.

50. **Answer: C**

    Explanation: In the given scenario, enabling hard drive encryption would be the best security practice. Hard drive encryption ensures that the data stored on the laptop's hard drive is protected by encrypting it with a strong encryption algorithm. This helps safeguard sensitive information even if the laptop is lost, stolen, or accessed by unauthorized individuals. By encrypting the hard drive, the data remains unreadable and inaccessible without the appropriate encryption key or password.

    Incorrect: Option A, PIN-based login, might provide an additional layer of security, but it does not offer the same level of protection as hard drive encryption when it comes to data confidentiality.

    Option B, quarterly password changes, is a good practice in general, but it may not be the most effective security measure for protecting data on a laptop that could be lost or stolen.

    Option D, physical laptop lock, is a physical security measure that helps prevent theft of the laptop, but it does not address the protection of data stored on the laptop's hard drive.

51. **Answer: D**

    Explanation: The fact that there is construction activity in the surrounding offices and the desktop not responding to the ping indicates that the most likely cause of the issue is a disconnected network cable. The construction activity might have caused physical disruption to the network infrastructure, resulting in the cable becoming disconnected.

    Incorrect: Option A is incorrect because the issue is specific to the user's desktop and not the DHCP server.

    Option B is incorrect because if the firewall was blocking network access, the ping request would not reach the desktop at all.

    Option C is incorrect because if the user's account was locked, they would still be able to connect to the network but might face authentication issues.

52. **Answer: A**

    Explanation: If the website has been verified to be online, the most likely cause of the issue lies with the user's browser. By deleting the browser history, any cached data or cookies that might be causing conflicts or preventing access to the website can be cleared, potentially resolving the issue.

    Incorrect: Option B is incorrect because clearing the DNS cache is more relevant for resolving issues related to domain name resolution.

    Option C is incorrect because flushing the ARP cache is more relevant for resolving network connectivity issues.

    Option D is incorrect because enabling JavaScript in the browser is not directly related to accessing a specific website.

53. **Answer: C**

    Explanation: To ensure files and user preferences are retained and perform the operation locally while migrating one station at a time, the most efficient method would be an in-place upgrade. An in-place upgrade allows the seamless transition from Windows 7 Pro to Windows 10 Pro while preserving user data and settings.

    Incorrect: Option A is incorrect because a master image is a pre-configured system image that is typically used for deploying multiple identical machines simultaneously.

    Option B is incorrect because a clean install would involve wiping out the existing operating system and user data, which goes against the requirement of retaining files and preferences.

    Option D, a server-based remote network installation (WDS), involves deploying the new operating system from a network location. This might not meet the requirement of performing the operation locally.

54. **Answer: A**

    Explanation: When there is a risk of data loss from lost or stolen laptops, the best recommendation is to enable full disk encryption. Full disk encryption ensures that even if the laptop falls into unauthorized hands, the data stored on the hard drive remains inaccessible without the encryption key.

    Incorrect: Option B is incorrect because while regular laptop backups are important for data protection, they do not directly address the risk of data loss from lost or stolen laptops.

    Option C is incorrect because while biometric authentication can enhance security, it may not be feasible for all laptop users and may impact user convenience.

    Option D is incorrect because while mandatory laptop tracking software can help in locating lost or stolen laptops, it does not directly protect the data stored on the laptops.

55. **Answer: C**

    Explanation: To achieve the highest level of wireless network security, the technician should implement WPA3. WPA3 is the latest security protocol, and it provides strong encryption algorithms and enhanced protection against unauthorized access. It offers improved security features compared to its predecessors, such as WPA2 and WEP.

    Incorrect: Option A, Wi-Fi Protected Setup (WPS), is incorrect because it introduces potential security vulnerabilities and should be disabled to ensure better security.

    Option B, Temporal Key Integrity Protocol (TKIP), is incorrect because it is an old security protocol that is less secure than WPA3.

    Option D, Wired Equivalent Privacy (WEP), is incorrect because it is an outdated and easily compromised security protocol.

    Option E, Media Access Control (MAC) filtering, is incorrect because it alone is not sufficient for providing comprehensive security and can be bypassed by attackers.

56. **Answer: B**

    Explanation: To address the reported slow performance and constant solid activity light on the hard drive, the FIRST step should be to use Performance Monitor to analyze resource utilization. This tool provides real-time monitoring and insights into the computer's performance, allowing you to identify any specific processes or applications that might be causing the slowdown.

    Incorrect: Option A is incorrect because checking Services in Control Panel primarily focuses on managing and configuring system services, not monitoring resource utilization.

    Option C is incorrect because running System File Checker is used to scan and restore Windows system files' integrity, which is not directly related to the reported performance issue.

    Option D is incorrect because Event Viewer is primarily used to review system events, logs, and errors, but it may not provide immediate insights into the resource utilization causing the slow performance.

57. **Answer: C**

    Explanation: Based on the symptoms described by the user, the most likely cause of the issue is a virus. Viruses are malicious software programs that can replicate and spread, causing various disruptions to the normal functioning of a computer system. In this case, the unauthorized opening of applications and browser redirects are common signs of a virus infection.

    Incorrect: Option A, keylogger, is incorrect because a keylogger is a type of software that records keystrokes on a computer, often used for malicious purposes like capturing sensitive information. While it can be a potential security concern, it does not directly explain the symptoms mentioned by the user.

    Option B, cryptominers, is incorrect because cryptominers are programs that are designed to use the computing power of a device to mine cryptocurrencies. While they can cause performance issues, they typically do not manifest in the form of unauthorized application openings or browser redirects.

    Option D, malware, is incorrect because malware is a general term that encompasses various types of malicious software, including viruses. While malware can indeed cause the reported symptoms, the specific term "virus" is a more accurate and suitable answer in this scenario.

58. **Answer: E**

    Explanation: To mitigate the issue of frequent micro power outages, the technician should utilize an uninterruptible power supply (UPS). Unlike surge suppressors that protect against voltage spikes, a UPS provides temporary power during short outages, ensuring the continuous operation of critical electronic devices. A UPS consists of a battery that automatically engages when a power outage occurs, supplying power until normal power is restored or allowing a controlled shutdown. This safeguards the connected equipment against potential data loss, hardware damage, and disruptions in productivity.

    Incorrect: Option A, surge suppressor, primarily protects against voltage spikes and power surges but does not provide backup power during outages.

    Option B, battery backup, is another term for Uninterruptible Power Supply (UPS), making it the correct answer in this scenario.

    Option C, CMOS battery, provides power to the computer's motherboard to retain BIOS settings but does not address power outages.

    Option D, generator backup, is a larger-scale solution typically used for extended power outages and is not necessary for short micro-outages.

59. **Answer: B**

    Explanation: In macOS, the default GUI and file manager for organizing, searching, and accessing files and folders is Finder. It provides a user-friendly interface and various features to navigate through the filesystem, perform file operations, and manage the overall file hierarchy.

    Incorrect: Option A, Disk Utility, is a utility in macOS used for disk management and performing tasks like formatting, partitioning, and repairing disks. It is not the default GUI and file manager.

    Option C, Dock, is a macOS feature that provides quick access to frequently used applications and files. While it is an essential component of the macOS interface, it is not the default GUI and file manager.

    Option D, FileVault, is a built-in encryption feature in macOS that protects data on the system's disk. However, it is not the default GUI and file manager in macOS.

60. **Answer: D**

    Explanation: The FAT32 filesystem format would be the best choice for ensuring the read and write compatibility of USB flash drives across several generations of Microsoft operating systems. FAT32 is a widely supported filesystem that can be accessed by various operating systems, including older versions of Windows, macOS, and Linux. It offers excellent compatibility and allows easy file sharing between different platforms.

    Incorrect: Option A, APFS (Apple File System), is the default filesystem used by Apple devices running macOS. While it provides advanced features and improved performance for macOS systems, it may not offer the same level of compatibility across different versions of Microsoft operating systems.

    Option B, ext4, is a popular filesystem used primarily in Linux operating systems. While it offers robust features and performance for Linux systems, it may not be as compatible with older versions of Microsoft operating systems.

    Option C, CDFS (Compact Disk File System), is a read-only filesystem format commonly used for optical disks. It is not suitable for USB flash drives and does not support write operations, making it incompatible with the requirements of the question.

61. **Answer: C**

    Explanation: The reason the malware is still present on the system even after performing a System Restore is that the malware has compromised the System Restore process itself. Malware can sometimes infiltrate and infect critical system files, making it difficult for the System Restore to fully eliminate the malicious software. In such cases, the malware can persist despite the restoration of previous system settings.

    Incorrect: Option A: Stating that a system patch disabled antivirus protection and the host firewall is incorrect because disabling these security measures would not explain why the malware is still present after a System Restore.

    Option B: Mentioning that the system updates did not include the latest anti-malware definitions is incorrect because it does not explain why the malware survived the System Restore process.

    Option D: This option suggests that the malware was installed before the creation of the System Restore point is incorrect because the System Restore is designed to revert the system to a previous point in time, regardless of when the malware was initially installed.

62. **Answer: A**

    Explanation: In this scenario, the most likely violation is the end user license agreement (EULA). The EULA typically specifies the terms and conditions for using the software, including limitations on the number of installations or the type of edition that can be used. If the technician discovered multiple copies of the home edition software installed on computers, it suggests a violation of the EULA by exceeding the permitted number of installations or using the software inappropriately.

Incorrect: Option B, personally identifiable information (PII), refers to sensitive information that can identify an individual, such as their name, address, or social security number. PII is unrelated to the violation described in the question.

Option C, digital rights management (DRM), pertains to technologies or measures used to protect copyrighted content from unauthorized distribution or use. It is not directly relevant to the violation of installing multiple copies of home edition software.

Option D, open source agreement, refers to the terms and conditions of using open source software, which typically allows users to install and distribute the software freely. It is not applicable in this scenario as the violation is related to proprietary home edition software.

63. **Answer: B, D**

    Explanation: Preserving data from a hard drive for forensic analysis requires meticulous attention to detail and adherence to proper procedures. The two options that should be given the MOST consideration in this context are chain of custody and data integrity.

    Chain of custody is essential in maintaining the integrity and credibility of digital evidence. It involves documenting the custody, control, and transfer of evidence from the time it is acquired until it is presented in court. By ensuring a clear and unbroken chain of custody, the authenticity and admissibility of the preserved data can be upheld.

    Data integrity refers to the assurance that the preserved data remains unaltered and uncorrupted throughout the forensic analysis process. Measures such as using write-blockers, making bit-for-bit copies of the hard drive, and employing hash algorithms can help verify the integrity of the data. This is crucial for ensuring the accuracy and reliability of the forensic findings.

    Incorrect: Option A: Licensing agreements are legal agreements that govern the authorized use of software or intellectual property. While important in the broader context of software usage, they are not directly related to preserving data for forensic analysis.

    Option C: Incident management documentation pertains to recording and managing information about security incidents or breaches. While incident management is important for handling security events, it is not directly related to preserving data from a hard drive for forensic analysis.

    Option E: Material safety data sheet (MSDS) contains information about the hazards and handling of specific chemicals or substances. While relevant in certain contexts, MSDS is not directly related to preserving data from a hard drive for forensic analysis.

    Option F: Retention requirements refer to the guidelines or regulations governing the retention and storage of data. While important for data management and compliance purposes, retention requirements are not directly related to preserving data specifically for forensic analysis.

64. **Answer: A**

Explanation: The most likely tool a technician would use to remotely connect to a Linux desktop is Secure Shell (SSH). SSH is a widely used protocol that provides secure remote access and control to Linux systems. It allows technicians to establish a secure command-line connection to the remote Linux desktop, enabling them to perform troubleshooting tasks, execute commands, and administer the system remotely.

Incorrect: Option B, VNC, is incorrect because while VNC can be used for remote desktop access, it is not natively designed for Linux and may require additional setup or compatibility measures. Option C, Remote Desktop Protocol (RDP), is incorrect because RDP is primarily used for remote access to Windows-based systems and is not natively designed for Linux. Option D, TeamViewer, is incorrect because although TeamViewer is a popular remote support tool, it is not specifically designed for Linux and may require additional installation steps or compatibility considerations.

65. **Answer: A**

Explanation: The social engineering attack being attempted in this scenario is known as an "evil twin" attack. In an evil twin attack, an attacker sets up a rogue Wi-Fi access point that mimics a legitimate network, often using a similar or identical SSID. The intention is to deceive users into connecting to the malicious network, enabling the attacker to intercept sensitive information or perform other malicious activities. It is important for users to be cautious when connecting to public Wi-Fi networks and verify the legitimacy of the network before joining.

Incorrect: Option B: Impersonation involves pretending to be someone else or a trusted entity to deceive individuals. While it can be a form of social engineering, it is not specifically related to the Wi-Fi network situation described.

Option C: Insider threat refers to an attack or security breach caused by someone within the organization who has authorized access. It does not directly relate to the Wi-Fi network situation described.

Option D: Whaling is a type of phishing attack that specifically targets high-profile individuals, such as executives or senior management, to trick them into revealing sensitive information. It is not directly related to the Wi-Fi network scenario described.

66. **Answer: B**

   Explanation: The most likely reason for the system not utilizing all the available RAM is that it is running on a 32-bit operating system. 32-bit operating systems have a maximum RAM capacity of approximately 4 GB, and any RAM installed beyond that limit will not be recognized or utilized. In this case, even though the technician installed 8 GB of RAM, the system's 32-bit operating system can only address and utilize up to 4 GB of RAM. To fully utilize the installed 8 GB of RAM, the system would need to be upgraded to a 64-bit operating system.

   Incorrect: Option A: Missing updates may affect system performance, but it is not directly related to the issue of RAM utilization.

   Option C: Malfunctioning RAM modules could cause issues, but in this case, the discrepancy is more likely due to the limitations of a 32-bit operating system.

   Option D: BIOS updates generally do not impact the recognition or utilization of RAM. The issue lies with the operating system's capacity.

67. **Answer: D**

   Explanation: The best method for returning the computer to service after a malware infection is to first reinstall the OS to ensure a clean and fresh installation, removing any traces of the malware. This step eliminates any infected files and configurations that may remain. Next, flashing the BIOS is recommended to restore the firmware to its original state, removing any malware that may have infected the BIOS. Finally, scanning the computer with on-premises antivirus software will help identify and eliminate any remaining malware threats, providing an additional layer of protection.

   Incorrect: Option A is incorrect because scanning the system with a Linux live disk may not be the most suitable method for removing malware from a corporate network computer as it may not have the necessary security and compatibility features.

   Option B is incorrect because flashing the BIOS and reformatting the drive alone does not address the malware infection. Without reinstalling the OS, the infected files and configurations may persist.

   Option C is incorrect because degaussing the hard drive is not an appropriate method for removing malware. Degaussing is the process of erasing magnetic media and is typically used for data destruction purposes, not for malware removal.

68. **Answer: A**

    Explanation: The most appropriate solution to address the issue of abnormally large desktop icons after a software patch deployment is to roll back the video card drivers. Video card drivers are responsible for rendering graphics on the screen, including the desktop icons. If the recently installed video card drivers are incompatible or causing display issues, rolling back to a previous version can restore the proper functionality and size of the icons.

    Incorrect: Option B, restoring the PC to factory settings, is an extreme measure that erases all user data and settings, reverting the system to its original state. This action should only be considered if other troubleshooting methods fail to resolve the issue.

    Option C, repairing the Windows profile, might address user-specific settings or configurations but is unlikely to resolve the issue with the desktop icons. The problem is more likely related to the video card drivers rather than the user's profile.

    Option D, reinstalling the Windows OS, is an extreme solution that should only be considered as a last resort. It involves reinstalling the entire OS, which can be time-consuming and may result in data loss. This action is unnecessary for resolving an issue with desktop icons and should be avoided unless all other options have been exhausted.

69. **Answer: D**

    Explanation: The term that defines the extent or boundaries of a change is the scope. The scope outlines the specific objectives, deliverables, and limits of a change project or initiative. It helps define what is included and excluded within the scope of the change, ensuring a clear understanding and effective management of the project's goals and boundaries.

    Incorrect: Option A, impact, is incorrect because it refers to the consequences or effects of a change, rather than specifying the range or boundaries of the change.

    Option B, purpose, is incorrect because it refers to the reason or objective behind the change, rather than its extent or boundaries.

    Option C, analysis, is incorrect because it pertains to the examination and evaluation of data or information, rather than defining the extent of a change.

70. **Answer: C**

Explanation: To troubleshoot connection issues with a third-party USB adapter, a technician should utilize the devmgmt.msc tool. devmgmt.msc, also known as Device Manager, allows technicians to view and manage hardware devices connected to a computer. By opening Device Manager, the technician can verify if the USB adapter is recognized by the system and check for any associated driver issues. They can then proceed to update or reinstall the appropriate drivers, ensuring compatibility and resolving any connection problems.

Incorrect: Option A, taskschd.msc, refers to the Task Scheduler, which is used for managing scheduled tasks and automated processes on a computer. It is not directly relevant to resolving connection issues with a USB adapter.

Option B, eventvwr.msc, represents the Event Viewer, a tool used to view system logs and monitor system events. While it can be valuable for troubleshooting, it is not specifically designed for addressing USB adapter connection issues.

Option D, diskmgmt.msc, pertains to Disk Management, a utility for managing disk drives and partitions on a computer. It does not directly address problems with USB adapter connectivity.

71. **Answer: D**

Explanation: In this scenario, the most likely malware type being used is a keylogger. Keyloggers are designed to clandestinely record keystrokes made by users, capturing sensitive information such as passwords, credit card details, and other confidential data. By surreptitiously logging user input, keyloggers enable malicious actors to obtain unauthorized access to valuable information.

Incorrect: Option A, cryptominers, is malicious software that exploits computer resources to mine cryptocurrencies. While they can affect system performance, they are not directly associated with capturing user input.

Option B, rootkits, is stealthy malware that allows unauthorized access and control of a system while concealing its presence. While they can provide unauthorized access, they do not specifically focus on capturing user input.

Option C, spear phishing, refers to a targeted form of phishing, where attackers deceive individuals into divulging sensitive information through deceptive emails or messages. Although it involves social engineering tactics, it does not directly involve capturing user input.

72. **Answer: C**

Explanation: The best method for physically destroying SSDs that contain sensitive information is shredding. Shredding involves using specialized equipment to physically break the SSD into tiny pieces, rendering the data completely irretrievable. This method ensures the highest level of data destruction and mitigates the risk of unauthorized access or data recovery attempts. It is a recommended practice for organizations that handle sensitive information and need to comply with data privacy regulations.

Incorrect: Option A, overwriting, is a method of securely erasing data from storage devices by overwriting it with random or predefined patterns. While overwriting can be effective for traditional hard drives, it is not as reliable for SSDs, as they employ wear leveling and other techniques that make it challenging to ensure complete data eradication.

Option B, low-level formatting, is a process that prepares a storage device for initial use by configuring its filesystem structure. However, it does not guarantee data destruction and should not be relied upon as a secure method for disposing of SSDs containing sensitive information.

Option D, deleting, refers to the act of removing data from a storage device. However, similar to wiping, standard deleting methods may not be sufficient to securely destroy data on SSDs. SSDs utilize wear leveling and other technologies that make it difficult to guarantee complete data removal solely through deleting.

73. **Answer: C**

Explanation: To integrate Linux servers and desktops into Windows Active Directory environments, the correct option is C, Samba. Samba is an open source software suite that provides interoperability between Linux/Unix-based systems and Windows-based systems. It allows Linux servers and desktops to join Windows Active Directory domains, enabling seamless integration and sharing of resources such as file and print services.

Incorrect: Option A, yum, is incorrect. yum is a package management command used in Linux distributions to install, upgrade, or remove software packages. It is not specifically related to integrating Linux systems with Windows Active Directory.

Option B, CIFS, is incorrect. Common Internet File System (CIFS) is a network file-sharing protocol used by Windows operating systems. While it can be utilized for file sharing between Windows and Linux systems, it is not primarily used for integrating Linux systems into Windows Active Directory.

Option D, chmod, is incorrect. chmod is a command-line utility used in Linux and Unix systems for setting access permissions on files. It does not have a direct role in integrating Linux systems with Windows Active Directory environments.

74. **Answer: D**

    Explanation: Before being granted login access to the network, a new employee must sign the acceptable use policy (AUP). The AUP outlines the rules and guidelines for utilizing the organization's network and technology resources. By signing the AUP, the employee acknowledges their understanding and agreement to abide by the policies set forth, ensuring responsible and secure use of the network.

    Incorrect: Option A: This is a document providing information about the properties, handling, and potential hazards of chemical substances. It is unrelated to network access.

    Option B: The EULA is a legal contract between the software provider and the end user, outlining the terms and conditions for software usage. While important, it is not directly related to network access.

    Option C: UAC is a security feature in operating systems that helps prevent unauthorized changes to the computer system. It is not a document that needs to be signed for network access.

75. **Answer: C**

    Explanation: To address the issue of an application failing to launch and displaying an error message indicating the need for repair, a technician should utilize the "Programs and Features" utility in Windows 10. This utility allows users to manage installed programs, including repairing or uninstalling problematic applications. By accessing "Programs and Features," the technician can initiate the repair process for the application in question, resolving the launch issue.

    Incorrect: Option A: The Device Manager utility in Windows 10 is used to manage hardware devices and their drivers, not for repairing applications.

    Option **B:** The Administrator Tools typically consist of various system management utilities, but they do not specifically address application repair.

    Option D: While the Recovery utility in Windows 10 allows for System Restore and troubleshooting, it is not directly involved in repairing specific applications.

244 Solutions

76. **Answer: C**

    Explanation: When it comes to creating a secure tunnel that hides IP addresses and provides enhanced security for network traffic, the protocol of choice is the virtual private network (VPN). VPNs establish an encrypted connection between the user's device and a remote server, ensuring that all data transmitted between them remains confidential and secure. By routing network traffic through this encrypted tunnel, VPNs effectively protect the privacy and integrity of the data while concealing the user's IP address.

    Incorrect: Option A, DNS, is responsible for translating domain names into IP addresses. However, it does not provide the necessary encryption and security measures to establish a secure tunnel for network traffic or hide IP addresses.

    Option B, IPS, is a network security technology that detects and prevents malicious activities within a network. While IPS plays a crucial role in network security, it does not specifically create tunnels or hide IP addresses to secure network traffic.

    Option D, SSH, is a cryptographic network protocol that provides secure remote access to systems and secure file transfers. While SSH offers encryption and security for remote access, it does not specifically establish a tunnel for hiding IP addresses and securing all network traffic like a VPN does.

77. **Answer: B**

    Explanation: In this scenario, it is crucial for the technician to consult the corporate policies regarding the handling of sensitive information and off-site repairs. Corporate policies provide guidelines and procedures to ensure the protection of sensitive data during such situations. By checking the policies, the technician can make informed decisions on how to proceed with the repair process while maintaining the security and integrity of the sensitive information.

    Incorrect: Option A, remove the hard disk drive (HDD) and then send the computer for repair, may result in the loss of necessary data or make it difficult to diagnose and fix the issue effectively. It is important to follow established procedures to protect the data.

    Option C, delete sensitive information before the computer leaves the building, might be an option in certain cases, but it is essential to refer to corporate policies to determine the appropriate action to take.

    Option D: While obtaining authorization from the manager is important in certain situations, it is necessary to check the corporate policies first to ensure compliance with established procedures and guidelines for handling sensitive information.

78. **Answer: C**

   Explanation: To effectively manage documentation while creating a full inventory of the company's IT hardware, a technician should utilize asset tags and IDs. Asset tags and IDs provide a unique identification system that helps track and categorize each piece of hardware accurately. By affixing asset tags and assigning IDs to the equipment, the technician can easily associate specific hardware with corresponding documentation, such as purchase details, maintenance records, and warranty information. This ensures efficient inventory management and facilitates future hardware tracking and troubleshooting.

   Incorrect: Option A, checklist for new user setup, is not directly related to documentation management for IT hardware inventory. It pertains to the onboarding process of new users and their required setup procedures.

   Option B, user information, primarily refers to personal data and profiles of individual users. While user information may be useful for some aspects of IT management, it is not directly related to documentation management for hardware inventory.

   Option D, procurement life cycle, focuses on the overall process of acquiring new hardware, from the initial request to final deployment. While documentation is involved in the procurement life cycle, it does not specifically address the management of documentation for hardware inventory.

79. **Answer: D**

   Explanation: The user in this scenario is experiencing a social engineering attack known as vishing. Vishing is a type of attack where the attacker attempts to deceive individuals by phone calls, pretending to be a trusted entity such as a bank representative. They aim to extract sensitive information, such as account details or personal data, from unsuspecting victims. It is important for users to be cautious and never provide personal information over the phone unless they can verify the legitimacy of the caller.

   Incorrect: Option A, phishing, is a social engineering attack that typically occurs through email or fraudulent websites, aiming to trick users into revealing sensitive information.

   Option B, smishing, is a social engineering attack that occurs through text messages (SMS), where attackers deceive users into disclosing personal information or clicking on malicious links.

   Option C, whaling, is a specific type of phishing attack targeting high-profile individuals or executives within organizations, with the goal of obtaining sensitive information or access to valuable resources.

80. **Answer: B**

    Explanation: To manually set an IP address on a computer running macOS, the technician should use the "ifconfig" command. The "ifconfig" command allows the configuration and management of network interfaces, including the assignment of IP addresses.

    Incorrect: Option A, "ipconfig," is the command used in Windows operating systems to view and manage IP configurations. It is not applicable to macOS.

    Option C, "arpa," is the Address and Routing Parameter Area (ARPA) used in the context of the domain name system (DNS) and is not for setting IP addresses manually.

    Option D, "ping," is a command used to check network connectivity and latency by sending ICMP Echo Request packets. It does not configure IP addresses.

81. **Answer: C**

    Explanation: The correct term used to indicate that a vendor no longer supports a product, including the discontinuation of patches and updates, is end of life (EOL). When a product reaches its EOL, the vendor ceases to provide further support, leaving users without access to patches, updates, or technical assistance. This indicates that the product is no longer actively maintained or developed.

    Incorrect: Option A, AUP, stands for acceptable use policy, which refers to a set of rules or guidelines outlining acceptable behavior when using a particular service or resource. It does not indicate the end of vendor support for a product.

    Option B, EULA, stands for end user license agreement, which is a legal contract between the software vendor and the end user, specifying the terms and conditions of software usage. It does not indicate the end of vendor support for a product.

    Option D, UAC, stands for User Account Control, a security feature in Windows operating systems that prompts users for permission when performing certain system-level changes. It does not indicate the end of vendor support for a product.

82. **Answer: B**

   Explanation: WPA2 offers an advantage over WPA3 in terms of greater backward compatibility. WPA2 has been widely adopted and implemented in a vast array of devices, including older ones. When upgrading to WPA3, some older devices might not support the newer protocol, leading to connectivity issues. Therefore, opting for WPA2 can ensure that a wider range of devices can still connect securely to the network.

   Incorrect: Option A: This is not accurate. WPA3, compared to WPA2, offers a higher level of security due to its enhanced encryption methods and protection against some vulnerabilities.

   Option C: WPA3 has improved resistance to brute-force attacks through features such as Simultaneous Authentication of Equals (SAE), making it more secure against such attacks compared to WPA2.

   Option D: This is not the main advantage of WPA2 over WPA3. The support for larger device networks is not a defining feature when comparing the security advantages of these two protocols.

83. **Answer: A**

   Explanation: High disk usage with no specific application identified could indicate malware or a virus. Running a full antivirus scan is the first step in addressing this issue.

   Incorrect: Option B: Updating the graphics card driver may improve graphics-related performance issues but is unlikely to resolve high disk usage.

   Option C: Increasing the virtual memory size is not the first step in troubleshooting high disk usage.

   Option D: Clearing the browser cache may improve web browsing performance but is unlikely to resolve system-wide high disk usage.

84. **Answer: C**

   Explanation: WPA2 is the most secure option listed here. It provides strong encryption and is recommended for securing wireless networks.

   Incorrect: Option A: WEP is outdated and considered insecure.

   Option B: WPA is an improvement over WEP but not as secure as WPA2.

   Option D: WPS is a convenience feature, not an encryption method, and can have security vulnerabilities.

85. **Answer: A**

    Explanation: The "No bootable device found" error suggests that the computer is unable to find a bootable operating system. Checking the boot sequence in BIOS to ensure the correct boot device is selected is the first step in resolving this issue.

    Incorrect: Option B: RAM issues may cause startup problems but are less likely to result in this specific error message.

    Option C: Graphics card drivers do not typically affect the boot process.

    Option D: Internet connectivity is unrelated to boot errors.

86. **Answer: B**

    Explanation: When a device fails to connect to a Wi-Fi network, the first thing to check is the network password. It's possible that the user entered the wrong password.

    Incorrect: Option A: Bluetooth settings do not typically affect Wi-Fi connectivity.

    Option C: Cellular data usage is unrelated to Wi-Fi connectivity.

    Options D: App updates do not impact Wi-Fi network connections.

87. **Answer: C**

    Explanation: IMAP is designed for accessing emails from multiple devices while keeping them synchronized. It's the preferred choice for this scenario.

    Incorrect: Option A: POP3 downloads emails to a single device and doesn't synchronize them.

    Option B: SMTP is used for sending, not receiving, emails.

    Option D: HTTP is used for web browsing, not email access.

88. **Answer: B**

    Explanation: The symptoms of sluggish response time and an excessive number of ads are indicative of a bootleg/malicious application on an Android device. Such applications often contain adware or malware that can slow down the device and display unwanted ads. It's essential to identify and remove such applications to resolve these issues.

    Incorrect: Option A, developer mode enabled, typically does not cause sluggishness or excessive ads. It's more related to the development and debugging of apps.

    Option C, limited Internet connectivity, might cause some issues, but it wouldn't directly lead to sluggishness and excessive ads.

    Option D, unexpected application behavior, could be a result of a malicious application, but it doesn't directly explain the high number of ads and sluggish response time.

89. **Answer: A**

    Explanation: Fake security warnings appearing on an Android device could be a result of installing applications from untrusted sources or downloading APK files from unreliable websites. Such sources may contain malware or adware that triggers fake security alerts. It's crucial to install apps only from trusted sources such as the Google Play Store to prevent this issue.

    Incorrect: Option B, data-usage limit notification, is unrelated to fake security warnings.

    Option C, root access/jailbreak, could introduce security risks, but it's not directly related to fake security warnings.

    Option D, application spoofing, refers to deceptive practices related to app identity, not fake security warnings.

90. **Answer: B**

    Explanation: Limited internet connectivity can occur due to various reasons, such as network issues or incorrect Wi-Fi settings. While security concerns might be related, the primary issue here is connectivity rather than a specific security threat.

    Incorrect: Option A, developer mode enabled, is unlikely to directly cause limited internet connectivity.

    Option C, high network traffic, might slow down the connection but is not the primary cause of limited connectivity.

    Option D, leaked personal files/data, is unrelated to limited internet connectivity.

91. **Answer: C**

    Explanation: Unexpected application behavior can be caused by security concerns related to the source of Android packages (APKs). If users download and install APKs from untrusted sources, they risk installing malicious or poorly developed apps that can lead to crashes and other issues.

    Incorrect: Option A, high network traffic, can affect app performance but is not the primary cause of unexpected behavior.

    Option B, no internet connectivity, is unrelated to unexpected application behavior.

    Option D, root access/jailbreak, can introduce security risks but is not the primary cause of unexpected app behavior.

92. **Answer: D**

   Explanation: The persistent appearance of fake security warnings and a high number of ads, even when not using any applications, suggests the presence of a bootleg or malicious application on the device. Such applications often display ads and trigger fake security alerts as part of their malicious activities.

   Incorrect: Option A, limited internet connectivity, wouldn't directly cause fake security warnings and excessive ads.

   Option B, unexpected application behavior, could be a result of a malicious application, but it doesn't directly explain the high number of ads and fake security warnings.

   Option C, developer mode enabled, is unlikely to directly cause fake security warnings and ads when not using applications.

93. **Answer: D**

   Explanation: Exceeding data usage limits when not using data-intensive apps can be indicative of application spoofing. Malicious apps or malware may consume data in the background, simulating legitimate app usage. Identifying and removing such spoofed apps is crucial to resolving this issue.

   Incorrect: Option A, high network traffic, might increase data usage but is not the primary cause of exceeding data limits.

   Option B, data-usage limit notification, is a notification feature and not the cause of excessive data usage.

   Option C, root access/jailbreak, can introduce security risks but is not the primary cause of data overuse in this context.

Index

A

airdrop: 66
algorithms: 91
amplify: 34
android: 22, 26, 69
anecdotes: 90
antenna: 68
antistatic: 82
antivirus: 84, 93
anti-virus: 41, 46, 58-64
assert: 90
attack: 39, 42-44, 49, 62
attacks: 33, 42, 48, 50, 66
automation: 51, 92
autoplay: 17, 49
autorotate: 67

B

backup: 25-27, 73, 78-81, 84-85, 91
backups: 26, 28, 71-72, 77-78, 80, 91
bandwidth: 66, 85
banking: 37, 44, 55
bare-metal: 79

baseline: 3, 24
batteries: 84
battery: 66-67, 69-72, 84-85
bitlocker: 2-4, 16, 18, 26, 45-47
blocked: 49
blocker: 55
blocking: 34, 53, 63
bluetooth: 1, 15, 19, 66-67
boards: 81
bollards: 35
bootable: 27
booting: 27
bootleg: 70
breach: 43, 71
breached: 35
breaches: 65, 91
brightness: 34, 66
broadcast: 32, 54
browser: 13-14, 21, 41, 44-45, 55, 59, 61, 63-64, 92-93
browsers: 33, 55, 92
browsing: 18, 55
built-in: 15, 95

C

cables: 15, 62, 81
calibrate: 68
camera: 90
cardholder: 88
cartridges: 84
cellular: 1, 19
certmgr: 10, 12
checklist: 53
chemical: 83
chkdsk: 8
chrome: 75
circuit: 81
classified: 52
cleanup: 11, 83, 85
client: 1-2, 17, 19, 26, 28
command: 6-7, 13, 17, 27-28, 30-32, 62
commands: 5-9, 11, 31-32
compliant: 35, 49
comptia: 1, 33, 57, 73
computer: 2-3, 6-7, 9-12, 14-15, 19, 23, 25-27, 37-40, 46-47, 53, 57-62, 64, 73, 77, 81-83, 85, 89, 91, 93-95
computers: 23, 25-26, 43, 45, 48, 57, 85
computing: 3, 73, 94-95
configure: 1-2, 15-17, 19, 28, 33, 41, 45-47, 49, 53-55, 64
configured: 13-16, 18, 24, 45-46, 53-54
console: 45, 60
control: 1, 12-17, 21, 25-28, 34-37, 45-46, 49, 64, 69, 92
customer: 1, 6, 17, 19-23, 35, 38, 46, 55, 74-76, 89-91
customize: 28

D

database: 44, 46-47
datacenter: 22
dcdiag: 9
deactivate: 47
dealing: 40, 91
debugging: 69, 92
default: 5, 13-15, 32, 36, 45, 47, 51, 54-55, 60, 64, 95
defender: 13-14, 18, 40, 46-47, 50
defragment: 11
degaussing: 52
department: 8, 12, 18, 25-26, 31, 38, 40
deploy: 8, 21-23, 53
deskside: 4
desktop: 1-3, 6, 12, 14, 17, 23, 25, 28, 30, 37, 57, 59, 62, 91, 94-95
device: 4, 6, 10-13, 15-16, 21, 27, 45, 50-51, 54, 58-60, 66-72, 84-85, 89
devmgmt: 10, 12
diagnostic: 12
diagrams: 75, 89
dialog: 46
dictionary: 44, 49
diskpart: 8, 11
display: 10, 13, 15, 54-55, 62
document: 83
documents: 28, 37, 42, 52-53, 74-75, 91
domain: 2, 7, 17-18, 34, 36, 38, 50, 57, 73-74
driver: 41, 61, 88
drivers: 11, 13, 58-59
drives: 24, 31, 39, 43, 49, 52
dropbox: 76
dumpster: 42-43
dvd-rw: 4
dynamic: 53

E

easier: 38, 91
easily: 81
eating: 90
edinburgh: 31
edition: 3-4, 20-21, 23
editions: 1-2
editor: 6, 9-10
educate: 65-66
educated: 64
educating: 65
education: 40-41
effect: 60
effective: 7, 21, 40, 48-50, 54, 57
efficient: 23, 73
effort: 3, 10
electrical: 85
electronic: 83-84
element: 77
elevates: 31
eliminate: 4
e-mail: 4, 6, 26
emails: 41, 89
embedded: 21, 33, 50
empathy: 89
employed: 35, 48
employee: 10, 43, 50
employees: 34, 48, 51, 74, 88, 90
enable: 2-3, 41, 45-46, 48-49, 53-55, 64, 67, 91
enabled: 11, 16, 33, 50, 66
enables: 67
enabling: 54, 69
encounter: 20
encounters: 61
encrypt: 47-48, 91
encrypted: 4, 45-46, 70-72
encrypting: 34, 39, 46, 74

encryption: 2, 16, 18, 38-39, 45-47, 50-51, 54, 71, 84, 88, 91
endpoint: 40
end-user: 1, 87
end-users: 5
enforce: 36, 49
enforced: 9, 48
engineer: 4, 21, 23, 44
engineers: 20, 43
enhance: 65, 69, 73
enhanced: 66, 70-72, 78, 93
ensure: 1, 10-13, 15, 21, 25, 34-39, 41, 45-50, 52, 55, 57, 64-65, 73-74, 82, 84-85, 89-90
ensures: 55, 64, 80, 86-87
ensuring: 50, 73, 81, 88
entered: 27
enterprise: 1-2, 6, 33
enters: 31
entire: 40, 79
entity: 84
entries: 11, 44
equipment: 4, 21, 34-36, 52, 76, 81-85
equivalent: 3
ergonomic: 82
errors: 57, 61-62
escalation: 86
eventvwr: 9
evidence: 8, 86
example: 29, 74-76, 78, 88-90
examples: 48
exception: 18
excessive: 11, 70-71, 83, 93
exchange: 67
excluding: 78
executable: 69
executing: 11, 65, 93
execution: 93
executive: 11, 36, 42

exhibiting: 41, 64
expensive: 19, 79
experience: 17, 22, 71, 93
expertise: 89
expiration: 48, 83
expired: 59, 63
exploiting: 39, 48
explorer: 25, 36
extend: 11, 69
extensible: 45, 48
extension: 55
extensions: 64, 93
external: 12, 14, 21, 26, 35, 39, 49, 68, 79

F

favorite: 75
feature: 2, 16, 18, 24, 26-28, 36, 45, 48, 53, 64
features: 1-2, 9, 13-14, 17, 24-25, 28, 37, 40, 53-54, 69-70, 72, 91
feedback: 17, 75, 77-78
fencing: 35
figure: 29
file-level: 79, 81
filesystem: 22, 30, 45
filevault: 26
filtered: 46
filtering: 53
filters: 40
finance: 8, 41, 46
financial: 76, 83, 88
finder: 25, 27
firewall: 13-14, 18, 41, 46-47, 50, 62-63, 84, 93
firewalls: 41
firmware: 48, 53, 68-69
flushdhcp: 18

flushdns: 18
folder: 8, 13, 18, 27-28, 30-31, 37, 45-46
format: 21, 23, 25, 69
freely: 88
freezes: 69
frequency: 88
frequent: 61-64, 66, 68-70, 72, 93
frequently: 49, 61-62, 68
functional: 81

G

gaming: 17, 53
generate: 31-32, 48
generated: 41, 43
generating: 34
genuine: 41, 43, 55
geofencing: 51
glasses: 82
glitch: 64
global: 32
gloves: 82
google: 5, 32, 75
gossiping: 90
government: 12, 52, 88
gpedit: 6
gpresult: 6-9
gpupdate: 8-9
graphical: 30
graphics: 20, 61
grounding: 83
guidance: 2, 34, 48, 57, 74
guidelines: 77, 83
guides: 75

H

hacking: 33
handling: 74, 81, 83, 86, 88, 92-93
hardware: 1-2, 10, 13, 15, 20-21, 24-25, 41, 60-61, 75, 78, 81-83
helpdesk: 11, 73-74
hibernate: 14
hijacking: 39, 63
hosting: 35
hostname: 4, 19

I

icloud: 26
identify: 1-2, 7, 9-11, 25, 27-28, 58, 73, 83, 91
identity: 34
images: 24, 69
inspection: 40
install: 4, 11, 15, 19-20, 23-24, 31, 33, 55, 59, 61, 63, 67-69, 83
installed: 3-4, 10, 13, 15, 18-19, 25, 46, 55, 64, 66
installing: 22, 27, 40-41, 61, 63, 83
instance: 53
insulated: 82
integrated: 20
integrity: 8, 38, 86, 91
interface: 7, 18-19, 21, 30-31, 36, 46, 48, 53, 68, 70, 95
internet: 13-14, 16, 18, 27, 38, 41, 43, 46, 53, 62-63, 70, 95
interpret: 57
inventory: 22, 75-76, 78
inverter: 85
invest: 21
ipconfig: 4-7, 17-18, 32
iphones: 66
irrelevant: 90
isolated: 65
issues: 13, 20, 32, 51, 57, 59-62, 64, 66, 69, 76-78, 93

J

jargon: 89
javascript: 91-92
joined: 2, 36

K

k-blocks: 30
keyboard: 14
keylogger: 39
keyloggers: 41-42
keystrokes: 39
knowledge: 1-2, 33-34, 57, 73-76

L

labels: 76
ladder: 82
launcher: 18
launching: 62, 68
leaked: 70
logging: 28, 43, 59, 91
log-in: 37
lowercase: 47
low-memory: 59

M

macbook: 26-28
machine: 11, 26-27, 89
magnetic: 52
magnetized: 81

memory: 3, 12, 19-20, 49, 59, 68, 93
methods: 23, 28, 33-34, 37-39, 50, 52, 57, 60, 73, 79-80, 84, 89-90
microphone: 90
microsoft: 1-4, 9, 11-12, 17, 24-25, 33, 45, 75-76, 94
mobile: 1, 16, 22, 33, 37, 50-51, 57, 66-72, 89
modify: 9, 45, 87
modules: 58
monitor: 10, 14, 24, 27, 50, 76, 87, 94
msconfig: 6, 9-10
msinfo: 9-10
multicast: 32

N

navigating: 68
nbstat: 5
nbtstat: 6, 8
near-field: 67
negative: 79
netstat: 4-5, 7-8
network: 1, 3-7, 13-14, 16-19, 23-24, 28, 30, 32, 36-40, 45-46, 48, 50, 53-54, 59, 62, 64, 66, 68-71, 74-75, 84-85, 88, 93-95
networking: 1, 17, 32
networks: 1, 33, 51, 53-54, 77
nslookup: 5-8, 32
number: 16, 27-28, 30, 35, 40-42, 70, 88
numbers: 47

O

object: 8, 38
offers: 38, 50, 91
office: 10, 14, 33, 42, 53, 57, 75, 94-95

official: 2, 25, 34, 57, 74
offsite: 80
outage: 60
outages: 85
outdated: 58-59, 63, 72
outgoing: 41
output: 5, 15, 17, 28-32, 46

P

password: 2, 16, 27, 37, 42, 44, 47-50, 55, 74, 86, 91
passwords: 27, 34, 39, 41, 45, 48-49, 54, 75, 88
payment: 35
payments: 37, 40
payroll: 10, 48
photos: 66
photoshop: 75
pop-up: 40, 55, 64, 71
printer: 12, 18-19, 28, 42, 91
printers: 4, 12, 15, 18, 43, 84
printing: 12, 75
privacy: 2, 16, 45, 47, 50, 73-74, 86-88, 91
private: 17-18, 91, 94-95
project: 14
prompt: 2, 13, 17, 30, 49, 62, 71
prompted: 2, 46, 61, 64
protocol: 30, 38, 51, 53, 94-95
protocols: 33, 38, 73
python: 91-92

Q

quarantine: 65
-query: 7

R

radius: 38
re-install: 41, 47, 61-64, 66-68
remote: 1, 3-4, 6-7, 19, 23, 25, 30,
    33, 41, 43, 73, 94-95
remotely: 3, 94-95
rendered: 52
rendering: 52
repair: 23-25
repairs: 60
reporting: 74
reports: 9, 12, 17-18, 41, 44, 59,
    62, 67-68, 74, 76
resource: 10, 93
resources: 6, 12, 16-17, 31, 37, 59, 61, 92-93, 95
rushing: 77
-rw-r-----: 28
-rw-r--r--: 31

S

safety: 73, 81-83
salesforce: 76
scanfile: 62
scanner: 34-35
scannow: 8, 62
scenario: 1, 4, 6, 9, 12, 15, 17, 19, 23,
    33, 39-40, 45, 47, 52-53, 55, 57-58,
    62, 64, 66, 69, 73-74, 79,
screen: 9, 13, 16, 47, 49-51, 58, 61-62, 66-67, 69
screened: 53-54
screens: 74
script: 7-8, 36-37, 44, 93
scripting: 44, 73, 91-92
server: 3, 5, 7-8, 13-14, 16, 21-22, 24, 29,
    31, 35-36, 44, 46-47, 53, 94-95

servers: 22, 35, 43
service: 3, 10-11, 13-14, 17, 20, 29,
    31, 35, 37-38, 40-43, 46, 50, 53,
    59-60, 62-63, 76, 78, 89, 91
servicenow: 75
services: 1, 10, 13, 38, 51, 60, 76
session: 29-30
sessions: 17
setting: 16, 18, 20, 49, 54, 90
settings: 1, 3-4, 9, 13-17, 19, 23, 28,
    33, 37, 40-41, 45, 49-50, 53-55,
    58-60, 62, 67-69, 79, 84, 92-93
shutdown: 9, 25
signal: 54, 71
sign-in: 17
spoofing: 43-44, 69
spyware: 40, 42
storage: 7, 11, 15, 19, 21-23, 36-37, 45,
    52, 67-68, 70-71, 79, 84, 91
strategies: 78
streamline: 22
strict: 21
syntax: 29
synthetic: 80
system: 1-6, 8-11, 13-17, 19-25, 28,
    30, 34, 36, 39, 46-47, 53, 57-70,
    74-79, 81, 85-86, 92-94
systems: 1-3, 22, 40, 51, 57, 65, 71-77, 84, 92

T

tablet: 43
tablets: 54
tailgating: 43
tailor: 1
tracert: 5, 8, 32

tracking: 39
trackpad: 28
transit: 74
translator: 55

U

ubuntu: 19, 21, 29-32
unix-like: 92
update: 7, 14, 44, 46, 59-64, 67-69, 93
updates: 10, 21, 53, 57-58, 61, 63-65, 70-72, 90
upgrade: 1, 3-4, 20, 23-25, 61, 67-68
upload: 53, 91
username: 44
usernames: 88

V

vector: 43
vendor: 10, 20, 46, 52, 55
verify: 7-9, 64
version: 4, 20, 22, 26, 64, 67, 92
vestibule: 35-36
virtual: 3, 90, 94-95
viruses: 39-40
voltage: 85
volume: 24, 84

W

webcam: 13
webpages: 14
website: 44, 55
websites: 4, 34, 55, 63
wep-psk: 54
whaling: 42
window: 13, 27, 32
windows: 1-9, 11-26, 31, 33, 36-37, 40-41, 45-47, 49-50, 55, 57-62, 65, 92, 94
wireless: 19, 33, 38-39, 53-54, 84
workforce: 19, 22, 38
workgroup: 17-18
wpa-psk: 38

Z

zero-day: 43-44

www.packtpub.com

Subscribe to our online digital library for full access to over 7,000 books and videos, as well as industry leading tools to help you plan your personal development and advance your career. For more information, please visit our website.

Why subscribe?

- Spend less time learning and more time coding with practical eBooks and Videos from over 4,000 industry professionals
- Improve your learning with Skill Plans built especially for you
- Get a free eBook or video every month
- Fully searchable for easy access to vital information
- Copy and paste, print, and bookmark content

At www.packtpub.com, you can also read a collection of free technical articles, sign up for a range of free newsletters, and receive exclusive discounts and offers on Packt books and eBooks.

Other Books You May Enjoy

If you enjoyed this book, you may be interested in these other books by Packt:

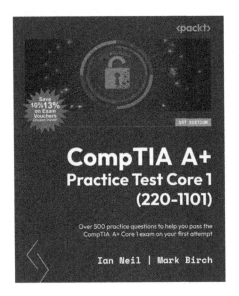

CompTIA A+ Practice Test Core 1 (220-1101)

Ian Neil and Mark Birch

ISBN: 978-1-83763-472-9

- Install and configure laptop hardware and components
- Compare and contrast common networking hardware and protocols for wireless networking
- Select and install storage devices
- Deploy and configure multifunction devices/printers and settings
- Troubleshoot problems related to motherboards, RAM, CPU, and power
- Summarize aspects of client-side virtualization and cloud computing concepts

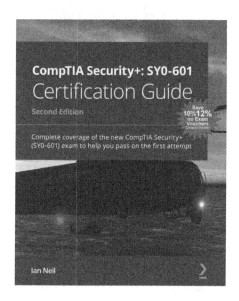

CompTIA Security+: SY0-601 Certification Guide - Second Edition

Ian Neil

ISBN: 978-1-80056-424-4

- Master cybersecurity fundamentals, from the CIA triad through to IAM
- Explore cloud security and techniques used in penetration testing
- Use different authentication methods and troubleshoot security issues
- Secure the devices and applications used by your company
- Identify and protect against various types of malware and viruses
- Protect yourself against social engineering and advanced attacks
- Understand and implement PKI concepts
- Delve into secure application development, deployment, and automation

Share Your Thoughts

Now you've finished *CompTIA A+ Practice Test Core 2 (220-1102)*, we'd love to hear your thoughts! Scan the QR code below to go straight to the Amazon review page for this book and share your feedback or leave a review on the site that you purchased it from.

`https://packt.link/r/1837638896`

Your review is important to us and the tech community and will help us make sure we're delivering excellent quality content.

Coupon Code for CompTIA A+ Exam Vouchers and Labs

Coupon Code for 13% Off on CompTIA A+ Core 2 (220-1102) Exam Vouchers

Take advantage of the **13% discount** by following the below instructions:

1. Go to `https://www.testforless.store/comptia-a`.
2. Click the **Buy Now** button.
3. Add the **exam voucher** to your cart.
4. From your cart, verify your credentials and product details. Then, proceed to **check out**.
5. The **13% discount** is already applied. No promo code is required.

> **The discount for the exam voucher is only available in USD. If you are purchasing from other regions, the purchase will still be made in USD. Vouchers can only be used in the countries associated with the currency in which they are purchased. View the CompTIA's Currency restrictions** (`https://wsr.pearsonvue.com/vouchers/pricelist/comptia.asp`) **for further clarification.**

Coupon Code for CompTIA A+ Core 2 (220-1102) Labs

Get CompTIA A+ Core 2 (220-1102) Labs for **$135 $90** and improve your skill set through practice. Access labs for 12 months from the date of purchase and get hands-on experience in a variety of exam tasks and scenarios.

Take advantage of the labs discount by following the instructions below:

1. Go to `https://www.testforless.store/acore2`.
2. Click the **Get Now** button.
3. Add the **lab** to your cart.
4. From your cart, verify your credentials and product details. Then, proceed to **check out**.
5. The discount is already applied. No promo code is required.